Marketing Your Library's Electronic Resources

Marketing Your Library's Electronic Resources

A how-to-do-it manual for librarians®

SECOND EDITION

Marie R. Kennedy and Cheryl LaGuardia

facet
publishing

Published by Facet Publishing,
7 Ridgmount Street, London WC1E 7AE
www.facetpublishing.co.uk

Facet Publishing is wholly owned by CILIP: the Library and
Information Association.

First published in the USA by the American Library Association,
2017.
This UK edition 2017.

British Library Cataloguing in Publication Data
A catalogue record for this book is available from the British
Library.

ISBN 978-1-78330-267-3

Printed and bound in the United Kingdom by Lightning Source.

Contents

Part I: How to Design Your Marketing Plan

Contents

Contents

Illustrations

Figures

Tables

Preface

Why write a book about e-resource marketing? We met at the 2010 Library Assessment Conference, Building Effective, Sustainable, Practical Assessment, in Baltimore, Maryland. Marie was giving the presentation "Cycling Through: Paths Libraries Take to Marketing Electronic Resources," and Cheryl was in the audience, listening (avidly) while noticing that all the other attendees were (rightly) taking down Marie's every word.

Why was everybody listening so hard? Because, as every frontline librarian knows, if our patrons really knew and understood how much we make available to them online, they wouldn't go to alternative information providers to do their research, and they wouldn't wonder where "all that money" for libraries goes: they'd use the resources to their fullest potential and clamor for more, as well as for more funding for the library so they can access more online. But our patrons don't know about all that we've got because our online systems don't make e-resources very accessible, and "marketing" has, until fairly recently, been an alien word, and practice, in libraries.

Discovery: Not There Yet

Besides, "Discovery systems will make our patrons aware of our e-resources," you say? They haven't so far. Although some contenders in the ring show promise for increasing awareness of online resources for researchers better than did the older, clunkier catalogs, they haven't knocked us out with their delivery yet—and it doesn't look like they will in the near future. We know that most of our patrons don't reach our electronic resources through a library system, but rather through a web browser; relying on a service like a discovery or federated search system to connect our resources to our patrons isn't a feasible solution to this problem of awareness. Simply making our patrons aware of resources doesn't really solve the problem in the long term either, given the number of resources available. The value of marketing an electronic resource means that the library knows its patrons well enough to say, "Out of all of these available resources, it's this one; this is the one you want." A discovery system won't ever succeed at that level because a system doesn't know our patrons like we do.

So we need to get the word out about our amazing wares, and getting that word out involves more than making some handouts to place at service desks. Getting the word out effectively means creating strategic marketing programs.

Getting the Word Out at Your Library

We perceive a considerable need among library users for greater knowledge about the e-resources purchased for them. Based on that need, we librarians must make it our business to market our e-resources to patrons (rather than just add new e-resources to our web portals and hope for the best). "If we build it [subscribe to it] they will come" may have worked for a baseball field in Iowa (Gordon and Gordon 1989), but it is not a successful marketing strategy for library e-resources, as most of you reading this book know. Getting the word out means developing a strategy to talk to your library patrons about how the resources you have selected for them can have an impact on their lives, from providing a trusted answer to a quick question to offering nuggets of inspiration to carry them through on a long-term project of their own design.

Value, Not ROI

ROI (return on investment) has been a library buzz-acronym in the recent past. The concept places a business construct on institutions that are inherently not businesses, but community organizations (i.e., libraries). An Internet search of the term returns results that are distinctly focused on a commercial business model. If you'd like to read more about how ROI relates to library impact/valuations, check out the ALA online bibliography "Return on Investment (ROI)" (American Library Association 2016).

Literal ROI studies don't make a lot of sense to us because those measures are based on corporate production values alien to a library's mission of service. However, qualitative measures of a library's impact make a ton of sense, and we support Jim Neal's arguments in his ACRL (Association of College & Research Libraries) paper "Stop the Madness: The Insanity of ROI and the Need for New Qualitative Measures of Academic Library Success" (Neal 2011).

We reaffirm Neal's thesis that the "academic library needs to be present to anyone, anywhere, anytime, and anyhow," although we feel his statement can apply more broadly to *all* libraries (Neal 2011, 425). In his paper, Neal argues that libraries and librarians must be more entrepreneurial, and in that process, we should

> ask ourselves fundamental questions. Can we offer additional
> information or transaction services to our existing customer

base? Can we address the needs of new customer segments by repackaging our current information assets or by creating new business capabilities through the Internet? Can we use our ability to attract customers to generate new sources of revenue? Will our business be significantly harmed by other companies providing some of the same value we currently offer? How do we become a customer magnet through electronic commerce? How do we build direct links to new customers? How do we take away bits of value digitally from other companies? Can we use the Internet as both a tool for global learning and scholarly communication and for technology transfer and entrepreneurial activities? (428)

If you examine all of Neal's questions, you'll note that every one of them intimately relates to library electronic resources—their selection, acquisition, accessibility, and ubiquity. We believe the libraries that are able to answer Neal's questions informedly, based on their users' needs and expectations, are the libraries that will thrive in the "mutable future" Neal foresees.

The "Competition"

It can be very useful for us to consider our services in a new light, to be more entrepreneurial, and to borrow business tactics when they will serve us well to further our mission. A recent study has shown us that our patrons will turn to "rogue" (read: not entirely legal) resources for their information needs if they perceive it is more convenient than using library resources (Hollandsworth et al. 2016). This study is alarming from an ethical standpoint; we want our patrons to choose the best resources, and to arrive at them legally. We find this statement from Neal's (2011) paper to be highly relevant to our discussion:

> Advancing the entrepreneurial imperative will demand a commitment to the tools of the trade, and these include business plans, competitive strategies, and venture capital. (429)

Hmmm. Business plans and competitive strategies. Would that be marketing plans, perhaps? It would!

The Hope in Building Community

You will notice as you read through this book that we put a lot of emphasis on knowing your library patrons. It is easy to silo yourself during your workday in the library, focusing on the tasks at hand. Let this book reaffirm for you why you likely joined the profession of librarianship: to engage your patrons with library materials that satisfy their information needs. We prompt you throughout the book to de-silo yourself, if at reading this book you find yourself to be so, and get back to building community, to learning what makes your library patrons tick. In this book we describe the marketing process as an intentional conversation, and you're the one to start the conversation. Participating in the network of library users is a hopeful use of your time, and a particularly meaningful one, with all the stressors out there in today's world.

The Who, What, When, Where, Why of Your E-resource Marketing Plan (Not Necessarily in That Order)

Now that you know why we wrote this book, let's consider why a marketing plan for your e-resources makes sense and how you will put one together. Before you undertake an e-resources marketing plan, you need to clearly identify what its purpose is, who will be involved in it, what its component parts will be, how you're going to implement it, when you're going to implement it, how you're going to assess its success, and when and how you'll revise it once it's been implemented.

Sound like a lot of work? It can be, but these are the very steps and processes we're going to lay out for you in this book—whether yours is an academic, public, school, or special library. Follow these steps and you'll save tons of time, effort, money, and headaches while increasing the use of your vital library resources and making your patrons happier and more successful. You'll also have a plan that is fully accountable to your library administration and your library stakeholders.

By reading this book, you will learn the terminology used by marketing experts. If the idea of marketing itself is intimidating, remember that the goal you're after—the "why"—is to form an intentional partnership with your library patrons. Our goal is to help you make a plan to develop that partnership, and that plan just happens to be called "marketing."

What Is Marketing?

For our purposes, we define the "marketing" in *Marketing Your Library's Electronic Resources* to be a combination of getting the word out about what our libraries offer in the way of e-resources, describing what those resources can do for various clientele, getting feedback from our clientele about their knowledge and use of the library e-resources, and being responsive to their needs after having gotten their feedback. So marketing, to us, is an ongoing circular process of planning, engagement, and assessment. The end game is to begin to develop relationships with your library patrons that are sustainable and meaningful.

We have micro- and macrogoals for this book. The microgoal is to give colleagues the specific means of developing, implementing, and assessing marketing plans for e-resource collection management. The macrogoal is to maximize the awareness of library e-resources among researchers and thereby increase the acknowledged value of libraries to their community—be it a school, town, college, university, office, or think tank. Our target audience is broader than just those librarians directly involved in collection development or managing electronic resources. As you read this book, you'll see that it's our belief that just about everybody in a library needs to be involved, in some way, with marketing e-resources.

How the Book Is Organized

Once you accept our premise that, for a variety of reasons, libraries need to develop and implement marketing plans, the chapters here flow pretty naturally. We focus on e-resource marketing plans, but our basic strategies are applicable to many other library services. In part I, we begin in chapter 1 with describing how you can determine the purpose of your plan—this will drive the rest of the process. Please do take the time and effort to zero in on your purpose in creating a marketing plan. It may sound like a no-brainer, but it is important for you to articulate your goals well at the beginning; this will give you guideposts along the way and will enable you to decide, at the end of the first marketing cycle, if you achieved what you set out to do and what you need to revise to achieve, or continue, a successful plan.

In chapter 2 we provide detailed specifics on how to go about developing a plan for your library, much of which is based on studying who your patrons are and what they need from you. Chapter 3 is all about taking action and putting your plan into practice. Note well that a large part of implementing your plan involves employing measurements and assessment tools along the way, as well as doing everything with an eye toward writing a report about the entire project.

Accountability is even more of a current-day library mantra than marketing, so as you implement your plan, keep the written report you'll do at "the end of the tunnel" firmly in mind. We demonstrate how to write the report in chapter 4 and point you to seven examples of marketing plan reports in part II for you to examine. We even have included a marketing plan report template that you can download (from www.alaeditions.org/webextras) and fill in as you go along. If you follow the advice in chapter 5, you'll have plenty to write about in the report because you will have assessed the dickens out of your plan and have lots of qualitative and quantitative data to back up your statements.

Chapter 6 brings the process full circle by discussing how to take stock of the project, revise and update it, and then implement and assess the revisions—as we said, it really is an ongoing circular process.

In part II, you'll find some sample library marketing plan reports. We love the plan presented in example 1 because it is for an all-digital library. Where you would normally have competing interests in marketing with print materials, that is not the case with NOVELny, and its marketing plan gives you a chance to imagine what it would be like to market electronic resources in an all-digital environment. Example 2 is a collaborative marketing plan report from a public library. To see the behind-the-scenes work that went into designing its formal plan report, check out the presentation at http://njla.pbworks.com/f/NJLA+Promoting+Online+Resources+Barber.pdf for the SWOT example and communication strategies. We include example 3 to show what a library with strong partnerships can accomplish. Example 4, from a consortium of community college libraries, expertly outlines the hopes the libraries have for their patrons by completing a marketing plan and by identifying desired behaviors and attitudes. Example 5, a university marketing plan report, has as its opening line, "While plans are not usually followed to the letter, the planning process is indispensable as it enables us to answer basic questions about what we do and why we do it." The bottom line about this process is that it will result in your learning much more about your clientele and in your being able to serve them better than ever before when it comes to providing electronic resources. Example 6, from an Irish institute of technology, provides a very full marketing plan, of which electronic resources are a component; the plan even includes a SWOT analysis. Example 7 uses the marketing plan report template we have provided with this book (at www.alaeditions.org/webextras), filled in so that you can see the process of this university's plan for a specific streaming video product.

So our goals are ambitious, and our target audience is large: essentially, the entire library community. We trust you'll judge for yourselves how well we meet these goals, and if we reach our audience, through this book.

What's New Since the First Edition

We have learned so much from you since the writing of the first edition of this book and are grateful to those of you who took time to write to us about your experiences with the book, and to those who wrote reviews of the book. All of your feedback has been folded into this edition.

One of the things we heard from you is that it was helpful to see marketing plans from libraries, so that you didn't feel like you needed to reinvent the wheel while creating your own. We agree that viewing different approaches to developing marketing plans can be valuable and so have included three more marketing plans in this edition. One of the marketing plans uses the brand-new marketing plan report template we've created for you (download it from www.alaeditions.org/webextras) to help you get to your own final marketing plan faster. Let us know how you like the template and what tweaks to it you would suggest for a future edition.

Looking outside of our own home libraries, the world of e-resource management continues to move forward. The usage statistics standards group that we all rely on to compare the usage of one e-resource to another, Project COUNTER, is currently working on a draft of a new Code of Practice (and related SUSHI protocol), Release 5. To engage librarians in the development of these standards, and to provide a mechanism for asking questions about the use of them, a community website on usage, Usus (www.usus.org.uk), has been developed. Take a look for yourself to see how you might want to participate with this online community.

The TERMS (Techniques for Electronic Resource Management) group is in the process of reconvening to revise its work on the steps involved in managing e-resources. Visit the group's Facebook page at www.facebook .com/groups/174086169332439, if you want to stay up-to-date with its progress.

There are lots of options to stay engaged with e-resources and marketing. As you find new opportunities you think we should know about, drop us a line! We enjoy observing and learning how to interact with the changing world of electronic resources right alongside you.

REFERENCES

American Library Association. 2016. "Return on Investment (ROI)." Accessed December 5, 2016. www.ala.org/research/librariesmatter/ taxonomy/term/129.

Gordon, Lawrence, and Charles Gordon, prods. 1989. *Field of Dreams.* Directed by Phil Alden Robinson. Based on *Shoeless Joe* by W. P. Kinsella (Houghton Mifflin, 1982). Universal Pictures. 107 min.

Hollandsworth, Bobby, Michael Levine Clark, John McDonald, and Jason Price. 2016. "Access to Freely Available Journal Articles: Gold, Green and Rogue Open Access across the Disciplines." Presentation at the Charleston Conference, Issues in Book and Serial Acquisition, Charleston, SC, November 3. http://sched.co/85dw.

Neal, James G. 2011. "Stop the Madness: The Insanity of ROI and the Need for New Qualitative Measures of Academic Library Success." In *Declaration of Interdependence: The Proceedings of the ACRL 2011 Conference, March 30–April 2, 2011, Philadelphia, PA*, 424–429. Chicago: American Library Association. www.ala.org/acrl/sites/ala .org.acrl/files/content/conferences/confsandpreconfs/national/2011/ papers/stop_the_madness.pdf.

Acknowledgments

We are grateful to be part of a community of librarians that moves the profession along through collaboration and innovation. Our thanks to all of you who have participated in the development of this book through your reviews of the first edition and contributions to this newest one.

Part I

How to Design Your Marketing Plan

Determine the Purpose of Your Marketing Plan

Have you ever gone grocery shopping without an ingredient list and ended up spending time reading the nutrition label on a box of cereal you're not really interested in? You meander through the aisles, notice the items with the sale signs, and get sucked into putting cans of organic tomatoes (two-for-one special!) into your cart, along with a five-pound bag of flour (because you think you may be low on that staple). At the checkout lane you notice that your cart is full of stuff, but none of it forms a meal. You spend $30 but you're not really sure what you bought, and you forgot to get the milk, which was the whole reason you went shopping. Hey, it happens.

A shopping list for a food shopper is like a marketing plan for electronic resources in a library. It keeps a library focused, without a wandering eye in the cookies aisle. Shopping without a list once in a while may be fine for an individual, but it's no way for a library to do business. You know that your best week's shopping is when you have a menu in mind and are shopping for ingredients; you leave satisfied, knowing that what you paid for will sustain you. The same is true for a marketing plan for electronic resources in a library. The effort a library puts into making a plan for marketing electronic resources directs the library to speak with one message, creates a community or culture of marketing, and empowers patrons to know that the electronic resources they use are the most effective. Dillon (2003) calls developing this kind of culture a "marketing-aware organization," and it happens "when an entire organization devotes its efforts to more effectively serving the customer" (120).

What You Can Discover about Your E-resources Right Now

When you put together your grocery list, you probably take stock of what you already have in your pantry and note what's lacking, listing items you know you'll need for the week's menu. When reviewing your library's electronic resources, you may ask yourself the following questions: What resources are already in the virtual pantry of my library? What are the staples of electronic resource management here at my fingertips that will give me information about the use and value of our electronic resources? There are three easy methods to help you learn about your e-collection right now: usage statistics, cost, and cost-per-use.

Usage Statistics

Does your library measure how many times your electronic resources are used? If you don't look at usage statistics or don't gather this kind of data, you're missing a potentially valuable piece of information. By examining usage statistics, you may find that the e-journal you were sure would be heavily used isn't as popular as you thought it would be. Alternatively, the usage statistics may confirm what you suspected all along! Knowing how many times an electronic resource is accessed is an important data point because it tells you how much your collection is being used and if you are collecting the right resources for your patrons. Libraries have measured the use of print journals for years, with varying methodologies and success. Fortunately, the process of measurement is already in place for electronic resources because it's inherent in the system. All we have to do is choose to gather the data.

If you already collect usage statistics, then you are aware of the wealth of information you can glean about your e-resources. Many vendors provide usage statistics every month. If you compile them into an annual report, you can note such trends as in which months are your e-resources most heavily used, which are your most-used resources, and, a possibly critical statistic depending on the state of your library budget, which e-resources have low use or aren't used at all.

The best available standard for counting the use of an e-resource is called "COUNTER." The COUNTER (Counting Online Usage of NeTworked Electronic Resources) standard allows you to compare the "use" of one e-journal, database, e-book, or multimedia resource with the "use" of another (COUNTER 2017). A "use" of an e-journal, according to the COUNTER standard, is defined as a successful full-text article request. This means that a patron found the article, perhaps browsed the abstract, and also believed it to be relevant enough that he or she clicked on the HTML or PDF link to read, save, or print the full text of the article. Knowing that this is a standard measurement, you can be sure that when you download the COUNTER Journal Report 1 (JR1) for an e-journal, the numbers provided will allow you to compare the "use" of that e-journal to another.

The definition of "use" according to the COUNTER standard obviously does not capture the myriad ways your electronic resource collection is used, but it is the cleanest way to compare the performance of one e-journal/database/e-book/multimedia resource to another. Other kinds of statistics can help assess the use of your collection, such as proxy server statistics, OpenURL resolver statistics, and non-COUNTER e-journal usage statistics, but these are not standardized, and you can't compare them against each other. If you're just beginning to think about assessing the use of your electronic collection, we recommend that you stick with the standard COUNTER statistics because they are the most reliable and will tell you the number of times the resources were actually used.

How to Get COUNTER Usage Statistics

COUNTER usage statistics are free to access, view, and download. To look at the statistics, or to download them to your computer for further manipulation, ask your vendor for access to an administrative site where the statistics are stored, or ask the vendor to e-mail the monthly reports to you. Not all vendors will be able to supply you with usage statistics, and not all vendors will be able to provide you with COUNTER statistics because the vendor is not "COUNTER-compliant." COUNTER statistics are typically available in a format that can be opened in Microsoft Excel, so they are easy to view and sort. COUNTER has standardized the reporting of usage statistics for many formats of licensed electronic content. For electronic journals, you can access reports showing the number of full-text article requests by month and journal (Journal Report 1, or JR1), the number of successful full-text article requests from an archive by month and journal (Journal Report 1a), the number of turnaways (access denied because the library is not subscribed to the content requested) by month and journal (Journal Report 2), and the number of successful full-text article requests by year of publication and journal (Journal Report 5). With each new release of COUNTER the types of reports have increased. With Release 4 there are eight possible reports for e-journal content alone. To view how visually accessible the design of the reports is, see figure 1.1 for a sample JR1 report in Microsoft Excel.

There are similar COUNTER reports for databases, e-books, and multimedia resources. The reports are typically available in CSV, XML, HTML, or PDF format. The reports can be viewed online or downloaded. Some

Journal Report 1 (R4)	Number of Successful Full-Text Article Requests by Month and Journal													
<Organization name>														
<Institutional Identifier>														
Period covered by Report:														
2016-01-01 to 2016-05-31														
Date run:														
2016-06-23														
Journal	Publisher	Platform	Journal DOI	Proprietary Identifier	Print ISSN	Online ISSN	Reporting Period Total	Reporting Period HTML	Reporting Period PDF	Jan-2016	Feb-2016	Mar-2016	Apr-2016	May-2016
Total for all journals	Springer	SpringerLink					5624	580	2632	466	1806	1090	1727	535
3 Biotech	Springer	SpringerLink	10.1007/1:	13205	2190-572X	2190-5738	2	0	1	0	2	0	0	0
3D Printing in Medicine	Springer	SpringerLink		41205		2365-6271	0	0	0	0	0	0	0	0
3D Research	Springer	SpringerLink	10.1007/1:	13319		2092-6731	0	0	0	0	0	0	0	0
4OR	Springer	SpringerLink	10.1007/1(	10288	1619-4500	1614-2411	0	0	0	0	0	0	0	0
AAPS Open	Springer	SpringerLink		41120		2364-9534	0	0	0	0	0	0	0	0
AAPS PharmSciTech	Springer	SpringerLink		12249		1530-9932	0	0	0	0	0	0	0	0
ADHD Attention Deficit and Hyperactivi	Springer	SpringerLink	10.1007/1:	12402	1866-6116	1866-6647	3	0	3	0	1	2	0	0

FIGURE 1.1 COUNTER Report Sample

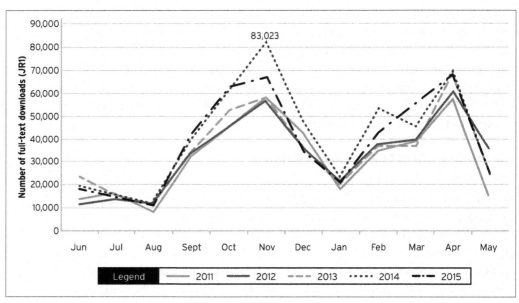

FIGURE 1.2 COUNTER Usage Data over Five Years

vendor platforms allow you to e-mail the file to yourself on a certain date each month.

Because this type of usage statistic is standardized, it can be informative for showing trends over time. Figure 1.2 shows five years of data taken from a single university library's JR1 COUNTER reports. All of the CSV files from vendors were combined, split into the academic library's fiscal year, and put into a line chart to show usage by month. The usage pattern matches what one would expect at a university on a semester schedule, with e-journal usage peaking each year during the busy fall semester research month of November and the busy spring semester research month of April. We have highlighted in this figure the month of November 2014 to show the largest number of full-text article requests (83,023).

In addition to usage trends over time, you can see which individual e-journals are used the most. If you combine all the COUNTER reports you gather into one Excel file and then sort by the Total PDFs column, you will get a rank order of the e-journals that get the most use. You can perform this sorting procedure with a new combined file every year to see which e-journals your patrons use the most over time. If you discover that newspaper titles are consistently in the top five on your list after three or four years of performing this kind of ranking, you may decide to add more newspaper content to your collection or possibly seek archive files of your most popular newspapers for historical content.

You may choose to gather your own COUNTER statistics, which requires that you log in to the administrative sites of all of your vendor systems to construct and download a usage report, but some libraries have found this workflow to be time-consuming. Instead, those libraries have opted to use commercial systems to gather the statistics on their behalf.

These systems charge an annual fee to store all of the usernames and passwords for your accounts and will perform the work of logging in to those systems to download usage statistics and create reports for you. Some electronic resource management systems (ERMSs) can perform similar activities, though at this point in development the commercial platforms are more robust than ERMSs in the types of COUNTER reports that can be managed in them.

There have been great strides in the automation of gathering COUNTER reports, using a protocol called SUSHI, an acronym that stands for Standardized Usage Statistics Harvesting Initiative (NISO 2017). This protocol allows systems to automate the retrieval of usage data, saving the time and effort of library staff. The commercial systems mentioned earlier make use of the SUSHI protocol, as do some ERMSs. As COUNTER reports continue to be developed, so do the retrieval mechanisms of SUSHI. The future development of the standard and protocol depends on the active involvement of librarians like you, and if you would like to learn more or ask questions, visit Usus, a website about usage for librarians, at www.usus.org.uk. At that site, you will find "Friendly Guides to COUNTER Reports" (under "Hints and Tips") to help you get started with usage statistics.

Cost

Another data element to assist you in the review of your e-collection is the cost of a resource. Your library is certainly tracking how much it spends annually on subscriptions to electronic resources, and you can use this information to help you put the cost of a resource in context with the rest of your collection. You can answer questions like, "How does the cost of this one electronic journal from Vendor A compare to the cost of an electronic journal of similar scope from Vendor B?" If Vendor A provides content similar to the journal from Vendor B, you may decide that your collection needs only one.

In addition to examining the costs of electronic resources during the current year, you can use your cost data to look at trends over time. You may notice that Vendor A seems to increase its subscription costs about 7 percent each year, whereas Vendor B has historically raised its costs only 1 percent. Knowing that this is a trend, you may choose to purchase more content from Vendor B if it is relevant and of a quality suited to your collection.

Some specialized individual e-journals cost tens of thousands of dollars annually, and being able to pull those into a list to sort by most expensive can be helpful to your collection development staff. Understanding the cost of one journal compared to another in the same area of interest is important when thinking about your patron needs. Does the e-journal that costs $10,000 per year give significantly more value than the one on the same topic that costs $500 per year? Discussions about which e-journal is the more valuable one should clearly be more nuanced than considering the single factor of price, but it is an important objective element to note.

Authors' Note

The COUNTER examples presented in this book are based on Release 4 of the standard. As libraries continue to demand more granular, accurate data, the COUNTER working group continues to tweak the language and requirements to adjust for new formats of electronic content. Release 4 (2014) is the current version of the standard and includes reports for gold Open Access journals and multimedia reports. COUNTER reports will show you which elements of your e-content are being used and which could be used more. Those with low usage may be good candidates for a marketing campaign.

Cost-Per-Use

Merging subscription price data with use statistics for your electronic resources can tell you how much it costs each time your patrons download an e-journal article, read an e-book chapter, or perform a search in a database. Calculating cost-per-use is simple to do and returns a rich data point for you to think about. It is usually calculated as $A \div B = C$, where A is the annual subscription cost, B is the number of uses in that subscription year, and C is the resulting cost-per-use. An electronic journal that costs 100 USD and is used fifty times costs 2 USD for each use. When you calculate the cost-per-use, you may be amazed at how inexpensive frequently used electronic resource subscription fees are and at how those resources that are infrequently used seem to cost so much more.

Cost-per-use data is especially pertinent during subscription renewal season. If you discover that the cost for each use of an electronic resource is very high, you may consider contacting the vendor with this data to support a request to lower your subscription cost. You may also consider stopping the subscription in favor of having your patrons request the material via interlibrary borrowing, which may be far less expensive for your library. Alternatively, you may decide that despite the cost of the resource it is the best one in its content area for your patrons, and this may be the resource you will choose to promote during your marketing campaign to try to increase its use.

We have discussed several kinds of data that you can gather about your electronic collection—data that is easy to visualize and present to others in a chart or figure. The use, cost, and cost-per-use data are important indicators of how your electronic resources are being accessed, but such data is missing key contextual information, that being how and why your patrons are choosing to access or not access those resources.

As you examine the usage statistics for an electronic resource, you may discover that it is hardly used at all, although you thought for certain it would be very popular with your library's young adult population. Why would this be? Could it be that your young adult population doesn't know about the resource? Could it be that young adults don't find the content useful? Could it be that they really love the content but hate the user interface, choosing instead to seek similar information from a different, more pleasant-looking source? The data you've gathered so far, on cost and use, can't answer these questions, but it can influence how you get the answers.

Advanced Data Considerations

There has been emphasis recently, as the information marketplace becomes more competitive, on the need for libraries to demonstrate their value. Librarians are learning how to tell the extended stories of their institutions, to talk about the impact libraries can have on their patrons' lives, and are making strides toward teaching themselves to manage and use data to tell those stories. There have been several published examples of libraries tying usage of the library to student attainment, and often e-resource usage data is a part of those examples (see Davidson, Rollins, and Cherry 2013 and Stone and Ramsden 2013 for more on this). In an article on e-resource usage, Samson (2014) describes the process she used to merge usage data with specific patron demographic data, to be able to track how much different kinds of library patrons were using e-resources over time. We consider attempts like these to be advanced topics but wanted to be sure to mention them to you as options, in case you have the resources and desire to complete analyses like these.

When you're making your shopping list, you don't write on it the things you already have in the pantry; you write down the things you're missing. Now that you know you have usage statistics, cost, and cost-per-use on your virtual pantry shelves, what things are you missing? What more do you need to know about the environment and impact of your library's electronic resources? Let's look into this further.

Speak with One Message

Engaging with your patrons is an essential step toward learning if your library is providing the electronic resources they find useful. The sentence you just read seems obvious, doesn't it? But this fundamental, practical process is often a weak point for libraries. Libraries have traditionally been good communicators with their patrons about factual things, like changes in hours, notifications of special author events, and alerts that requested items on hold are ready to be picked up. These transactional kinds of communications can effectively be expanded to include the voice of strategic marketing for electronic resources.

Many of the communications between patrons and library staff, via e-mail, text, mail, flyers, or in person, are casual, question-and-response in nature. Think about how your communications might change if they included a simple, intentional message. When shopping at the department store Kmart, for example, the cashier will hand you your bag of purchased items and say, "Thank you for shopping at Kmart." You may have noticed a sticker on the cash register at Kmart with the word "TYFSAK" on it, and wondered what it meant. TYFSAK is an acronym to remind cashiers to say the standardized thank-you message. That quick, strategic saying was designed to convey to the customers that their patronage was appreciated. How might you convey something like this when communicating about your electronic resources?

If communications like that which we just described seem a little heavy-handed, don't worry. The thing to take away from the example is that all Kmart staff are on board with speaking with one message, and that message is to convey appreciation to their customers. The message is in line with their mission, and it is intentional. Creating a marketing plan for your electronic resources allows a library to develop a communication style about those resources that resonates with and reinforces the mission of the library. It can be conveyed through a standardized saying like "TYFSAK," it can be something subtler, or, depending on your goals, it can be bolder.

Part of a typical marketing plan involves evaluation and assessment, and this is a natural place to insert a request for patron feedback. Developing a cyclical request for interaction and feedback from your patrons will allow for comfortable information gathering about your electronic resources. If your patrons know that you are going to be asking them about their use of and desires about electronic resources, they will grow to expect this style of communication, and pretty soon you will be able to answer the "why" questions that the usage statistics and cost data couldn't tell you about the young adult e-resource mentioned in the previous section.

Creating a strategic communication plan, including asking questions of your patrons that are likely to provide you with actionable information, is what marketing is all about. Communicating about too many things or with too many different voices can be confusing. A marketing plan helps keep communications steady and on target. The messages are deliberate. The process becomes like the shopping list, keeping your messages clear and focused and away from the cookies aisle.

Everybody Does the Marketing

If your library's intention is to speak with a consistent message, it is easy to see why marketing is everybody's job. If you decide that marketing your library's electronic resources is a priority for your library, it is important that everybody in the library prioritizes it, too, in order to be effective. If your library staff are on board with the message you're trying to convey about electronic resources, it is easy for them to communicate effortlessly in their everyday contacts with patrons, regardless of mechanism (e-mail, in person, etc.).

The quote attributed to David Packard (of Hewlett-Packard), "Marketing is far too important to be left to the marketing department," means that in order for a library to speak with one message, communications can't be tightly controlled in one department but rather have to be part of everyday conversation among all library staff. Dubicki (2007) believes that "the success of any marketing program relies heavily on involvement and commitment from the entire library staff" (7). This style of communications management turns a traditional administrative hierarchy on its head, prioritizing patrons and empowering staff—not just administrators—to speak for the library.

Surely there will be those of you reading who work in libraries with dedicated outreach and communications staff, and the people serving those functions may be the coordinators of general marketing efforts for the library. Traditionally, though, those marketing efforts have not included electronic resources. This broadening of the scope of what "marketing" means is an exciting proposition, and the people in the roles of outreach staff are likely to embrace the opportunities to have more interactions with patrons through a new focus on electronic resources. If you are in a position to raise this idea with your outreach staff, prepare yourself for their enthusiastic response.

If frontline staff act as spokespersons for the library's electronic resources, it is important that they be thoughtfully prepared to answer questions about those resources. Brannon (2007) notes that her library realized, "Patrons will trust confident, knowledgeable staff more, and find more satisfaction in their use of the library with proper assistance" (43); as a result, the library decided to focus attention on staff education. When you think about the people who work at the service points in your library, would you say they're knowledgeable about the electronic collection? Would they benefit from learning more about it?

The team approach to marketing electronic resources allows for collaborations that might not happen given the traditional management hierarchy usually found in a library. Such a team will naturally include your collection development staff because they are most aware of recent purchases for the library that may be selected with a particular user group in mind. It can include your cataloging staff, if you have decided to focus on the cataloging record as a promotional tool, and it will seek affirmation and cheerleading from your management staff. Because your circulation staff and reference staff interact directly with patrons, they will also be part of the team in your library's marketing plan. Metz-Wiseman and Rodgers (2007) note that the team approach to marketing in their libraries "was an opportunity for librarians and library staff to provide leadership beyond the traditional hierarchy" (20).

Developing a plan for the marketing of electronic resources should be embedded in the library's mission and tied in with other marketing plans that may already exist. As you work within the existing structure of policy documents like your library's mission statement and begin to build a team of people knowledgeable and enthusiastic about the possibilities inherent in electronic resources, you will be effecting a cultural change. Changing culture to include something new will take some time. Be patient and enjoy the process and your small successes along the way.

When Does the Marketing Happen?

You may be wondering when in the management life cycle of an electronic resource you should begin marketing. The ideal scenario is to have a plan in place at the time a new e-resource is licensed for the collection, so that all the communication is geared toward gathering data that will be needed for assessment at the time of annual renewal of the subscription. In practice, parts of your marketing plan will be occurring at multiple points in the life cycle of an electronic resource, for new or existing resources in your library collection. Let us examine the illustration of this life cycle of an electronic resource in figure 1.3, developed by Oliver Pesch, and discuss where marketing may occur throughout it.

At the top of the image is the beginning of the management life cycle of an electronic resource, *acquire.* At this point in the life cycle, the collection development team for the library has made the intentional decision to add the resource to the collection and the acquisitions team begins the process by requesting information from the provider about the particulars of the resource, regarding cost, length of subscription, and any rights and restrictions of use. Ideally at this time, the acquisitions team, in collaboration with the collection development team, will also ask the vendor or publisher for any marketing or outreach materials related to the resource. The collection development team already has in mind who the expected users of the resource will be, and so asking for targeted communication material for that user group at the time of the acquisition is reasonable. Publishers will customize promotional materials for your library, often even agreeing to insert your library's name or logo on posters or bookmarks. Just ask your account

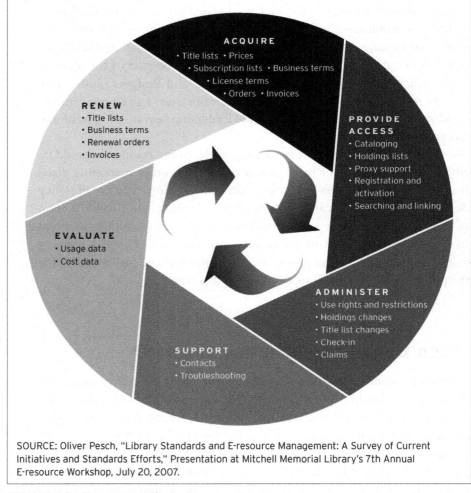

SOURCE: Oliver Pesch, "Library Standards and E-resource Management: A Survey of Current Initiatives and Standards Efforts," Presentation at Mitchell Memorial Library's 7th Annual E-resource Workshop, July 20, 2007.

FIGURE 1.3 E-resource Life Cycle

salesperson for any customizations; he or she will be eager to partner with you so you get the most out of the resource.

At the next step in the life cycle, *provide access,* a librarian adds the resource to the inventory of the collection by noting it in the catalog. Where the librarian chooses to link the resource, how to describe it in the catalog and any related portals, and where to provide documentation of how the resource may be used can all be considered part of the marketing process. If the expected user group for this resource is senior engineers in an off-site research lab, then it would be reasonable that the librarian would make sure that the proxy access is functional, there is a brief summary of the contents of the resource in the monthly e-mail announcement to the lab of the library's new acquisitions, and a link to the resource on that lab's specialized database portal page (e.g., on a LibGuide). At the time the resource is activated, the librarian can plan to disseminate to expected users any flyers or communication material delivered by the provider.

At the *administer* step in the life cycle of an electronic resource, a librarian annotates the catalog record with any rights or restrictions regarding how it may be used. Libraries typically negotiate the broadest possible use for their patrons at the time a resource is licensed, and conveying to patrons how the resource may be used is often a requirement of the license agreement. In the catalog record (or linked license record, if an ERMS is in use), the library can enter statements like these: "This resource may be downloaded, printed, and saved for future use," "This resource may be linked from Blackboard," or "This resource may be used in a course pack." Statements like these guide the patrons as to how they may legally and ethically use the content licensed on their behalf. Having this information available for patrons means that patrons can more confidently use the library's resources; in this way, transparency of license terms subtly acts as a marketing tool.

At the *support* step in the life cycle of an electronic resource, the library really has a chance to shine. We know from experience that even the most stable electronic resources act up occasionally, and the speed and manner in which the library chooses to respond to trouble reports is all part of marketing. Creating a mechanism to solicit feedback from patrons about their experiences with electronic resources is a marketing decision (if you have a mechanism in place, it conveys to a patron that you care about his or her experience in the library). The concept of *support* goes beyond troubleshooting; it can look like advocacy. For example, if you notice that patrons consistently get tripped up at the same spot while downloading an e-book, the library can communicate this problem to the provider and work together with the provider to facilitate a change or work-around for the downloading of e-books. Advocacy means that you are giving a voice to the concerns of your patrons in your communications to the providers of the content the library licenses.

Another way to think about support is by providing help before a patron asks for it. Publishers will very often create quick-start guides or getting-started videos for their products. Linking to these use guides from the catalog record may be just the thing your patrons need to jump-start their use of a new e-resource.

In the *evaluate* step in the life cycle of an electronic resource, price and use come into play. Since these types of data usually inform a renewal decision, a library may choose to develop a communication plan for greater use of an electronic resource if existing usage data is low. If usage is low and cost is high, then the library may design marketing of that particular resource to bring usage up to meet the expectations of its high cost. If usage of an electronic resource is lower than expected and the resource has already been widely advertised, it may be time to consider not renewing it.

In the *renew* step in the life cycle of an electronic resource, typically a year's worth of effort comes to fruition, with a decision to renew or cancel a subscription. It may be at this point that the library launches a marketing plan, if expected usage of the resource is low but the collection development team believes that it might just need one more year to get on the radar of the anticipated user group.

The illustration of the management life cycle of an electronic resource, in conjunction with our comments on marketing steps that occur throughout it, should give you a sense of the investment a library makes when subscribing to or purchasing an electronic resource. For an electronic resource to be a useful addition to the library collection, it must be considered consistently throughout its life cycle.

Be Mindful of Competing Interests

If you agree that having a plan for communicating is reasonable, you'll probably understand why sporadic attempts or one-time events for marketing electronic resources will fail over time. Consider this scenario, a description of a possible one-time event. You decide to design an electronic resource vendor day in the library, and twelve vendor representatives come and give away a bunch of flyers, handouts, and other treats. You don't seek feedback, but you get anecdotal commentary from patrons that they enjoyed the event. What have you learned about your patrons or their use of your electronic resources from the event? Not much! If the event doesn't fit into a larger plan, then it doesn't give usable information about where to focus your next efforts. The event ends up competing as "noise" against all the other events going on in the library, soon to be forgotten by your patrons.

Now suppose you create a one-question survey that asks your library patrons to list five e-resources in the library they'd like to know more about and then design an electronic resource vendor day in the library based on the survey responses. The vendor setup is the same as in the previous scenario, but now there are only five vendors, and they each have a computer screen at which they demonstrate how to use their companies' e-resources in addition to giving away quick-start guides, flyers, handouts, and treats. Before this event, you've downloaded usage statistics on those five resources to gauge their performance until now. One month after the vendor day, you gather a similar set of statistics for comparison to see if there is an increase in the use of those resources that may be attributed to the vendor day training sessions.

The cash cost for the setup of these two vendor days is the same, as is the staff effort. Which do you suppose was more worth the money and time in the long run? The vendor day with training and patron interaction is the more valuable. The patrons who visited your library on that day now have five resources in mind that rise above all the others, which will help them narrow their options the next time they seek information at your library. They know where to begin—with the possible five they now know, thanks to the vendor day you hosted—rather than being overwhelmed by the 250 databases to which your library subscribes.

The Evolving Formats and Methods of E-content Delivery

The publishing world has certainly expanded its scope in recent years, shifting the way it delivers content to meet the demands of online users. Consider, in just the past few years, the rise of streaming-video options, the multitude of types of e-readers, and the acceptance of the Open Access model for scholarship. As the formats and methods of e-content delivery continue to change, we are presented with an excellent opportunity for marketing.

Everybody knows the library is the place to come to ask questions, often about new technology gadgets or things they've heard about in the local news but about which they would like to know more. As your collection grows with new types and formats of e-resources, consider it as an opportunity to connect with your patrons in a way you haven't done so before. When librarians talk about libraries "being relevant," that's really what we mean; we, and our libraries, are a part of our patrons' lives, adapting and flourishing right alongside them.

Marketing Makes Your Patrons Smarter

If your library's mission is to create a patron experience that leaves patrons satisfied and empowered, then developing a marketing plan is right up your alley. Marketing is a way to share knowledge; it synthesizes information into a gift for your patrons to open and use immediately. Through marketing, your patrons will learn which e-resources are right for their information needs, getting them to where they want to be, faster. There are innate advantages to using electronic resources, such as the convenience of finding resources at one site (a computer terminal or mobile device), the possibility of accessing the content from outside the library, and so forth, which can be

For Further Information

If you would like to look at an example of the inner workings of a marketing team in a library setting, check out the minutes of the Rutgers University Libraries Marketing/PR Team at www. libraries.rutgers.edu/rul/staff/ groups/marketing-pr/minutes.shtml. You'll find that the Rutgers team members have been working since 2007 on the topic of marketing and promotion, and their experience may give you some guidance on how to develop your own team and meeting agendas.

satisfying and empowering. Depending on the expertise of your patrons, a simple communication plan to bolster confidence in using the technology of electronic resources may be enough to situate them for marketing for a particular e-resource.

Pursuing a marketing plan for your library's e-resources can create purposeful users of those resources because it educates patrons about why they should choose one over another and what benefit they can gain from using this one over that. Marketing communicates that you understand the value of the resources your library has, and you are passing on that value to your patrons.

The focus of this book is on patron-centered marketing, which is considered "the current best practice and undoubtedly the future of marketing" (McDonald and Wilson 2002, 222). The rest of this book will guide you through the components of a marketing plan, with special attention paid to getting to know your patrons as well as to assessing your marketing attempts in order to know if your marketing is satisfying their needs. The next chapter, chapter 2, is where you'll begin to synthesize what you already know about your patrons, and you'll get some guidance about what to do in order to discover more about them and their use of your library's e-resources.

Gather the Troops

We've said here that marketing works best as a team, and you may be asking yourself who should be directing that team. Who needs to be at the leadership table for your e-resources marketing plan to work? Studies have shown that the ideal working group size for a project like this is five or six people; any more than this and the productivity per person wanes. If your ultimate goal is for everyone in the library to be involved in the marketing plan, then your ideal marketing leadership team would be composed of the people who are the most connected to others in your library; their connectedness to others provides an instantaneous communication stream to most staff. Your marketing leadership team is the group that will work most closely with you in developing your library's marketing plan, and as a practicality, the team will be composed of people who have time to commit to the task or have marketing or outreach as part of their job descriptions.

When people are invited to collaborate on a process—to help make decisions from the outset of a project—the more invested in a successful outcome they will be. It is in your best interest, therefore, to develop your team early. Metz-Wiseman and Rodgers (2007), who describe their marketing leadership team development process at the University of South Florida in detail, found that "the team approach, with a combination of librarians and support staff, allowed for engagement at all levels" (22). Their team was self-selected, and members served five-year terms; they called themselves the Marketing Team. They found that the "task of a focused, intense, continuous marketing program could not be sustained beyond five years with a dedicated group of volunteers" and noted that team members dropped out after their initial five-year term (Metz-Wiseman and Rodgers 2007, 23). When constructing your own team, keep this in mind as you seek volunteers and perhaps limit the length of time that your team will devote to leading the marketing. You can read more about sensitivity to time management in the next chapter (see Action Plan, in the Components of a Marketing Plan section).

We love the idea Carol Anne Germain (2012) discussed in her article about putting together a whole marketing group just to highlight her library's movie collections. In the article, she suggested throwing a "movie brainstorming party" and inviting "students, bibliographers, and other individuals who have expressed interest in movies and your collection" (172). She proposed that this group of enthusiasts would likely brainstorm a relevant list of marketing strategies she could then implement to promote the use of the film resources.

Are you wondering about the potential composition and membership of your marketing team? Below is an example from Gumberg Library at Duquesne University regarding the organization of its current Electronic Resources Review Committee (ERRC). We especially like the diversity in type of librarian represented on the committee; it appears to be designed to maximize a range of perspectives in regard to marketing.

ELECTRONIC RESOURCES REVIEW COMMITTEE (ERRC)

Charge

In an effort to build and maintain a collection of electronic resources that supports the academic and research needs of the students, faculty, and staff of Duquesne University, the Electronic Resources Review Committee (ERRC) will investigate, discuss, develop, and propose strategies related to the use and management of electronic resources, including current subscriptions, requests for new purchases, and cancellations. The ERRC may also conduct research on commercially available digital products and related systems and investigate requests for print as well as electronic journals. The ERRC will establish criteria for evaluating titles for the purposes of continuance or cancellation. This group should consult with stakeholders, including liaisons and faculty, documenting recommendations made to the University Librarian.

Composition

The committee will be made up of the Electronic Resources and Discovery Librarian, who will chair the committee; the Head of Collection Management; the Acquisitions Librarian; the Outreach and Communications Librarian, and up to two (2) additional faculty librarians. Liaison Librarians will be consulted when resources directly relating to their liaison departments are considered for purchase or cancellation.

Membership

Charlotte Myers, chair—Electronic Resources and Discovery Librarian

Tracie Ballock—Head of Collection Management

Kirsten Ostergaard—Acquisitions Librarian

Christie Kliewer—Outreach and Communications Librarian

David Nolfi—Health Sciences and Assessment Librarian

Gesina Phillips—Digital Scholarship Librarian

Meeting Schedule

Meetings will happen about once a month, with additional meetings called as necessary. Periodically the group will report to and/or consult with the Liaison Librarians in an effort to both disseminate and gather information.

Previous incarnations of the ERRC have presented at a conference about the development of their organizational structure; the presentation slides are available at https://smartech.gatech.edu/handle/1853/10400.

As you pull your team together, use the library's mission statement as an organizing principle. We know that successful marketing campaigns are part of a larger marketing plan or institutional mission (Duke and Tucker 2007; Kotler and Levy 1969). Woods (2007) notes, "A good marketing plan should be based on the library's mission statement, strategic goals and initiatives" (108). Kennedy (2010), however, discovered that less than one-third of libraries reported their e-resource marketing campaigns as part of a larger marketing plan. With this in mind, review the library's mission before you gather your team and begin your marketing plan in order to increase the chances for success.

The elements of the marketing plan outlined in the next chapter will keep your marketing plan aligned with the other activities of your library. The process of developing a marketing plan will take some time, so proceed with patience. Calkins (2008) notes, "It would be nice if you could simply sit down and, in a few hours, develop a marketing plan that would lead to guaranteed great results. Unfortunately, this is not the way things go" (70). The good news is that you have a team to work with you, which makes all the difference. With your troops gathered and your library's mission in mind, you are ready to begin developing your marketing plan for electronic resources.

References

Brannon, Sian. 2007. "A Successful Promotional Campaign—We Can't Keep Quiet about Our Electronic Resources." *The Serials Librarian* 53 (3): 41–55.

Calkins, Tim. 2008. *Breakthrough Marketing Plans: How to Stop Wasting Time and Start Driving Growth.* New York: Palgrave Macmillan.

COUNTER. 2017. "The COUNTER Code of Practice." Accessed April 17. www.projectcounter.org/code-of-practice-sections/general -information.

Davidson, Karen S., Stephanie H. Rollins, and Ed Cherry. 2013. "Demonstrating Our Value: Tying Use of E-resources to Academic Success." *Serials Librarian* 65 (1): 74–79.

Dillon, Dennis. 2003. "Strategic Marketing of Electronic Resources." *The Acquisitions Librarian* 14 (28): 117–34.

Dubicki, Eleonora. 2007. "Basic Marketing and Promotion Concepts." *The Serials Librarian* 53 (3): 5–15.

Duke, Lynda M., and Toni Tucker. 2007. "How to Develop a Marketing Plan for an Academic Library." *Technical Services Quarterly* 25 (1): 51–68.

Germain, Carol Anne. 2012. "'Reel' Marketing for Your Movie Collections and Film Resources." *Public Services Quarterly* 8 (2): 171–7.

Kennedy, Marie R. 2010. "Cycling Through: Paths Libraries Take to Marketing Electronic Resources." Paper presented at the Library Assessment Conference, Baltimore, MD, October 27. http://digitalcommons.lmu.edu/librarian_pubs/3.

Kotler, Philip, and Sidney J. Levy. 1969. "Broadening the Concept of Marketing." *The Journal of Marketing* 33 (1): 10–15.

McDonald, Malcolm, and Hugh Wilson. 2002. *The New Marketing: Transforming the Corporate Future.* Oxford: Butterworth-Heinemann.

Metz-Wiseman, Monica, and Skye L. Rodgers. 2007. "Thinking Outside of the Library Box." *The Serials Librarian* 53 (3): 17–39.

NISO (National Information Standards Organization). 2017. "Standardized Usage Statistics Harvesting Initiative (SUSHI) Protocol (ANSI/NISO Z39.93–2014)." Accessed April 17. www.niso.org/workrooms/sushi/.

Samson, Sue. 2014. "Usage of E-resources: Virtual Value of Demographics." *The Journal of Academic Librarianship* 40 (6): 620–5.

Stone, Graham, and Bryony Ramsden. 2013. "Library Impact Data Project: Looking for the Link between Library Usage and Student Attainment." *College and Research Libraries* 74 (6): 546–59.

Woods, Shelley L. 2007. "A Three-Step Approach to Marketing Electronic Resources at Brock University." *The Serials Librarian* 53 (3): 107–24.

Fashion Your Marketing Plan

This chapter introduces you to nine components of a marketing plan for electronic resources. There are different ways to approach marketing, quickly evident in the results of any web browser search. The components presented here are an amalgam of those most often used in marketing. In today's competitive world for library monies, we think it is especially important to be deliberate and transparent about your marketing in the evaluation process. To highlight the dual aspects of the component usually called "evaluation"—measurement and assessment—we discuss them separately.

This chapter outlines what to be thinking about during each phase and what action needs to be completed to address each component. You will notice that each component leads to the next, creating a cycle. We suggest you read this chapter through to get a sense of the scope of work for each component. Then read through chapter 3, where we show how libraries have made decisions at each of the steps. Armed with the information presented in this chapter (the "how-to"), coupled with the practical advice presented in chapter 3 (the "evidence"), we believe you will be well on your way to constructing an admirable plan for marketing your library's electronic resources.

Components of a Marketing Plan

The components of a marketing plan are usually visualized as a circle, beginning with *project description* as the first step and ending with *assessment* feeding back into *project description* as a new cycle of marketing begins. See figure 2.1 for a visual representation of the marketing cycle used in this book.

You can see from figure 2.1 that each component leads to the next. Having a clearly stated goal for a marketing plan should lead to choosing a strategy to achieve that goal, and identifying how to measure the strategy will ultimately tell a library if the campaign has helped to reach the goal. The

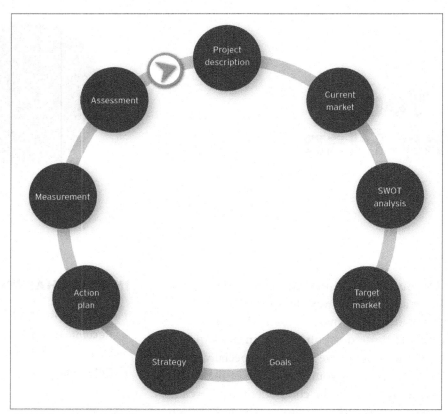

FIGURE 2.1　A Marketing Cycle

TABLE 2.1　Marketing Cycle Components and Definitions

COMPONENT	DEFINITION
Project description	Describes the thinking behind why the library embarked on a marketing campaign
Current market	Notes if a resource is currently being used and what other products are like it; also describes the environment in which it is used
SWOT analysis	Identifies strengths, weaknesses, opportunities, and threats that the library has as a result of this resource
Target market	Identifies the user group(s) that will be the focus of the marketing
Goal(s)	Explains what the library hopes to gain by marketing
Strategies	Identifies the approach(es) to achieve the goal(s); also decides which marketing techniques are appropriate for the stated goal(s) and how their use will be measured
Action plan	States how the strategies will be carried out (This code is not used itself but rather is comprised of timeline, staff, and budget.)
Timeline	How long the marketing campaign will run or how long each component of the plan will take
Staff	Who will work on the marketing campaign
Budget	How much money the marketing campaign will use
Measurement	Determines the degree to which the strategies achieved the stated goal(s)
Assessment	Determines if the measurement of the strategies provides enough evidence to take the next step in the marketing cycle

next sections of this chapter will guide you through each of the components in the cycle, directing you to gather data or consider something about your library's environment. See table 2.1 for a description of what each component of the marketing plan will contain. Before you begin working with your team, we suggest that you read through all the components on your own first to determine what you can accomplish yourself and what help you will need from your team. Make notes in the margins of this book as you move through to identify the components you'll need help with or want to be sure to address in your own marketing plan.

As you and your team move through each of the components, take notes throughout the process. If you write on a whiteboard, photograph the board or transcribe the content at the end of your meetings. If someone on your team is charged with note taking, save those notes in a shared space accessible to all team members. You will later use all of the brainstorming and thinking that you do during the components of developing your marketing plan when you construct the written report for your library's administration or stakeholders. If you prefer to get yourself organized at the outset, download the blank template for the marketing plan report that comes with this book from www.alaeditions.org/webextras. Chapter 3 provides examples of each of the components as well as guidance in what to do and what to avoid at each step.

Project Description

The first step in developing a marketing plan is to externalize your reasons for wanting to market your e-resources. You and your team likely have already been mulling over why you want to communicate with your patrons about e-resources, and this first step is an attempt to put all of those thoughts down on paper so that you are organized and in agreement about why you're launching a marketing plan.

In the project description you will identify four things: why you want to market your e-resources; what is needed to accomplish your plan; how much the plan will cost; and how long the plan will take to complete. At this point in the development of your marketing plan, you will be able to address firmly only the first part of the description, the "why." As you develop the other components, you will return to revise the project description, but from the beginning, you should be as clear as you can about the "why." Identifying the reason(s) why you want to market your e-resources will help to define the rest of your marketing plan, so be thoughtful about the process. If you need to convince anyone at your library that your e-resources need to have a marketing plan, the project description is your selling point. Imagine your library director stepping onto the elevator with you right as the doors are closing. She turns to you and asks, "What's this I hear about your proposing a marketing plan?" Now's your moment! You have ten seconds to respond, before the elevator arrives at the director's floor. You respond, "Yes, we need to market our electronic resources in order to [insert your "why" here]."

Brannon (2007) demonstrates the impetus for her library to embark on developing a marketing plan:

> After double-checking the statistics on the library's fifty databases, and looking at three or four years' worth of data, I saw the overall trend was that the numbers were heading down, slowly and surely. I knew to expect certain periods of low-usage. Summer months rarely yield high statistics for electronic resources; December is also traditionally low. The library's other statistics were great: circulation was high, door counts were up, and reference transactions were rising. The time had come to pay attention to our databases. (42)

You can see that Brannon is concerned that use of the subscription databases is trending down. You would expect, then, that her library's reason for wanting to develop a marketing plan is to reverse the trend and increase use. The stated reason for why your library is embarking on a marketing plan can be as simple as this.

Current Market

Identifying whom your library serves, what your library provides, and how your library currently provides services is an essential step of describing your current market. A "market" in this case can be considered your setting, so this step describes your library's current environment. This step is sometimes referred to as an "environmental scan" and answers these six questions: Who are our library patrons? Where is our library? What are the information concerns of our library patrons? How are we currently serving those information needs? What are our current electronic resources? Where are our electronic resources? Put together, describing your current market answers this question: Who are we serving?

Lee (2003) asserts that understanding the current market is the essential step in a marketing plan and describes a formal process for gathering information about the needs of the patrons. She suggests that "laying the marketing foundation" by knowing what library patrons want will help to guide a library in choosing an appropriate strategy. Identifying the current market can be described as "pre-marketing" because when you are completing this step, the marketing goals don't come into the picture. Instead, during pre-marketing the library focuses on taking an objective look at the library the way it exists at this moment.

Who Are Our Library's Patrons?

Describing your current market can be a simple data-gathering step, perfect for those of you who like to make lists. You've probably got the answers to most of these questions already. Focusing first on the question of who your library patrons are, your ILS (integrated library system) will tell you how many active patron records you have, and you likely have a gate count for patron visits. You may have "hit" statistics for your library webpages to tell you how many times your website is being visited and which pages are visited most often. Do you include demographic information about your patrons in your library's annual report? Where else do you already have stored information about your library patrons?

We tend to define the current market based on user "clusters," that is, types of patrons who fall into natural categories. In chapter 1 we mentioned young adult patrons, which describes a group of library users with similar characteristics of age, social interests, and so forth. There may be clusters you haven't considered, such as hobby clusters, research interest clusters, and kind-of-book clusters. This type of user segmentation may allow for customized communications. When you connect with groups in a positive way, they are likely to share the goodwill they feel toward you with their friends; this supplements the library's marketing efforts by enlisting patrons' "word-of-mouth marketing."

According to an OCLC (2010) report, library patrons are changing quickly, demonstrating dramatic shifts in use of electronic resources in the years since the report was initially published. In the category "use of e-journals" alone, teens (aged fourteen to seventeen years) decreased their use of e-journals from 35 to 20 percent between 2005 and 2010 (a 28 percent decrease), while in that same time frame young adults (aged eighteen to twenty-four years) increased their use of e-journals from 24 to 38 percent (a 58 percent increase). The demonstration of such a difference in the use of e-journals by patron type reaffirms the notion that your "current market" of today will not be your "current market" of tomorrow.

Where Is Our Library?

Your library obviously doesn't exist in a vacuum but rather is put in context with its location relevant to its surroundings. Where it is situated can tell you a lot about your current market. Are you the only library within 100 miles? Are you in the middle of a college campus? Are you housed in an elementary school or perhaps in an office within a law firm? Is your library in an urban or rural area? How is your library funded—by the county or city or privately?

What Are the Information Concerns of Our Library's Patrons?

To answer this question, you should head to your Information Commons to ask for reference desk consultation statistics. Does your reference staff gather data on the kinds of questions being asked? Can you identify the methods your patrons use to ask questions—via IM chat, text messaging, or e-mail, in person, or on the phone? Does your federated search or discovery service software provide you with a list of keywords that your patrons type into the main search box? Perhaps your ILS provides the keyword, subject, or title searches your patrons perform in your online catalog? Does your Google Analytics account show you how many times your patrons check your library website's "Get Help" or "FAQ" page?

We discussed usage statistics in chapter 1, and here is another place they come in handy. What are the top fifty e-resources your patrons use? If the top ten are all current online newspapers, for example, then this may tell you that your library patrons are concerned with getting the most recent information on a variety of worldly topics. If the top ten are all science journals, then this may tell you that your library patrons are concerned with information about a variety of scientific topics. The point we are trying to make here is that your existing usage statistics can tell you a lot about the current market in your library by helping you to identify the information concerns of your patrons.

How Are We Currently Serving Those Information Needs?

Can you identify the ways you are currently serving information needs? This should be a fun process, identifying all of the ways your library conveys information to your patrons. Does your library have a public website? Is your catalog online? Do you create customized webpages for particular topics of interest? Does your library have a blog? How about a newsletter (print or e-mail)? Do you have a staffed information desk? Do patrons instead ask for information at the circulation desk? Are your service points staffed with people who speak the primary language(s) of your patron population? How many directional or informational signs are in your library? If you have a public website, does it have a frequently asked questions page? Is the telephone number or e-mail address listed on the webpage?

Because methods of electronic communication are so pervasive, you might assume that everyone knows how to use computers efficiently for their information needs. According to the ERIAL (Ethnographic Research in Illinois Academic Libraries) Project, however, not even current university students are efficient searchers for research information (Kolowich 2011). If the group you would expect to be the most technologically savvy isn't, what might this say about your other library patron populations? There may be barriers to getting to electronic information that you would not expect, and assessing patrons' technological competence through observation, as described in the ERIAL Project (www.erialproject.org), is one way to discover if what you think you know about how you are serving your patrons via e-resources is actually true.

In an electronic environment, accessibility and usability are real issues. There's the physical accessibility issue of how a patron maneuvers himself or herself to a computer terminal to use electronic resources. How does your library provide access to patrons who have physical limitations or challenges? Then there's the content accessibility issue of how a publisher has designed the user interface for its resource. Has the resource been configured so that it is compatible with screen-reading software, or does the publisher offer a large-print or text-to-audio feature? Libraries need to consider if they are equitably serving their entire patron population, and the way we provide access to electronic resources is part of that consideration.

What Are Our Current Electronic Resources?

Another thing to identify about your current market is easy: List all of the electronic resources your library makes available. How many of those are databases, how many are e-journals, and how many are e-books? Do you offer audiobooks, music download options, or streaming videos? It is likely that you already include this kind of data in an annual report, so this is a perfect reuse of that data. It tells you how big your collection is and how diverse it is by type and subject area.

You could take this a step further and consider how many resources would be appropriate for each of your patron "clusters" (kinds of user groups). Could you map the list you made of your patron types to each of your resources? Might you discover that you've got loads of e-resources for your entry-level medical students, for example, but have just a few that would satisfy the continuing educational needs of your practicing doctor population? Food for thought!

Where Are Our Electronic Resources?

The last piece to identify about your current market gives you another opportunity to make a list: Where are all of your library's electronic resources mentioned? The answer to this question may seem silly or obvious: "Everywhere!" But where, specifically?

Within the library, in one-on-one interactions is a good place to begin thinking about the answer to this question. Your instruction librarians surely mention electronic resources during learning sessions with students, but which resources do they mention? Do they mention the same resources in each learning session, or do they mention different ones depending on the session? Are there instruction librarians who mention more resources than others? Do they tend to mention one resource along with another resource, like a suite of resources for students to use? At service points is another likely place the library's electronic resources are discussed. Do your Information Commons desk staff keep track of the questions asked and which resources are mentioned in response? How about at other service points in the library? Do your Circulation desk or Special Collections front desk staff ever get questions from patrons about e-resources?

Within the library, linked from management systems is another good source for you to consider. Does your library have a federated search or discovery layer? If so, are your electronic resources listed there? How about an e-resource portal or A–Z list? Does your library use the LibGuides service? Which electronic resources are mentioned in your LibGuides? Are there e-resources to which your library subscribes that are *not* mentioned in a LibGuide? Has your library established a link via Google Scholar to get your patrons connected to library content when they conduct a Google Scholar search? Do you have other systems in place that connect with your library's e-resources?

Outside of the library is another location to think about in terms of where your e-resources may be lurking. Does your college have a learning management system? Often faculty will link to articles or e-books they want their students to read. If you work in a research environment, there may be lab assistants out there who are building a collection of links to your electronic resources that the research team uses for ready reference. Maybe your community writing center maintains a list of your library's e-thesauri and language dictionaries for its writers to use.

Thinking about all the places your library's electronic resources are linked to or mentioned is exhilarating, isn't it? Those resources are deeply embedded in your community, and this step of listing them can make you really appreciate those connections (or possible future connections).

SWOT Analysis

SWOT is an acronym for a process of evaluating strengths, weaknesses, opportunities, and threats. A SWOT analysis sounds like an intimidating thing to do, but you're doing parts of it already. How many times have you quietly cheered to yourself when a patron said, "Thanks for helping me to find the article that saved my research," or when you made a mental note to talk to the collection development librarian because you noticed that your e-collection seems to have some overlap in content? You're evaluating all the time, and a SWOT analysis simply formalizes that process. A SWOT analysis has two parts, internal factors and external factors. This analysis is designed to help answer the question, "What is helping us or getting in our way as we strive for our goal?"

Identifying these factors may seem subjective, and we agree that it is. We have already discussed why you will want a team to design your marketing plan, and this step is an illustration of why that is so. In addition to developing the analysis with your team, you may want to put together a brown-bag lunch session and brainstorm a SWOT list with all of your library staff so that you consider many perspectives. De Saez (2002) suggests completing your SWOT analysis in consultation with service staff because "[t]he gap in perceptions between senior managers and their staff as to what are strengths and what are weaknesses will usually surprise the staff less than the managers and emphasizes the need for collective ownership of the marketing effort through internal communication" (40). Performing a SWOT analysis may be intimidating because your team will be identifying weaknesses and threats. Depending on your library culture, instead of brainstorming in person with your library staff, you may choose to have them contribute to this analysis anonymously to get reliable data. You know best how your library will respond to a process like this.

Internal Factors

Examine internal factors to identify strengths and weaknesses of your library's environment related to electronic resources. As well as identifying the strengths and weaknesses from your own perspective, imagine what your patrons would consider your strengths and weaknesses to be. Better yet, rather than simply imagining what your patrons think, this is an ideal time to run patron focus groups to learn how much they know about your library's e-resources and how they came to find out about them; then you can incorporate these findings into the strengths and weaknesses wherever they apply.

When thinking about the strengths and weaknesses of the environment of your library, you may wish to consider the following topics and prompting questions as related to electronic resources:

Library culture: What would you say are the strengths and weaknesses of electronic resources in your library culture? Are electronic resources well used and accepted as part of your library collection, or are you still building support for their use?

Key staff: What are the strengths and weaknesses of your key staff related to electronic resources? Do you have a champion/cheerleader on your staff who always mentions e-resources to patrons or has particular expertise in instruction? Is that one staff person the only one in your library who is comfortable using e-resources? Ask your staff whom they go to for help if they have a problem with an e-resource; the person most frequently named is likely a "key" staff person.

Training: How are staff members currently educated in the use of e-resources? How does their training translate to the education of patrons in their use of e-resources?

Organizational structure: Do e-resources have a strong presence in the organizational structure of your library, or is the management of e-resources dispersed among many (or few) library staff? What would you say are the strengths or weaknesses about this structure at your library?

Financial resources: Is your library making appropriate allocations of funds for e-resources? Have you had to make any cuts to subscriptions or purchases of e-content in the past few years, or is your library spending more money recently on e-content?

Brand awareness: When patrons think of your library, do they think "e-resources"? Are e-resources linked from your library homepage or are they tucked away, several clicks from the main library webpage? Does your e-resource portal have a special name?

Innovation: Where is your library on the spectrum of innovation? Are you using mainly commercial products to manage the content of the e-collection, or are you using any open-source tools? Is your library bleeding edge or cautious? Do you employ a computer programmer? Do your staff tend to use computers to do their daily tasks, or are they more comfortable using notepads and pencils? Does your team view this as a strength or a weakness?

Collection: Is your e-resource collection centralized in one academic area? Does it focus heavily on only one patron group, or does it have something for everyone? Is there an e-collection that your library is known for? How much usage does it get? How many of what types of resources are used? Electronic resources are linked data. From where are yours currently linked—LibGuides, library website, other? Are they each linked to equally, or is one of your databases the go-to electronic resource when you're doing instruction?

Data structures: Does your library effectively use the electronic resources it has? Do your patrons have to hunt through webpages to find them, or are they displayed in a prominent place? Do you have a service quality feedback mechanism in place for patrons to report problems they encounter with your library's e-resources, like a "Report a Problem" form they can complete or a posted phone number to call?

You may want to address some of the these questions with your focus groups, especially the following: "Are electronic resources well used and accepted as part of your library collection, or are you still building support for their use?"; "Do your patrons have to hunt through webpages to find them, or are they displayed in a prominent place?"; and "Do you have a service quality feedback mechanism in place for patrons to report problems they encounter with your library's e-resources, like a 'Report a Problem' form they can complete or a posted phone number to call?" If you ask your patrons, they will almost certainly be happy to tell you what they perceive the library's strengths and weaknesses are in the area of e-resources. We have provided a book for you to read about how to design focus groups in the Recommended Resources section of this chapter.

External Factors

Examine external factors to identify opportunities and threats to your library's environment. External factors are issues that arise outside of your library's immediate environment that have an impact on how it does business.

When thinking about opportunities and threats to the environment of your library, you may wish to consider the following topics and prompting questions as related to electronic resources:

Technological change: Is your library well poised and eager to address changes in the technology related to e-resources? If a hot, new technology arose today would your library budget enable you to take advantage of it?

Patrons: Are your patrons eager to use your e-resources? Are they technologically savvy? Do they have their own e-devices like e-readers, smartphones, and laptop computers? Does your Information Desk staff get questions from your patrons about e-devices, or are they confident users of those tools without staff help? Is there a potential patron group that doesn't yet know about your fabulous collection of genealogy databases?

Competitors: What other organizations in your community provide access to electronic resources? Are there places your patrons go for information other than your library? What other electronic resources are your patrons using that might compete with resources your library subscribes to or owns? How do those other e-resources compare to yours? Does your library's e-resource collection stand out in a way that another organization's does not?

Library trends: What are the big issues and trends facing libraries as related to e-resources? Is your library a trend setter or a trend follower?

Vendors/suppliers: Are your library's vendors and suppliers of electronic information keeping up with the times? Are they innovators themselves? Which is your library's strongest partner, and how is that vendor viewed in the marketplace as a whole? Do your library vendors/suppliers know your staff on a first-name basis? Are your library vendors designing interfaces to content that are fairly accessible to all of your library patrons? Do their products work with assistive devices like screen readers?

Sociological changes: As society changes, does your library change with it? Is the electronic resource you subscribed to five years ago still relevant for your patron population of today? If a patron had an information need based on what he or she read in the newspaper headlines today, would your e-collection have that material?

Changes in research areas and hobby interests: Depending on the population your library serves, is your collection in tune with today's current hot fads? Perhaps instead it has a solid, classic collection?

A SWOT analysis is often viewed in a 2 × 2 matrix format, which helps you see all of the analysis at one time. This analysis, once past the brainstorming stage, should result in a bulleted list of five or six key points, as demonstrated in figure 2.2. Synthesizing what is likely to be a complex discussion into a simple matrix may seem superficial, but identifying your library's key strengths, weaknesses, opportunities, and threats is helpful for getting all involved on the same page.

There are models of assessment other than SWOT, such as the PEST (with a focus on the *political*, *economic*, *social*, and *technological* aspects), STEEP (with a focus on the *social*, *technological*, *economic*, *ecological*, and *political* aspects) (Bensoussan and Fleisher 2012), TOWS (a variation on the SWOT analysis, focusing on *threats*, *opportunities*, *weaknesses*, and *strengths*), and Porter's five forces analysis (Porter 2008). Feel free to consider the other models if you're not fond of the SWOT analysis. We have highlighted it here because it is common to see SWOT used in a library

Free SWOT Template

If you would like to download a SWOT template to help organize your points, we recommend using the web-based, free template at Gliffy (www.gliffy.com/uses/swot -analysis-software).

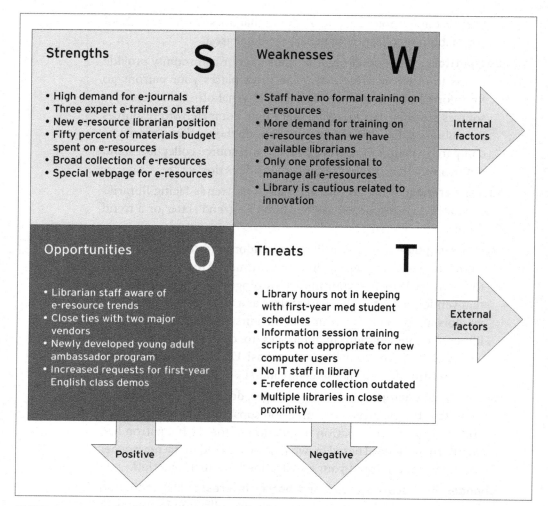

FIGURE 2.2   Example SWOT Analysis for a Library

environment. The goal of using a model of situational analysis like SWOT is to call attention to the environment in which your marketing plan will exist. Conducting an analysis like this will identify a lot of factors that a marketing plan will not be able to address, and that's okay. Understanding your library environment helps you to be realistic about what a marketing plan for e-resources can accomplish.

Target Market

In the earlier discussion about describing your current market we talked about identifying your library patrons by similar characteristics, grouping them into "clusters." This kind of grouping by age, social interests, education level, and so forth, helps to identify the kinds of people who use your library. It can be challenging, however, to identify clusters you may not have considered before, like hobby clusters, research interest clusters, and type-of-book clusters. Teens may be the obvious cluster to be interested in your online music collection, for example, but might you have a potential adult cluster that you haven't thought of trying to reach yet? The rise of maker-spaces in libraries calls attention to a cluster of people who prefer to create things on their own rather than rely on commercial solutions. Could this group have information needs that could be assisted by library e-resources? Do you annually welcome a new group of scientists to your institution that would benefit from having group instruction on a database you know they will need to use in their new jobs? Here is one more example of a possible cluster, or group, of patrons in an educational setting: Your student population is the apparent target for instruction sessions on using e-resources for course-related research, but might you have had a request or two from campus office staff to have instruction on the same resources even though their interests aren't course related?

Let's put some of this theorizing into practice with a brief exercise that will help you identify your target market. Make a list of all of your possible audiences for e-resources. When the list is complete (it's a long list, we'd bet, once you consider all the possibilities), rank your potential clusters by priority based on which group your library wants to reach first. Figuring out which group to address first is entirely up to you. You may decide that you want to reach as many people as possible and so will opt to prioritize a cluster you know is large in size, or you may decide that a small group of patrons you are already working with is the best group with which to begin your marketing. As you think through the options, one group will likely rise to the top of your list. This top-ranked group will become your target market, and for the rest of the marketing plan, this is the only group you'll be thinking about.

Let us assume for the moment that you decide that your library really needs to communicate with the first-year medical students on campus because the key e-resource they have to use just underwent a major interface change over the summer. How will you best communicate about the change to that group? You may ask yourself how well you actually know the first-year medical students as a group. You may know a few things, like the number of students who were admitted, but you may not have a clue about their backgrounds, technological capabilities, or even what style of communication methods they prefer. You can find out about them using both direct and indirect methods, with formal and informal approaches.

The descriptions and examples presented here are quite abbreviated, just to give you a sense of the range of possible formal methods for learning about your target group. In addition, we highlight some informal methods so that you can decide which approach best suits your needs. Perhaps you would benefit from a blend of both formal and informal approaches? See the Recommended Resources for Further Reading section at the end of this chapter for more suggestions on each of these methods.

Formal Approaches

CASE STUDIES

A case study recounts the factual details of a situation in order to objectively review actual behaviors of patrons in a setting. To use a case study to learn about patron use of e-resources, for example, one could put together a list of e-resources and ask a patron to find them on your library website. You would sit and record the patron's actions, or videotape the patron, or ask him or her to talk aloud while finding the resources. After you complete a few cases, review them for similarities of retrieval, for how patrons talk about their finding processes, and so forth.

SURVEYS

A survey is a series of questions given to patrons with a request to respond to each in order to gather feedback or information on a given topic. The same task as mentioned in Case Studies can be done via a survey, although the resulting information would be self-reported in a survey rather than viewed objectively by the person recording the actions in a case study.

PARTICIPANT OBSERVATION

The idea behind participant observation is that the person seeking information about a group takes a dual role, one as a member of the group (or plays a role in the group) and one as the outside observer. We can again use the e-resource finding task for this method, where the librarian (or the person charged with learning about the student population) is also an actual student and is therefore able to observe others doing the finding task as well as performing the task himself or herself.

COHORT STUDIES

A group of people with similar characteristics (usually age- or time-based characteristics) that move through a phase together are said to be a cohort, and longitudinal studies that examine external effects on a cohort over time are popular. If we use the e-resource finding task in a cohort study, we would examine how first-year students perform the task compared to second-year students, compared to third-year students, and so forth.

FOCUS GROUPS

A focus group is composed of a facilitator and an invited selection of people who meet to discuss a predefined topic. In using focus groups for e-resource marketing, a selection of participants from your target audience of researchers, using the e-resource finding task and a series of prompting questions from the facilitator, can reveal how your patrons go about finding your e-resources (or not finding them), what they know about shortcuts (if any), and tips—or criticisms—they have heard from others.

For Further Information

To stay up-to-date with the population's interaction with the Internet as a whole, read through the website of the Pew Internet and American Life Project (www.pewinternet.org).

Informal Approaches

With the rise of social networking sites like Facebook, Twitter, Instagram, and Pinterest, libraries have novel mechanisms for learning about their patrons. You can choose to approach the use of sites like these as broadcast tools, to share information about programs or updates to building hours or even to note a link to a new electronic resource added to the collection. This approach is practical but rather one-sided, and the posts to those sites may end up acting as "noise" in your patrons' busy lives—just another attempt to get attention. Another approach to the use of such sites is as an informal listening and conversation tool, a chance to get to learn about your patrons in a low-risk, unscripted way.

In their 2012 article, David and Sagun highlight a marketing strategy that includes, in addition to the traditional "e-mail blasts," the "use of social networking sites (Facebook and Twitter) to make announcements and *receive feedback from students*" (295; emphasis added). An unplanned success from their marketing strategy was the development of a book club "by the students whose attention[s] were caught because of the marketing and promotion activities targeted at the students" (295). That David and Sagun were willing to create a book club to respond to specific patron feedback, even though that was not their intent in marketing, is powerful, and it points to communication—that is, being open to responding to what your patrons tell you is important—as a key component of marketing.

While we have noted that social media sites can be used as an informal way to know your patrons, this doesn't mean the use is not strategic. In their excellent study, Young and Rossmann (2015) demonstrate that by evaluating their Twitter activity over the course of five years, they were able to categorize the types of users following/replying to their library Twitter account and the kinds of resulting interactions. Not surprising, given their academic community, the tweets receiving the most interactions (defined as those that were marked as a "favorite," retweeted, or replied to) were about student life and local community. By figuring out what the Montana State University Twitter users care about, their library is better poised to support the relationships they are building through that communication mechanism. In an intentional decision to participate in those relationships, the library now tweets about the topics that its patrons care most about. Young and Rossmann (2015) comment, "As library social media practice advances within the framework of community, it moves from a one-dimensional online broadcast platform to a multidimensional socially connected space that creates value for both the library and library users" (22).

■ ■ ■

Using a variety of these formal and informal methods, designed to spark communication, will keep you in touch with your patrons. The characteristics of your target group will change over time, so your marketing plan will always need to be flexible to account for this.

A benefit of learning about your target group of patrons is that you get to understand what is important to them, what kinds of things they like, and how they prefer to hear from the library. In your marketing, you can show them what you've learned. When choosing images for your marketing materials, for example, Ramsey (2014) suggests, "Make sure you're considering the diversity of your users when choosing images. By seeing themselves depicted in library marketing, patrons may feel more comfortable in your library" (81). At Ramsey's library, while putting together marketing materials to celebrate Elvis week, they chose an image of an Elvis impersonator who looked like one of the university's undergraduate students. This is a savvy approach to relaying to your target group that you "get" them.

If you like thinking about potential ways to know your patrons, we suggest you read chapter 2, "Understanding Users of Online Resources," in Curtis and Scheschy's (2005) library-focused book. In that chapter, the authors discuss the pros and cons of some of the methods mentioned here as well as alternatives to these methods.

Goals

Assuming your library has already defined for itself what its mission is, what its core ideology is, the goals for your marketing efforts related to electronic resources should align themselves with that larger mission. Collins and Porras (1996) visualize this alignment as the yin-yang symbol, with "core ideology" in one half and "envisioned future" in the other. They suggest defining your goals as an "envisioned future," which consists of two parts: a long-term goal plus "vivid descriptions of what it will be like to achieve the goal" (Collins and Porras 1996, 73). They say that the description should be "vibrant, engaging, and specific" so that the goal is easily conveyed to others and they are equally energized by the possibility. "The envisioned future should be so exciting in its own right that it would continue to keep the organization motivated even if the leaders who set the goal disappeared" (Collins and Porras 1996, 75).

If you had to define what the mission of your library's electronic resource program would be, what would you say? Defining the smaller mission (answering the questions, "Why do we have all of these electronic resources?" and "What do we hope we're doing for our patrons by having them?") in relation to the larger mission (the library's stated mission) can help to define the goals for marketing your library's electronic resources. In her book, Wallace (2004) gives excellent guidance on writing a mission statement, tips that can easily be adapted to writing the goal(s) of your marketing plan for electronic resources. One of her most powerful tips is, "Be specific about what you aim to accomplish [and] limit yourself to three key points" (Wallace 2004, 15).

If you identify three key points for your goals, then one way to define those points is to think of them related to time. Imagine the third point as your destination, or what you hope to have accomplished by the time your marketing is complete. The first point will serve as a milestone on the way to your last point. The second point will serve as your midpoint milestone. Where do you want to be? Think big! Is it possible what you propose can be transformative for your library? Absolutely, especially if it means you're assisting your patrons in becoming smarter, confident users of your electronic content.

There is surely a predictive element to setting your goals. How do you know the goals are attainable? We're not suggesting that your goals surpass what you can reasonably achieve. Following along in the next steps of developing the marketing plan will define your path to the goals. If it turns out that as you develop the rest of your marketing plan you discover that the action plan, which includes a timeline, staff, and budget, won't allow your goals to be realized, come back to this step and redefine your goals.

It will help you in the goals component of your marketing plan to be as specific as you can because in the future measurement component of the plan you will be prompted to develop a plan to measure your goals. At that step, you will be advised not to proceed with a stated goal if it can't be measured. Goals can be measured in all kinds of ways, so, for the moment, just try to focus on defining goals that are specific.

Strategy

Now that you've identified which group of patrons is your priority for this marketing plan and you've decided what your goal is, the next step is to decide how you're going to communicate with the group. The communication mechanism may already be obvious to you, based on the sleuthing you've done about your group. In this component of the plan, you will identify appropriate communication techniques to use with your target group. All of the techniques you choose will complement one another to form a strategy.

The good news about this step is that your library already has multiple communication mechanisms in place, and you identified these when you went through the current market component of planning and thought about how your library is currently serving information needs. You'll need to decide at this step if you want to use an existing communication mechanism or if your target group will demand something new. Perhaps you know, for example, that for your public library's marketing plan the target group will be senior citizens, few of them have access at home to the Internet, and you've noticed they always stop to read the flyers posted on the bulletin board at the front door of the library when they come for their weekly book group meetings. Although your library typically communicates with patrons via e-mail, this group may require an eye-catching flyer to tell them about the series of training courses you're preparing for them on how to use your library's reliable health e-resources.

As you think about how to get the desired information to your target group, you may identify more than one technique. Kennedy (2011) found that most libraries used more than one technique; in fact, the medical libraries in her research reported using an average of 12.6 marketing techniques in their e-resource marketing plans. Because using multiple techniques is accepted, if you're a librarian on the marketing team for the previously mentioned library that is targeting senior citizens, consider doing more than just providing a flyer on the bulletin board. Ask the book group meeting leader to announce the series of classes, prompt your circulation staff to mention it as they check out books to seniors, slip a bookmark with the dates and times of the training courses onto the chairs in the book group meeting room, send e-mails to those seniors who do have Internet access at home, and so forth. The techniques you choose should complement one another to reinforce your message.

Are you wondering how other libraries perform this step and which techniques work the best? Unfortunately, there is not enough published information yet about the marketing of e-resources to be able to point to a particular strategy or grouping of techniques as a best practice to attain a favorable outcome. The identification of best practices in marketing for electronic resources is a goal for future collaboration opportunities in our field of information and library science. There is some limited published information about the techniques libraries have actually used in marketing their electronic resources, and you can read in chapter 3 about the techniques in use at college, medical, public, and university libraries. You will see that they all used multiple techniques but were not able to identify which of them was the most successful.

Later in the process of developing your marketing plan, you will be prompted to make decisions about which measurements to use to inform your team of its successes and failures. You may begin to consider them now when choosing your marketing strategy: (1) Is the strategy appropriate for the goal? (2) How will you measure parts of the strategy to know if your marketing plan is succeeding or failing? If you are part of the public library team mentioned earlier, a simple measurement would be to ask the seniors who attend the classes how they found out about them. You could give them a list of all the communication mechanisms you used (flyer, book group meeting leader announcement, bookmark, circulation desk mention, e-mail, etc.) and ask the seniors to identify which of these convinced them to attend the classes.

Before the Internet, options for marketing communications were limited. Now there are many more. Consider as many of them as you can! Buczynski (2007) notes that it is difficult for libraries to move away from "a 'library as place' marketing mindset" (196), and it is evident from Kennedy's 2011 research that Buczynski's comment is true. The most frequently used marketing techniques for e-resources fall into the category of physical medium—or tangible items that libraries produce to try to connect patrons to particular e-resources. These items range from pens and pencils to banners and posters, all of which ultimately tie an electronic resource to the physical library. In his report on influencing the influencers, Row (2006) asks and answers, "'How can marketers efficiently spend dollars to influence word of mouth?' The answer is clear: 'web advertising'" (4). We expect the e-communications category of marketing electronic resources to become the norm over the next few years as libraries as a whole begin to understand how to better communicate with patrons who may never use the physical building of the library to access their resources.

At the time of publishing the second edition of this book, we have not read any marketing plans for licensed e-resources that rely solely on social networking tools like Facebook and Twitter, though surely they are now part of multitechnique approaches used in libraries. We did uncover two articles that highlighted attempts to market library-created resources (LibGuides and archival finding aids) using social media, and from them we learned that Facebook is a reliable source for views and click-throughs (Foster et al. 2010; Williamson, Vieira, and Williamson 2015). We know there are more of you out there who are using social media as part of your marketing strategy! A 2012 study of over 600 public libraries across the United States found that the majority of them had social media accounts and that of the social networks that were analyzed, libraries used Facebook the most (Library Research Service 2013). We hope some of you will get inspired to develop marketing plans that use social networking to market e-resources and then publish the results of your efforts. We are interested to learn alongside you what works for your communities of users.

Action Plan

Now we arrive at an exciting part, crafting all your decisions into a plan of action! In this step you will determine how long your marketing plan will take, who will be involved in the various steps of the plan, and how much your marketing plan will cost.

Timeline

Be reasonable when developing your time budget. Vasileiou and Rowley (2011) found that "lack of time is considered to be the largest issue in terms of e-book promotion" (635). If it is your largest issue, you will need to manage time appropriately and with consideration for all parties involved.

Two factors in developing a timeline are the short-term tasks and the whole picture. To help keep your timeline organized you can create a Gantt chart, which is a bar chart that tracks both tasks and the time it takes to complete each task. Seeing a complete project outline on one piece of paper or on one screen will help you to organize the amount of effort you want to give to each task and to view your project holistically. See figure 2.3 for an example of how your tasks and timeline can look in a Gantt chart. You can create a Gantt chart by using simple spreadsheet software. Begin by making a spreadsheet of thirteen columns. Enter each step in your marketing plan in its own row in the left column. Begin with the steps you've taken so far,

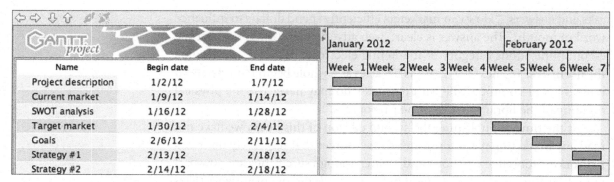

Name	Begin date	End date	January 2012				February 2012		
			Week 1	Week 2	Week 3	Week 4	Week 5	Week 6	Week 7
Project description	1/2/12	1/7/12	▬						
Current market	1/9/12	1/14/12		▬					
SWOT analysis	1/16/12	1/28/12			▬▬				
Target market	1/30/12	2/4/12					▬		
Goals	2/6/12	2/11/12						▬	
Strategy #1	2/13/12	2/18/12							▬
Strategy #2	2/14/12	2/18/12							▬

FIGURE 2.3 Timeline Plotted in a Gantt Chart

including a row for each of the following: developing your project description; identifying your current market; performing the SWOT analysis; identifying your target market; developing your goals; and choosing your strategy. Be sure to include all the components of the marketing cycle to account for them as you complete your plan.

In the remaining twelve columns, enter a calendar month as the heading for each column, starting with the month you began to design your marketing plan and ending one year from then. Mark an X in the spreadsheet cell next to each step in the marketing plan in the month you began to commit effort to that task. For example, you likely began to develop your project description early on, so it should get an X in the earliest month. If your project description took two months to fully complete, you should mark an X in two boxes. Make marks like this next to each task, one mark per month for the length of time you predict it will take you to complete the entire task.

In planning time, you will need to consider if any of the steps in your plan will be repeated. If, for example, you want to launch a marketing campaign in the fall and then repeat it in the spring, you should plan for that effort on the calendar as you are developing your timeline.

Another thing to consider is that some tasks are completed in one effort but others are ongoing. If you decide to use social media tools as a strategy in your plan, for example, you will need to schedule time for the initial development of the message and posting to the sites and will also need to schedule time to respond to those posts. You should decide before you begin how much time you want to devote to social media communications (e.g., a half hour per day or an hour per week), and then make sure you have the right people scheduled for the desired amount of time. Paying attention to what Kietzmann and Canhoto (2013) call "electronic word of mouth," or "eWoM," is critical for participating in a conversation that your patron wants to have with your library; a brief, canned, or nonexistent response to a question/concern posted on a social media site breaks trust between the library and the patron.

There are all kinds of computer software possibilities to assist you with this time management process, from Microsoft Office's Project to the free downloadable software called GanttProject (www.ganttproject.biz). For a low-tech approach, you can also draw the timeline on a whiteboard in your office or on a sheet of paper.

Once you've got all of the discrete steps planned on the calendar, note the earliest date and the latest date to give you a sense of how long the total project will take. Communicating the total length of time, as well as the time expected for all of the components of your marketing plan, will let your library's administrators know that your marketing team understands and values time as a cost in performing marketing for e-resources.

Staff

Collaborating with librarians and library staff is great because you get a wide set of opinions and attitudes mixed into your marketing plan. To keep that collaboration flowing and pleasant, you'll want to make careful decisions about how much and what kinds of things you're asking those collaborators to do.

As you develop this part of your action plan, consider who has been involved in the development process so far. For each of the tasks you identified in your timeline, assign at least one person to be responsible for completing that task. For the first pass of assigning people to tasks, you can choose your ideal person for each task. Now step back and look at all the people you've tasked. Are one or two people heavily tasked, while others have only a few responsibilities? To keep efforts balanced, go back and revise so that the distribution of tasks is dispersed. If you get stuck deciding who should be responsible for which tasks, ask for volunteers. Someone may volunteer to complete a task that you wouldn't have expected.

In addition to assigning tasks based on time, you'll need to consider which skills are necessary for completing the tasks and which team members have those skills. If you've decided that an Internet announcement of your community college library's series of classes on business e-resources is the way you'd like to communicate to your target group, for example, but you don't have anyone on staff who knows HTML, you may need to assign that task to a consultant, being sure to include his or her fee in your budget. If you already know you won't have money to cover a consultant's fee, consider partnering with a local group to assist you for free or using an alternative strategy.

There is support in the published literature for the notion that communication can be more effective when a library partners with an external group, and this may be something for you to pursue. Are there ways that the marketing plan you are putting together could be strengthened by collaborating with another office on campus or a local business? For example, you could say during your library instruction sessions, "If you need help with your writing, call the Academic Writing Center for an appointment." In exchange, during the one-on-one writing sessions at the center, the tutors would show the students how to navigate the library homepage to access your best writing e-resources (dictionary, citation guide, etc.).

To build successful partnerships takes a real commitment, and we direct you to page 7 of the ICMA (International City/County Management Association) report titled *Maximize the Potential of Your Public Library* (Carlee et al. 2011) for advice on how to cultivate partnerships with external organizations. The report offers such guidance as "manage expectations," "communicate frequently," "share success," and "be flexible," among others. The report is more broadly about innovation in public libraries, and the findings strongly support the creation of partnerships for innovative thinking about the future of libraries.

It is possible you will be called upon to collaborate on a marketing effort as part of a consortium to streamline the messaging across branches of libraries. In this kind of coordination, identifying key contacts at each of the branches will be an important consideration. We have seen two web-based portals for sharing resources for marketing in this kind of collaborative environment that we want to point out to you as possible tools to emulate: the New Jersey State Library has created a marketing portal for all of New Jersey libraries at http://njsldirect.org that has links to tools and ongoing marketing campaigns in the state; the libraries that are part of the Maricopa Community College District in Arizona have created a LibGuide at http://library.scottsdalecc.edu/database_marketing as a resource for all interested parties to use.

Budget

Lindsay (2004) found in a survey that "the library's annual budget does not usually include funding specifically for marketing" (10). Yours, however, will! Your budget will account for all of the costs of your marketing plan.

For this component, make a list of all of the costs down to the smallest available detail. Will you be making photocopies of a flyer? The cost of using the library's photocopier may be overlooked because you're not dropping coins into the machine, but it has a real cost. Find out from the library administration office how much the copier company charges per copy, and add it to your budget. Other office items to add to your budget are things that you plan to use that are already in your library's office supplies closet; if the items weren't already in the closet, you would need to purchase them. Add these items and costs to your budget.

Remember the example of the library that wanted to do an Internet announcement but didn't have staff expertise to code the HTML? Suppose you found a professional coder who wanted to do the work for you at no cost. Even though there isn't a charge this time, there may be future charges for changes to the webpage, or perhaps the coder won't be able to work for free next time. If your plan hinges on having the expertise of a coder, ask the coder for a fee and add it to your budget. You can note in your budget that the fee is donated.

We recommend that you add staffing time allotments to your budget. In your action plan, you've already assigned staff to tasks and you've given them an estimate of how much time they can expect to spend on their tasks.

You may choose to add to your budget "staff hours" and "librarian hours," with a simple count of number of hours for each. Since salary is often a private piece of information, even if it is known, we do not recommend including actual salary figures for the librarians and staff persons on your marketing team. By producing a simple count of the number of hours, you will convey to administration that the time committed to your marketing plan has a real cost associated with it without risking the confidentiality of the salary figures.

The budgeting process can take a while if you are thorough, and being as complete as you can will convince your library's administration that you value the library's funds allocated to your marketing plan for electronic resources. Once you have a documented budget, any revisions of your marketing plan in preparation for your next cycle of marketing will be much easier.

Normally, after you complete your action plan, you can put your marketing plan in motion. If you're reading this book for the first time, don't launch your marketing plan quite yet. Read through the rest of the components to see what you need to plan for as you're performing the marketing.

Measurement

When you were thinking earlier about which techniques to use to get to your marketing goal, we prompted you to consider techniques that allow some kind of measurement. In this component of the marketing cycle, you will commit to devising exactly how you will measure those techniques and a timeline for when you will take the measurement(s).

When you see the word *measurement,* do you automatically think of math? To successfully measure something doesn't mean you have to do it with numbers. This component is simply to prompt you to come up with some objective way to gather feedback about your marketing strategy. You can do this with numbers—for example, "How many flyers did we print, and how many do we have left after one week of putting them at the circulation desk?"—or you can do this with words—for example, "Did the patrons who participated in the hands-on database demonstration workshops report that they (a) didn't learn anything new, (b) learned what they expected to learn, or (c) learned more than they expected?"

The way in which you measure will be related to the techniques you identify in your marketing plan. Again using the example of the flyer, you won't gather much objective information about this technique beyond how many you printed and how many you have left. You may get some anecdotal feedback about the content of the flyer, but unless you plan to systematically seek feedback from patrons, the passing comments about the flyer will be just conversational. The hands-on database demonstration will provide you with many more measurement opportunities, but, of course, this technique is more difficult to accomplish. It's easy to pick up a flyer at the circulation desk, but it is a commitment to attend a training session in the library at an appointed time. Measurement possibilities for hands-on workshops are to hand out a quick questionnaire asking how participants heard about the workshop and what made them decide to attend or to provide short pre- and post-tests to gauge how much they learned in the workshop. We note these examples here to prompt you to consider that each marketing technique you choose should have a plan for an objective measurement at some point to tell you about the success or failure of the technique. We firmly believe that if you can't measure it, then you shouldn't do it. If you're going to be accountable for your marketing efforts, you have to be able to report back on how successful you've been.

We realize that sometimes it is difficult to know exactly what or how to measure. Broering, Chauncey, and Gomes (2006) remark on that by noting, "One of the most challenging parts of a service of this nature, involving multiple sites and diverse population, is to gather information and data to evaluate the program with some degree of uniformity" (3). If you get stuck, ask your team members, or a friend, for their ideas on how to accomplish the measurement. It is possible that the technique you've chosen is too complex? Can it be simplified so that the measurement you apply will actually tell you something?

If the strategy you select includes the use of social media, it is a good idea to consider what a relevant measurement will look like and how that measurement tells you if you are meeting your goal. We discovered a potential mismatch in the goal and measurement on a project done at the University of Alabama at Birmingham (Vucovich et al. 2013), in which the stated goal was about engagement but the measurements were about the numbers of posts viewed and the timing of those views. If the project's intended goal was to engage with patrons, we would have expected to see measurements about the numbers of comments, retweets, or discussions or some analysis of those discussions, things that would point to interactions between the patron and the library. We understand that arriving at an appropriate measurement for social media is tricky and may take some time to develop one that matches your goal, but as Howley notes in his 2016 article, "the paradox is that the significant measurement is all about the community—not libraries themselves" (14). Keep in mind that if you select social media as a mechanism, your posts there are about the e-content, which surely is about the library, but it is also about the connections between that content and your patrons, building that community.

Think of measurement as providing evidence of your good work. If you've set up a solid marketing plan, even if your hoped-for results aren't achieved, you've learned something, and this has value for your next marketing cycle.

Assessment

The final component in a marketing plan is to synthesize your marketing activities to see if your goal has been achieved. This assessment component allows you to determine if the path you laid out for your team was a success or a failure, with enough information gathered to tell you what the beginning of your next marketing cycle should look like. Throughout this process, you've been deliberate in the choices you were making to aid you in the pursuit of actionable knowledge. "Actionable knowledge" implies that what you've learned tells you how you should move forward, or take action, next. This final component answers the question, "Why have we done this, and how did we do?"

To complete this step, look again at your goals, strategy, and measurements. Ask yourself if those things combined tell you where you're headed in your next marketing cycle. If your goal was to increase usage of a particular database and your strategy included multiple techniques to get that usage increased and the statistics demonstrate that usage did, in fact, increase, where should you head in your next marketing cycle? Perhaps you're satisfied that usage was increased enough and you're ready to move on to something else in your next cycle, or perhaps usage did increase but you suspect it could increase even more; having data in hand can inform if you'll repeat the marketing plan with slight variations or if a new marketing plan is warranted.

Recommended Resources for Further Reading

American Marketing Association. "Marketer's Toolkit." Marketing Power, 2016. www.ama.org/resources/MarketingToolkit/Pages/default.aspx.

> We recommend viewing the videos linked from this toolkit from a major marketing organization in America.

Barbour, Rosaline. *Doing Focus Groups*. London: SAGE, 2007.

> For an authoritative resource on how to conduct focus groups, we recommend this book by the publisher SAGE, which is known for its methods-focused books. In this book, you will read how to form a targeted group of patrons and find out what they think about your library's electronic resources.

DeWalt, Kathleen Musante, and Billie R. DeWalt. *Participant Observation: A Guide for Fieldworkers*. Lanham, MD: Rowman and Littlefield, 2011.

> For those interested in objectively viewing a group of people while you are a member of the group, this book explores participant observation. The term *participant observation* means that you are a member of the group you are researching, which can be helpful in discovering information about the use of your library's electronic resources. For example, if you are a graduate student and you want to learn how to gather data on other graduate students' use of electronic resources, this is just the book to show you how to do it.

Fielding, Nigel, Raymond M. Lee, and Grant Blank, eds. *The SAGE Handbook of Online Research Methods*. London: SAGE, 2008.

> This book offers suggestions on how to gather data about the use of your library's electronic resources via online methods. Learn about online surveys, virtual ethnography, and other research methods conducted over the Internet.

Glenn, Norval D. *Cohort Analysis*. 2nd ed. Thousand Oaks, CA: SAGE, 2005.

> This Little Green Book by SAGE introduces you to the concepts behind cohort analysis and suggests appropriate methods for data gathering.

Gravetter, Frederick J., and Lori-Ann B. Forzano. *Research Methods for the Behavioral Sciences*. 5th ed. Belmont, CA: Cengage Learning, 2016.

> This textbook covers all the basics related to research design appropriate for libraries. It guides you through the processes of creating a research question and choosing appropriate methods and provides practical exercises for readers.

Hart, Judith L., Vicki Coleman, and Hong Yu. "Marketing Electronic Resources and Services—Surveying Faculty Use as a First Step." *The Reference Librarian* 32, no. 67 (2001): 41–55.

> This article provides a good, practical example of how you can get to know your target market in order to construct a more effective marketing plan. Before the authors moved forward in their marketing cycle, they sought to understand the existing use of electronic resources and the possible barriers to their greater use.

Naumes, William, and Margaret J. Naumes. *The Art and Craft of Case Writing*. 2nd ed. Armonk, NY: M.E. Sharpe, 2006.

> This text is for those interested in writing about how they are currently performing a task or project and learning how to make it more broadly applicable. The book demonstrates how to write a case study and provides examples.

Solomon, Laura. 2011. *Doing Social Media So It Matters: A Librarian's Guide*. Chicago: ALA Editions.

> This book gives you ideas to consider for how to engage your library patrons using social media and how to measure your efforts.

References

Bensoussan, Babette E., and Craig S. Fleisher. 2012. *Analysis without Paralysis: 12 Tools to Make Better Strategic Decisions*. 2nd ed. Upper Saddle River, NJ: FT Press.

Brannon, Sian. 2007. "A Successful Promotional Campaign—We Can't Keep Quiet about Our Electronic Resources." *The Serials Librarian* 53 (3): 41–55.

Broering, Naomi C., Gregory A. Chauncey, and Stacy L. Gomes. 2006. "Outreach to Public Libraries, Senior Centers, and Clinics to Improve Patient and Consumer Health Care—An Update." *Journal of Consumer Health on the Internet* 10 (3): 1–19.

Buczynski, James. 2007. "Referral Marketing Campaigns: 'Slashdotting' Electronic Resources." *The Serials Librarian* 53 (3): 193–209.

Carlee, Ron, Keith Strigaro, Elizabeth R. Miller, and Molly Donelan. 2011. *Maximize the Potential of Your Public Library: A Report on the Innovative Ways Public Libraries Are Addressing Community Priorities.* Washington, DC: International City/County Management Association. icma.org/Documents/Document/Document/302161.

Collins, James C., and Jerry I. Porras. 1996. "Building Your Company's Vision." *Harvard Business Review* 74 (5): 65–77.

Curtis, Donnelyn, and Virginia M. Scheschy. 2005. *E-journals: A How-To-Do-It Manual for Building, Managing, and Supporting Electronic Journal Collections.* New York: Neal-Schuman.

David, Lourdes T., and Karryl Kim A. Sagun. 2012. "Increasing Awareness and Use of the Library's Resources and Facilities through Relationship Marketing Strategies." *Library Management* 33 (4/5): 292–6.

De Saez, Eileen Elliott. 2002. *Marketing Concepts for Libraries and Information Services.* 2nd ed. London: Facet.

Foster, Mira, Hesper Wilson, Nicole Allensworth, and Diane T. Sands. 2010. "Marketing Research Guides: An Online Experiment with LibGuides." *Journal of Library Administration* 50 (5/6): 602–16.

Howley, Brendan. 2016. "Collective Intelligence and Libraries as Social Businesses." *Information Today* 33 (8): 14–15.

Kennedy, Marie R. 2011. "What Are We Really Doing to Market Electronic Resources?" *Library Management* 32 (3): 144–58.

Kietzmann, Jan, and Ana Canhoto. 2013. "Bittersweet! Understanding and Managing Electronic Word of Mouth." *Journal of Public Affairs* 13 (2): 146–59.

Kolowich, Steve. 2011. "What Students Don't Know." *Inside Higher Ed,* August 22. www.insidehighered.com/news/2011/08/22/erial_study _of_student_research_habits_at_illinois_university_libraries _reveals_alarmingly_poor_information_literacy_and_skills.

Lee, Deborah. 2003. "Marketing Research: Laying the Marketing Foundation." *Library Administration and Management* 17 (4): 186–8.

Library Research Service. 2013. "U.S. Public Libraries and the Use of Web Technologies, 2012." Posted November 18. www.lrs.org/2013/11/18/ u-s-public-libraries-use-web-technologies-2012.

Lindsay, Anita Rothwell. 2004. *Marketing and Public Relations Practices in College Libraries.* CLIP Note. Chicago: American Library Association.

OCLC. 2010. *Perceptions of Libraries, 2010: Context and Community.* Dublin, OH: OCLC. www.oclc.org/en/reports/2010perceptions.html.

Porter, Michael E. 2008. "The Five Competitive Forces That Shape Strategy." *Harvard Business Review* 86 (1): 78–93.

Ramsey, Elizabeth. 2014. "Using Slide Shows to Engage Patrons with Library Resources." *Pacific Northwest Library Association Quarterly* 79 (1): 79–83.

Row, Heath. 2006. "Influencing the Influencers: How Online Advertising and Media Impact Word of Mouth." DoubleClick.com. static.googleusercontent.com/media/www.google.co.jp/ja/jp/doubleclick/pdfs/DoubleClick-12-2006-Influencing-the-Influencers.pdf.

Vasileiou, Magdalini, and Jennifer Rowley. 2011. "Marketing and Promotion of E-books in Academic Libraries." *Journal of Documentation* 67 (4): 624–74.

Vucovich, Lee A., Valerie S. Gordon, Nicole Mitchell, and Lisa A. Ennis. 2013. "Is the Time and Effort Worth It? One Library's Evaluation of Using Social Networking Tools for Outreach." *Medical Reference Services Quarterly* 32 (1): 12–25.

Wallace, Linda K. 2004. *Libraries, Mission, and Marketing: Writing Mission Statements That Work.* Chicago: American Library Association.

Williamson, Felicia, Scott Vieira, and James Williamson. 2015. "Marketing Finding Aids on Social Media: What Worked and What Didn't Work." *The American Archivist* 78 (2): 488–513.

Young, Scott W. H., and Doralyn Rossmann. 2015. "Building Library Community through Social Media." *Information Technology and Libraries* 34 (1): 20–37.

Implement Your Marketing Plan

In chapter 2, we introduced you to the relevant concepts for each step in the process of developing your marketing plan for electronic resources. This chapter provides examples from real-world reports of how libraries have addressed each of the components of their marketing plans for electronic resources. The quotations from and summaries of these marketing campaigns are offered here as guidance for what to consider, what to strive for, and what to avoid as you make your own marketing plans.

Components of a Marketing Plan, with Examples

In this chapter, we follow the cycle of marketing and provide examples along the way of how libraries have taken action, to help you make the best choices at each component.

Project Description

A project description is the anchor in a marketing plan. It gives reason to the rest of the steps. A good project description contains these four components: the reasons you want to market your e-resources; what is needed to accomplish your plan; how much the plan will cost; and how long the plan will take to complete. Kennedy (2010) found that most libraries ably communicated that they were embarking on a marketing campaign, but most of them were missing the key components of a solid project description. Henderson and colleagues (2009) provide a brief example of their team's project description:

> Project Uncover Health Information Databases (UnHID) was designed to promote the use of the National Library of Medicine (NLM) consumer health information resources and databases

among students and faculty of the Morehouse School of Medicine Master of Public Health (MPH) Program and among the adults and high school students in the community adjacent to the school's campus. (136)

From this description we learn that the reason for the marketing plan is to "promote the use of" electronic resources. Without reading further we don't know why Henderson's team is driven to promote the use of the resources, and so the project description as stated loses some of its potential impact as a selling point. A statement explaining why the project team feels the need to design a marketing campaign would be an excellent addition to the project description.

Brannon (2007) clearly states why her institution is compelled to develop a marketing plan: "I knew why I wanted to promote the databases—spending over $30,000 a year on a product is too much to be overlooked for so long" (43). This simple reason alone gained the support of her institution's administration for her proposed marketing campaign. Note that Brannon's project description is missing the other practical components and would not be considered complete as presented; it is mentioned here as an example of how powerful a motivator the "why" in your project description can be.

Many of the case reports examined in Kennedy's 2010 research include project descriptions that simply note that the authors embarked on a marketing campaign, without providing the context of the stage-setting steps in a marketing plan. If the project description is an anchor for the rest of the plan, consider making it expansive and be sure to address the reasoning behind your plan.

Current Market

Hart, Coleman, and Yu (2001) documented doing some knowledge gathering about their patrons before embarking on a marketing campaign. They used a direct method: they surveyed a random sample of faculty and teaching staff. In chapter 2, you learned that one of the components of identifying your current market is to ask yourself how you are serving the information needs of your patrons, and discovering this was the intention of Hart, Coleman, and Yu's (2001) survey. They considered their study "the beginning of a marketing strategy for . . . electronic resources" (42), which we describe as *pre-marketing* in chapter 2. Their survey gathered some demographic information to assist them in clustering the responses: faculty rank, number of years of postsecondary teaching experience, and academic college.

Here are some other examples of how libraries identified their current market:

> Citing concern for their institution's cohort of distance learners, Edwards and Webb (1999) observe, "The University has a growing number of distance learners and many staff and students have access to the Internet from home. Electronic

services are a vitally important element of the distributed library service and, since 1996, access to electronic journal titles has risen from zero to around 4,000 titles" (277). You can see in this one statement that they acknowledge their concern for their distance-education students and at-home users and cite a three-year trend in the rise of their collection of electronic resources; when put together, this provides a comprehensive understanding of their library's current market.

Song (2006) identifies what her institution doesn't know about its international business students: "There was a concern that BEL might not be offering services that graduate business students actually needed the most. Only in-depth research would reveal what services they were hoping to receive, what services should be continued, and those that should be considered for termination" (72). The process of describing your library's current market will enable you to identify what you believe the information concerns of your patrons may be, and deliberately focusing on this aspect may demonstrate that you don't know enough about their needs and need more information.

In a section of a journal article describing the current market of their library, titled "The Situation," Thorpe and Bowman (2013) note, "The librarians have discussed whether usage data is a fair metric, since some resources receive more 'air time' because they are general and/or more familiar to the librarians. This prompted the librarians to wonder whether direct marketing campaigns for resources would have an effect on usage statistics" (102). This perceptive assessment of which e-resources may be the most commonly used at their regional campus university library demonstrates an understanding of the nature of higher education in their particular setting.

The Tacoma Public Library understands that the nature of its public library's outreach to small businesses in the community is changing due to the increase in the number of electronic resources and notes that increase as a strength:

> The library can remind its customers that it is as close as the personal digital assistant in one's pocket or purse, or laptop, not to mention the office computer. One no longer has to drive to the library building to seek information. The necessity for the business library to be solely in the central business district has been eliminated. Every branch library, even those in the farthest corners of the city, rather than just the central library, has the potential to be a business information center. (Pankl 2010, 100)

From these examples, we can see the attempts the libraries made to understand their current markets, describing their libraries' patrons, focusing on the information concerns of their libraries' patrons, and commenting on general characteristics of usage of their libraries. The description of your own library's current market will be more thorough than the examples presented here, which are provided as samples solely to demonstrate how libraries are actually completing the components of a marketing plan.

SWOT Analysis

As you identify your library's internal (strengths, weaknesses) and external (opportunities, threats) concerns, some issues will leap out as needing immediate attention while others that you identify you won't be able to do anything about. It will be tempting to focus on the ones that need attention, swaying your focus to problem solving rather than simply identifying the issues. The SWOT analysis process of your marketing plan development shouldn't be tied to resolving any issues. As you brainstorm with a group to develop the SWOT list, it is important to try to keep all issues neutral. Prioritization of possible changes can happen later, and this likely will be of concern to a group other than your marketing team. Clarifying that the goal of performing the analysis is to better understand the micro- and macroenvironments in which your library is situated may help the discussion with your marketing team stay on track.

Kennedy (2010) did not find any library that stated it performed a SWOT analysis as part of its marketing plan, but she found several clues in the articles she reviewed that suggested they were performed, as illustrated in the following quotes:

> Manda (2005) wonders about the dissemination of marketing information to key departmental liaisons in an academic environment, honing in on an existing threat (noncommunicative departmental gatekeepers) and a possible opportunity (other ways to disseminate information):
>
>> But do the gatekeepers who get this information disseminate it to others in their respective departments? This appears to be problematic. For example, the results of this study have shown that in some departments there are staff who are heavy users of PERI resources, but also there are staff members in the same departments who claim never to have heard of electronic resources. Other strategies, though not purely marketing techniques, through which users learn about electronic resources are training sessions and orientation programmes in the use of these resources. (275)
>
> Metz-Wiseman and Rodgers (2007) identify internal challenges related to library culture, staff, and financial resources:
>
>> Furthermore, it was sometimes difficult to accommodate the local interests, goals, and missions of all of the USF Libraries. There were significant differences in budgets, populations

> served, collections, and staffing that brought challenges to this process. Given the number of Virtual Library Teams, not every USF Library could afford to continue to have a representative on the Marketing Team. (23)

Roberts and Appleton (2003) describe external concerns related to technological change and vendors, as well as user expectations:

> Introducing electronic books as a new resource surprisingly does not come without its issues. For example, there are questions concerning the model of NetLibrary, i.e., it operates on a single user licence, and NetLibrary books (per copy) cost more than print books, although the actual way in which e-books are accessed and used needs to be taken into account. There are general considerations about maximising value for money, but models and prices of e-books are issues that individual libraries will have to address. A particular model and pricing structure may well be ideal for a specific user group (e.g. Edge Hill School of Health Studies' students), but not others. (85)

In the last example, the authors cite an external concern (a threat), the platform choice for e-book dissemination. If you conduct your own SWOT analysis, "vendor platforms" will surely be somewhere on your list. External concerns are very often treated as hands-off problems, issues that cannot be directly dealt with or readily addressed. Regarding publisher platforms, however, libraries may be able to move the item of "vendor platforms" from the "threat" column to the "opportunity" column. Some vendors welcome feedback related to platform development, user interface improvements, and licensing and purchase/subscription models for electronic content. Despite electronic content having existed for quite some time, publishers we have talked to have often expressed a lack of confidence in knowing how to attractively price their products or how to develop appealing subscription models for libraries. If your library is staffed with someone willing to discuss these topics in a collegial manner with your vendor representatives, changes can happen. In this way, a SWOT analysis item that would normally fall under "threat" could be stored under "opportunity." Knowing your user group, as the library in the aforementioned example does ("Health Studies students"), would put you at a real advantage when speaking with a vendor because you can comment on that specific group's characteristics and habits when describing how a particular platform change or alteration of pricing structure may benefit the group overall.

Although the examples described here illustrate that the libraries represented are thinking about possible strengths, weaknesses, opportunities, and threats, their subsequent commentaries in the journal articles suggest that their evaluations were not complete. We recommend taking the time to think through the issues, write down your conclusions, and share the results to ensure that those involved in marketing your library's e-resources are all on the same page.

We earlier suggested the use of the free Internet-based product Gliffy to help you visualize your SWOT analysis (see figure 2.2 in chapter 2), but you can use a simple office spreadsheet or word-processing software to create a 2 × 2 table to achieve a similar result. If you are interested in a low-tech approach, you could even make a list of your library's strengths, weaknesses, opportunities, and threats and then draw a SWOT analysis box by hand on a piece of paper or a chalkboard.

Target Market

The libraries that have published articles about their marketing plans for e-resources have generally done a good job of identifying one special patron group as the focus of their marketing efforts. For example, Brannon (2007) realized that "the library needed to focus on staff education first. You cannot promote a product you don't understand. Patrons will trust confident, knowledgeable staff more, and find more satisfaction in their use of the library with proper assistance" (43). As a result, her library focused marketing efforts on library staff.

Bartley, Gomibuchi, and Mann (2007) observe that "in order to cater for external customers' interests properly, organisations need to treat their own employees (internal customers) with similar care and attention" (489). Conduit and Mavondo (2001) used this association as a hypothesis and found that the relationship between an internal marketing orientation and a marketing orientation for the institution as a whole is supported, suggesting that the steps your library takes to create a culture of marketing that includes all levels of staff is worth the effort. You might want to consider focusing your library's first marketing plan on your own staff. Practicing new techniques in your own library first will give you an informal feedback mechanism as well as confidence to try the techniques on a larger, external group next.

Understanding that marketing via word of mouth is a powerful strategy, Millet and Chamberlain (2007) explain their attempt to market e-resources to their target market of peer tutors, who would then share that information with their first-year students during their regular communications and training sessions. They describe their target market as "a selective group; the cream of the crop" and "one of the obvious groups of opinion leaders at Trinity University, especially in regards to first-year students" (Millet and Chamberlain 2007, 103).

Because the kind of marketing strategy you will choose is specific for the group you identify, it is best to stay focused on just one target group. A few of the libraries that Kennedy (2010) studied identified groups that would clearly call for different types of marketing strategies; for example, Betz and colleagues (2009) chose "subject librarians, faculty members, researchers and students" (251). If we were to revise their plan, we would suggest that their target market be narrowed to just one of those groups. As you become savvier in your marketing, you will see that some strategies can apply to more than one target group, and the skeleton of one marketing plan can provide an outline for a new one. At the outset we suggest using a simple process, focusing on one target group, to make sure all the components are well considered. An example of a single focus can be found in Thorpe and Bowman (2013): "The task force, however, did decide to market EDS [EBSCO Discovery Service] to only undergraduate students. The unique research needs of graduate students require a separate, targeted message that is different from the one promoted to undergraduate students" (106).

You can even choose to focus your marketing efforts on groups within groups. We found a nice example of research done to discover which social networking sites international students at a university mainly use, in order to determine if there was a difference between their communication preferences and those of domestic students (Saw et al. 2013). Doing this kind of pre-marketing, to discover where international students are most likely to be receptive to library messages, is a savvy approach to learning about your target market.

We understand that there is variation within groups and that one message will not satisfy all the members of that group. There is recent interest in the idea of focusing your marketing efforts on your existing library fan base. People in your fan base are easy to identify; they're the ones in your Friends of the Library group, they turn up at your public presentations, and they're active members in your book groups. Your library's fans are already receptive to communications from you, and in return for your efforts, they are likely to share those communications with their friends. This makes a lot of sense for libraries. If your marketing plan focuses on a specific cluster of patrons, you may make your marketing go further if you can identify a library fan in that cluster with whom to directly communicate. You can learn more about this kind of marketing by investigating "relationship marketing," "one-to-one marketing," or "co-creation marketing" on the Internet or in published literature.

Goals

As you develop the marketing plan for your library, you will have some goals in mind for what you hope to accomplish. Having clear goals can be a real selling point when it comes to communicating with your library's administration. When you say to your library director, "We hope to raise the confidence of our library's senior population by providing hands-on instruction in our health-related e-resources so that they know how to find reliable health information," the director is likely to be impressed that you identified a specific group with a specific outcome in mind. This specificity gives others a tangible understanding of what you hope your efforts will produce. Having goals in mind and knowing your target group and how it fits into your environment (your current market) will guide your strategy, which is the next step in developing your marketing plan.

It may seem like having a clear goal before beginning a project is obvious, but two libraries in Kennedy's 2010 research do not report a goal for their marketing efforts. Cosgrove (2006) notes, "We did not develop a formal plan" (94), and he does not mention in the article why his team did what it did. Ellis (2004) comments, "We all want to make the most of our investments and resources" (57), but no other specific goal or hoped-for outcome is mentioned. Jumping into a marketing campaign without knowing why you are doing so doesn't give much hope for measurable success.

Bancroft and colleagues (1998) clearly describe their library's goals: "Specific goals of the survey were to: (1) assess users' needs and expectations, thereby allowing library personnel to prioritize expenditures, (2) apprise users of possible services and resources so that they would be able to make informed prioritizations, (3) encourage faculty and student input concerning library issues, and (4) document the needs of the library system" (216). This is a very clear statement of what the library hopes to get out of its marketing efforts. Their example is what Wallace (2004) had in mind when she said, "Be specific about what you aim to accomplish. . . . [L]imit yourself to three key points" (15). Let this example guide you in developing your own goals.

Strategy

To learn about the kinds of marketing techniques being used in libraries, we reviewed the published literature in the field of information and library science, focusing specifically on marketing electronic resources. We did not limit our search by date in order to gather the broadest group of articles from which to identify marketing techniques. We found twenty-three pertinent articles published between 1994 and 2009 (Kennedy 2010), and table 3.1 describes most of the techniques mentioned. Seeing the breadth of possibilities may help you to identify which you would like to use for your own marketing plan. There are obviously more techniques that you can use beyond those listed in table 3.1, but we thought it would be helpful to present the ones that libraries actually reported using.

To assess the marketing techniques, we grouped similar techniques into categories. Four general categories of techniques resulted: human interaction, e-communication, physical medium, and training.

- The techniques in the human interaction category are academic staff as collection developers; collaboration; collection policy; faculty/professionals as marketing tools; phone call/personal visit; students as marketing tools; surveys; and word of mouth.
- The techniques in the e-communications category are Blackboard; branding; e-mail (external); e-mail (internal); feedback form; home/off-campus access; mascot; online social network; screen saver; usage statistics; webpage alert; and webpage, customized.
- The techniques in the physical medium category are banners/ posters; bookmarks; calendar; flyers/brochures; giveaways;

TABLE 3.1 Marketing Techniques

CATEGORY AND TECHNIQUE	DESCRIPTION
Human interaction	
Academic staff as collection developers	Academic staff choose the e-resources that are added to the collection.
Collaboration	The library works with an organization outside the library to promote e-resources.
Collection policy	E-texts are a part of the collection development policy, and this policy is shared with academic staff.
Faculty/professionals as marketing tools	Faculty or professionals on campus tell colleagues and students about e-resources.
Phone call/personal visit	A library staff member calls on the phone or visits the home/office of a patron.
Students as marketing tools	Students on campus tell other students about e-resources.
Surveys	Patrons are asked questions about their uses of e-resources.
Word of mouth	A patron tells another patron about an e-resource.
E-communication	
Blackboard	An e-resource is promoted via the online classroom companion.
Branding	A specific effort is made to identify an e-resource as belonging to a library.
E-mail (external)	E-mail messages are sent to patrons.
E-mail (internal)	E-mail messages are sent to library staff.
Feedback form	The library has a mechanism to solicit feedback about an e-resource.
Home/off-campus access	Access to e-resources is available outside the library.
Mascot	A mascot for a marketing campaign is developed.
Online social network	Social networking software like Facebook or Instagram is used to alert patrons to e-resources.
Screen saver	E-resource descriptions are put on screen savers at public workstations in the library.
Usage statistics	Usage statistics are used to assess a marketing activity or are used as a marketing tool.
Webpage alert	An announcement of a new e-resource is posted on the library webpage.
Webpage, customized	A customized webpage is built to describe an e-resource.
Physical medium	
Banners/posters	Banners or posters are used to describe or promote an e-resource.
Bookmarks	Printed bookmarks include a marketing slogan or information about an e-resource.
Calendar	An annual calendar is created.
Flyers/brochures	Printed flyers or brochures announce or describe an e-resource.
Giveaways	Items such as pens, pencils, and notepads are given away to publicize an e-resource.
Incentives	Goods (e.g., gift cards) are traded for time spent in a training workshop.
Newsletter	A newsletter that is either exclusively about e-resources or consistently contains a section for e-resources is published.
Newspaper alert	An advertisement about an e-resource is placed in a newspaper.
Pins	Pins featuring a marketing slogan are worn by library staff.
Postcards/letters/direct mail	Materials are created to send to patrons.
Training	
FAQs	A webpage with frequently asked questions about an e-resource is created.
Native language education	Training for an e-resource is done in the patron's native language.
Patron training (group)	Patrons are trained on how to use an e-resource in a group setting.
Patron training (individual)	A patron is trained in how to use an e-resource in a one-on-one setting.
Slide shows/demonstrations	A demonstration of an e-resource is provided in an interactive or noninteractive setting.
Staff training (group)	Staff are trained on how to use an e-resource in a group setting.
Staff training (individual)	A staff member is trained on how to use an e-resource in a one-on-one setting.
Use guide	A guide is designed to instruct patrons on how to use an e-resource.

incentives; newsletter; newspaper alert; pins; and postcards/letters/direct mail.

- The techniques that relate to training are FAQs; native language education; patron training (group); patron training (individual); slide shows/demonstrations; staff training (group); staff training (individual); and use guide.

Figures 3.1 through 3.4 illustrate this categorization. It is clear from the figures that libraries do not choose to market consistently using one category of techniques over another but rather choose from all of them.

From the categories noted in figures 3.1 through 3.4, you can see that libraries use marketing techniques related to physical media (illustrated in figure 3.3) most frequently, with ten techniques used sixty-one times and flyers/brochures being the most frequently used (with twelve of the twenty-three libraries noting that they used this technique). E-communications are the second most frequently used (illustrated in figure 3.2), with twelve techniques used fifty-three times, of which e-mail (external) is the most frequent (used at ten of the libraries). Training is third (illustrated in figure 3.4), with eight techniques used forty-eight times, of which patron training (group) is the most frequent. Eight human interaction techniques are used thirty-nine times (illustrated in figure 3.1), with surveys being the most popular and ten of the twenty-three libraries noting that they used this technique.

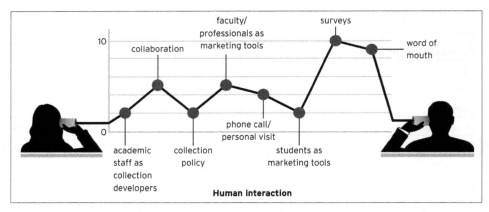

FIGURE 3.1 Human Interaction as Marketing Technique

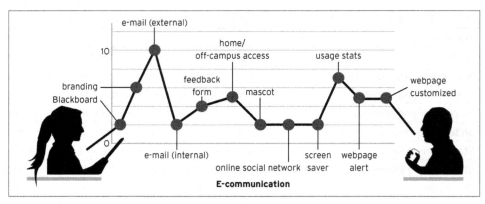

FIGURE 3.2 E-communication as Marketing Technique

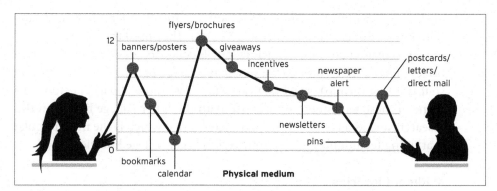

FIGURE 3.3 Physical Medium as Marketing Technique

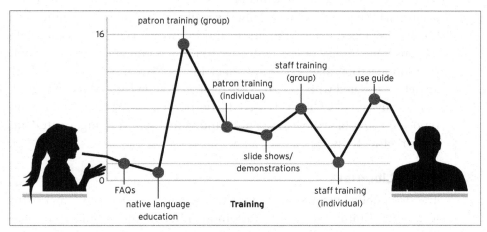

FIGURE 3.4 Training as Marketing Technique

The four most popular techniques overall were patron training in a group setting, flyers/brochures, e-mails to patrons, and surveys.

Four kinds of libraries are represented in the published literature about marketing electronic resources between 1994 and 2009—college libraries, medical libraries, public libraries, and university libraries. The next four sections discuss which techniques were used the most in these kinds of libraries.

College Libraries

Two publications were about marketing techniques for e-resources in college libraries. One mentioned having a budget for its marketing campaign. This library spent $137 on a postcard campaign as "a simple attempt to get the attention of our patrons" (Cosgrove 2006, 94). Of the thirty-eight unique marketing techniques, this library used only two: postcards/letters/direct mail and use guide; one of the postcards included a brief description of how to use an e-resource.

The other college library used ten of the thirty-eight marketing techniques to market NetLibrary e-books to their School of Health Studies students. They noted that "integration and contextualization do not simply mean 'placement,' i.e., e-journals on reading lists, linked within virtual learning environments, but rather are based upon interaction, an understanding of their role within the curriculum, and are linked to learning needs and outcomes" (Roberts and Appleton 2003, 84). They used the following techniques to market e-books: academic staff as collection developers; collection policy; FAQs; flyers/brochures; newspaper alert; patron training (group); staff training (group); surveys; usage statistics; and webpage, customized. None of these techniques overlapped with the other college library in this research, and as a result, it cannot be determined which is the most popular marketing technique for electronic resources at college libraries.

Medical Libraries

The five medical library institutions used an average of 12.6 marketing techniques (minimum, three; maximum, twenty-one). The most frequently used marketing technique among these libraries is patron training; four libraries reported using both group and individual training sessions with patrons. One library noted, "Effective training is one of the most valuable promotional tools of an electronic collection, because training helps to limit anxiety associated with electronic searching" (Kendall and Massarella 2001, 31). The five medical libraries used thirty-four marketing techniques. None reported using Blackboard, calendar, individual staff training, or students as marketing tools.

Public Libraries

The two public libraries in the analysis used an average of 13.5 marketing techniques (minimum, twelve; maximum, fifteen). The techniques used by both institutions are banners/posters, giveaways, incentives, staff training (group), and use guide.

These public libraries used twenty-five techniques. Neither institution reported using academic staff as collection developers, Blackboard, calendar, collaboration, collection policy, faculty/professionals as marketing tools, native language education, newsletter, online social networking, pins, screen saver, slide shows/demonstrations, or webpage alert.

University Libraries

The fifteen university libraries used an average of 6.73 marketing techniques (minimum, one; maximum, fifteen). The most frequently noted marketing technique is patron training (group), used in nine libraries. Among all libraries, thirty techniques were used. None of the university libraries reported using academic staff as collection developers, collection policy, e-mail (internal), FAQs, mascot, native language education, pins, or webpage, customized.

The finding that the university libraries in this study used the least number of marketing techniques was surprising. One would expect that because they are traditionally larger than public and medical libraries, they would also think more expansively about marketing (i.e., put more marketing techniques to use). In the sample of libraries represented in the analysis, however, Kennedy (2010) found this not to be true.

School and Other Special Libraries

Kennedy's 2010 research did not find any journal articles referencing marketing electronic resources in school or special libraries other than medical libraries, but this doesn't mean that those libraries aren't marketing their e-resources. Schrock's 2003 article in *Library Journal* (about a library media center program) suggests following up in-person library events such as book group meetings with an Internet forum so that face-to-face conversations can continue online. Schrock (2003) mentions using other communication techniques like webpages, press releases, newsletters, handbooks, how-to guides, pathfinders, and bookmarks for general marketing purposes. As found in other kinds of libraries, themed events are suggested as reasonable marketing techniques for school libraries. Ferriol (2007) outlines an entire school year of possible themed events in her presentation on marketing strategies for school libraries; they can all be tweaked to focus on your library's electronic resources. Pipkin and Kirk (2005) collected examples of uses of the American Library Association's "@your library" slogans in school library media centers across the United States, presenting a list of around 100. Most notably related to electronic resources are the slogans "24/7 access @your library," "Online resources @your library," and "Super search engines @your library." Though the "@your library" campaign was retired in 2015, the examples may still be relevant for your own marketing.

In a 1990 article, St. Clair notes that "[in today's special library,] effective library marketing includes combining the concepts of marketing, promotion and public relations, but it begins with a clear definition of the library's mission in the parent organization" (213). This affirmation that marketing efforts should be tied to the wider institution's mission has not changed in the years since the article was written. In Burkman's (2004) article about marketing her school library, she notes that "traditional library programs may fail because there is a lack of communication between the library and the people supporting the school" (43), and she discusses several practical techniques for conversation with target audiences, such as creating a family night in the library once a semester, flyers for parents about library policies and usage, teacher breakfasts, and public service announcements in the local newspaper to engage the local community. Brunner (2009) reaffirms the need for constructing opportunities to communicate with your constituents and recounts the efforts of her law library to design an annual themed event surrounding National Library Week.

In a 2014 article, Ramsey notes, "It might sound limiting to allow only . . . themes associated with the library's mission, but we have found that with a little creativity almost any sort of holiday or theme can be connected to the library" (80). She goes on to give three fun examples:

> December 5 is National Ninja Day, which we used to promote our resources connected to the science of body movement in the Kinesiology library guide. December is also the month for Festivus, the holiday initiated by George Costanza's father on the TV sitcom *Seinfeld*, which we used to promote our Philosophy

library guide. International Beer Day occurs August 1st, and while we don't want to promote alcohol use on campus, we can certainly question the health benefits of beer and direct our users to the Health Sciences Library guide. (Ramsey 2014, 80)

A Special Note on E-communications

It was surprising to learn from Kennedy's (2010) study that the most frequently used marketing techniques fell into the category of physical media, especially because what is being marketed is electronic in format. Row (2006) believes that the most efficient use of money to influence word-of-mouth marketing is via Internet-based advertising, so you may want to consider intentionally using electronic means like webpages, electronic newsletters, e-mail, and social networking sites to market your library's e-resources to make the most of your budget.

Ryan and Jones (2009) offer some great dos and don'ts of an e-mail marketing campaign. They comment on what to do and what to avoid in the design, content, delivery, and measurement of e-mail as a marketing technique. Some highlights include designing with your institution's brand/identity in mind; not cluttering e-mails with images, as some e-mail clients will strip them out; thinking of an eye-catching subject line that "clearly outlines what the e-mail is about" (144); getting someone else to proofread your copy; following up on sent e-mails that are returned to you with undeliverable notes to make sure your e-mail list is up-to-date; and paying attention to how people respond to your communications (whether they write back, whether you get a lot of "Please unsubscribe me" messages after an e-mail, etc.).

Options for e-communication tools have really expanded over the past few years, growing beyond the traditional e-mail newsletter. With the prevalent use of social media, it is important to think about using a voice and a style that are appropriate for your patrons. It is natural to think that if your communication is to a public library's young adult literature book club, then you would want to use language that is familiar to that group. Communicating with a voice that is familiar to the recipients of your message makes it more likely that they will respond. In addition to considerations of voice, you should also be thinking about style. Is your communication directive, like giving instructions for how to download an e-book from a new provider? If so, then an instructive and technical style works best here, with bullet points or numbered instructions to follow. It's a lot to juggle in your mind, to figure out how to communicate a voice and a style while using an electronic method like social media. You may want to create a social media subcommittee within your marketing team to coordinate these communications, to keep them on track and using similar voice and style over time.

Striking a Strategic Balance

In this section of the book, we have offered a wealth of possible marketing techniques and combinations of techniques. Thorpe and Bowman (2013) wisely comment, "In discussing these options, we realized that pursuing every communication option would be impractical for a small task force and could potentially oversaturate our audience" (107). Finding a balance among the options is a healthy thing for your marketing team to consider, especially if you are developing a long-term marketing plan.

Action Plan

Thus far you've been synthesizing quite a bit of information about your project, your library, your patrons, and your goals. The action plan is where you put all of these components together with a timeline, staff, and budget.

Timeline

In Kennedy's 2010 research, time is referenced in a variety of ways in seventeen of the twenty-three documents, all reporting only short-term time considerations, and only a couple identifying how long they expect their complete marketing plan to take. Of these, Turner, Wilkie, and Rosen (2004) are specific about a timeline for the entire marketing plan—"This team has prepared a three year strategy, for 2003–2006" (265)—while Delgado and Wood (2007) focus on the timeline for only the marketing campaign being described—"a month-long promotional campaign to promote Ex Libris SFX" (129). The documents describing activities in an academic setting tend to focus on the beginning of a school term as the start of the marketing campaign. A few are designed around a themed campaign, such as "Awareness Week 2002," "Orientation Week," and "Nursing Week" (Turner, Wilkie, and Rosen 2004; Woods 2007; Kendall and Massarella 2001). One library reports an understanding of the cyclical nature of marketing, noting, "Although the program is started with a timeline in mind, . . . the promotion never ends" (Brannon 2007, 51).

Delgado and Wood (2007) relay time information in hindsight, recounting how much they invested in each marketing technique they used. For example, they note that creating lapel pins took "2 weeks (2 hours for creation and 2 weeks in production)" and developing an Internet announcement took "2 hours" (Delgado and Wood 2007, 135).

Now that you have learned about putting the timeline for all the tasks in your plan into a spreadsheet, when you revise your plan, it will be easy to shift tasks around in the schedule to streamline the process for your next marketing cycle. It will give you a sense of how long the short-term tasks took as well as the big picture of how long the entire process took. Using a spreadsheet format, a whiteboard, or Gantt chart software like GanttProject (www.ganttproject.biz) will keep all of your tasks organized. A Gantt chart makes it easy to track whether you plan to repeat any of the tasks. If you plan on tweeting about the same electronic resource four times over a year, you can mark your chart in four separate months. Reusing wording from previous announcements is a time saver because there is only the initial time investment of its creation and then its planned reuse. Patrons may need to see/hear about a new electronic resource multiple times before it becomes familiar. Hearing about a resource too much, however, may have the opposite effect ("I'm sick of that commercial!," for example), so you'll need to think about how many times to repeat messages, and how often, so that your patrons are not oversaturated by the messages.

Staff

The people behind your marketing plan are the keys to its success. If you are tasking people with components of the plan, it is essential that you are clear about their roles. Account for *all* staff involved so that nothing falls through the cracks. If your plan involves designing flyers to hand out at an information session, think through all the steps of creating a flyer to determine if you will need assistance. Perhaps someone is an excellent designer and can make the flyer, and someone else knows a cut-rate photocopy shop, but nobody thought about who would go to the shop to place the order and pick it up. Forgotten tasks are likely to end up being taken care of by the coordinator of the marketing plan (this means you). Be considerate of others' time in this process but also consider your own efforts, especially if marketing is only a small part of your overall job description. You don't want to burn out because of time spent on unanticipated tasks or ruin goodwill with your marketing team by asking people to do things at the last minute.

We found in the literature that library staff at all levels can be involved in marketing tasks. Eighteen of the twenty-three documents in Kennedy's 2010 research mention the people involved in the marketing campaign. The people were generally not identified specifically with a role in the campaign but rather were described as part of an "ad hoc committee," "each assistant librarian," or "a combination of librarians and support staff" (Bancroft et al. 1998; Edwards and Webb 1999; Metz-Wiseman and Rodgers 2007). When you compose your own marketing plan, you do want to name specific people and their roles so that the work is distributed and those people know they are responsible for completing their tasks.

Betz and colleagues (2009) note that the level of effort per staff member may vary during the course of the marketing plan: "Initially, for the librarian, a high level of effort was required to organize the program; as time passed, the ongoing work was more clerical, with the librarian averaging two to three hours per week on the program" (252). You may find in your own plans that you will have many activities that require more time to complete in the beginning than later on, as the plan progresses and tasks shift into a maintenance mode.

Roberts and Appleton (2003) note, "We also had to ensure that we had the staff help and support in place, so all help desk staff throughout the campuses had to at least be aware of NetLibrary and had to be able to use it on a basic level" (85). Based on what you have learned in this section and in chapter 2, you would assume that Roberts and Appleton's team charged people with training, follow-up, and proof of competence with using NetLibrary at the basic level, although this was not mentioned in the article.

Sometimes your marketing team may align with external partners for events. You may choose to host an event for your law firm's new lawyers, for example. If you have designed the event to be an e-resources fair, in order to demonstrate all the electronic resources available to those new hires, you may want to partner with multiple vendors of law content. Identifying who at those vendors is the responsible party for contributing to the success of your event is an important consideration; include them (along with their e-mail addresses and phone numbers) in your staffing plan for this marketing event. Partnering on events like this, especially if those partners are local, is a great way to embed your library in the community it serves as well as benefit from marketing expertise your own team may not have.

Budget

Of the twenty-three institutions represented in Kennedy's 2010 research, twelve either report having no budget for marketing or do not mention budgeting. This is in keeping with Lindsay's (2004) finding that "the library's annual budget does not usually include funding specifically for marketing" (10). Of the five libraries that mention a specific budgeted dollar amount, the least is $137 (a postcard campaign) and the largest is $3,000 (laptops purchased for on-site marketing of electronic resources). Ellis (2004) comments, "Unfortunately, we do not have a special budget that can be used for marketing, so we had to think of marketing techniques we could afford with the general resources we have in the library" (57).

Betz and colleagues (2009) obtained sponsorship by Elsevier to support the payment of graduate student trainers as well as creation of instructional materials, leaving the library to pay for supervisory time. Broering, Chauncey, and Gomes (2006) received regional funding for their efforts to provide health information services to communities. If budgeting is a major concern for your library, consider collaborating with others or obtaining sponsors. Partnering with a business school to enlist students who are professionally minded to assist with designing and implementing your marketing plan may be another option.

Delgado and Wood (2007) share their advice about budgeting: "One of the lessons learned is that creativity has costs and that the budgeting needs to be overestimated; the final expenditures for the promotion exceeded the budget" (141). However, we caution you to be realistic about your budget, to not overestimate too much if you can help it. Represent what you think you will need in the budget. If your judgment is poor the first time you conduct a marketing plan, then that is all part of the learning process. You'll get better at budgeting with experience. Overestimating just to overestimate is not advised.

In chapter 2, you learned that items needed for your marketing plan may not have a visible cost but should still be noted in your budget. Brannon (2007) includes a sample budget, and in it she notes that three items are free, when in fact they have a real cost: "website promotions," "e-mails to patrons and community members," and "presentations to public" (55).

These deliverables have a cost for the library, in staff time and the tools needed (computer, software, etc.) for the development and deployment of these items. Instead of marking things like this as free in your own budget, consider noting the number of staff hours needed to complete the tasks. "E-mails to patrons and community members" may have a real cost of two staff hours. "Presentations to public" can be broken down further to include development time and actual presentation time, with the staffing level and number of hours noted for each.

Measurement

Although it may seem difficult to know how and what to measure related to your chosen marketing techniques, we have some great examples of how libraries have done just that. We present here practical examples in use at libraries that can help you plan to measure your own marketing techniques. Three kinds of measurements we have found in the literature include simple counts; questionnaires, surveys, and pre- and post-tests; and usage statistics.

Simple Counts

Sometimes all you need to know to tell if your marketing strategy is working is a simple count, a hands-off approach that doesn't require input from your patrons. Here is an example of counts of people and time: "The [Student Ambassadors] instructed almost 500 people in forty-four classes across fourteen months" (Betz et al. 2009, 252). If you are gathering simple counts for your marketing plan and it is your first attempt at marketing, as in this example, then the counts become your baseline data. When you run through your next cycle of marketing, you can compare the new counts to your first attempt. If your marketing goal is to increase attendance, here is an example that demonstrates success: "Overall, the program participants have increased to over 3,500 and class attendees to over 425 people as a result of the project extension to the new sites" (Broering, Chauncey, and Gomes 2006, 9). You could improve on this example by providing the previous numbers of participants and attendees to show the percentage increase. If this marketing was repeated, the library could begin to show trends over time for numbers of program participants (Is it going up or down from one year to the next?) and numbers of class attendees.

In an attempt to reach as many undergraduate music students as possible, a librarian at Hong Kong Baptist University staged a flash-mob-style promotional event. She positioned her promotion near the entry to the room where all undergraduate music students attended the required Music Assembly class. Her promotion reached 127 of the 141 students registered in that class. The stated goal for the promotion was to "promote electronic resources that are important to music undergraduates" (Lai 2015, 282). Given that the goal was simple, the measurement of a simple count is appropriate.

Here's one more example of a simple count that provides more information than one would expect: "Although the CD-ROM database questions being asked at the reference desk have decreased in number since the implementation of the mobile unit (to 8,355 for 1993), they have become more sophisticated in nature" (Parker-Gibson 1994, 126). We don't know how the level of sophistication was measured, or if it even was, but being able to notice that the quality of reference desk transactions changed is valuable data. It also shows an awareness on the part of the person counting the transactions; this is the kind of colleague you want working on your marketing team.

Questionnaires, Surveys, and Pre- and Post-Tests

You can gather feedback about your marketing techniques by asking your patrons for their input. The ways libraries reported doing this are via questionnaires, surveys, and pre- and post-tests. Gathering feedback can be done systematically by using the same questionnaire for everyone who enters the library on a given day, administering the same survey to a select group of patrons, or giving the same pre-test and post-test to patrons who participated in a class session or demonstration.

A LITTLE MARKETING/LIBRARY INSTRUCTION GOES A LONG WAY

Shelley Woods, User Education Coordinator at the Sheridan College Library (www.sheridancollege.ca), describes some of their efforts to market e-resources at Sheridan.

In 2010, Sheridan College Library Services redesigned their website to improve access to electronic resources. They achieved this by decreasing the amount of text, and adding images and Springshare program-related LibGuides to the site. A Summon federated search box was added to the top of the site allowing students to access 85% of the college's electronic resources with a single Google-like search. Since adding the Summon search box, hits to the library catalog (including e-books and streaming video) have increased considerably.

With 155 electronic resources, including databases, e-books, streaming video and online courses, continual training is necessary for library staff. A Coordinator position was created to identify and meet student information literacy and staff training needs. Training for staff is generally provided for any recently licensed or acquired electronic resource, new platform changes, and as specifically requested by staff. The training has been a combination of face-to-face instruction and webinars led by librarians and vendors. Ongoing staff training contributes to the quality of research and support services the library offers to students.

Student responses to a fall 2011 SurveyMonkey survey show students are more likely to search library electronic resources after receiving in-class instruction. Of the sixty-four students who completed the survey, only 46.9% had used the Sheridan College Library online prior to having classroom information literacy (IL) instruction. After having participated in a library IL session, 96.9% of respondents said they would be more likely to visit the Sheridan College Library online. Student comments support the notion that use of electronic resources will increase as a direct result of classroom instruction.

> The information provided about how to use data bases was excellent. I have never tried it before and it is really a very helpful tool provided by the college.

> I had no idea that I had access to all the resources through the Sheridan online library.

> Even though I used the library online before, that presentation provided me with more sources to use and showed me how to use them.

> The presentation was a great help in understanding all of the different online databases we have access to.

Course instruction often includes a feedback form, as described in this example: "The evaluations proved that the sessions were useful and well-received, and Brown felt that the mixture of 'too basic' and 'too advanced' on the feedback forms indicated that the level of sophistication of the classes was right on target" (Betz et al. 2009, 252). Pre- and post-tests, brief tests to determine what a patron knows about a resource before and after class instruction, are also used: "Formative and summative evaluations were carried out by an experienced evaluator" (Henderson et al. 2009, 136). To eliminate your own bias and achieve maximum objectivity, you can ask a colleague to administer and evaluate the tests.

The kind of information you will get from a questionnaire, survey, or test can be complex and often is valuable in providing nuances, such as *how well* your plan is succeeding. A simple count, as described earlier, won't tell you how well your patrons are performing in their mastery of a database. It will tell you only how many people were in the classroom. Choosing an appropriate measurement, therefore, is critical to gauging the success or failure of your chosen technique.

Usage Statistics

Very often the goal of a marketing plan for electronic resources is simply to raise the awareness and usage of a particular resource by a given target group. By demonstrating to group members why the database/e-journal/e-book can be valuable to them, a library may expect that its usage will increase. To determine if usage has increased, gather usage statistics before any marketing is done to establish baseline data, and then collect usage statistics during and after marketing to see if there is a difference. If you choose usage statistics as a measurement, be aware of the natural increases and decreases in the use of any electronic resource over the course of the calendar year, depending on external circumstances such as a busy season for a special library or midsemester/school-year projects coming due in a public library or academic setting. We recommend collecting an entire year's worth of usage statistics before any marketing is completed so that you can compare the time during and after the marketing technique has been employed with the same month in the previous calendar year. Brannon (2007) concludes that her library's marketing technique was "successful in raising database usage statistics" (52), but she does not tell us if the usage statistics increase because of the marketing or if perhaps they always rise during that time of year. The same is true about Turner, Wilkie, and Rosen's (2004) conclusion: "Usage rocketed following Awareness Week—from 43,000 distinct hosts in October to over 50,000 in November" (266). Having the comparative data may tell you if it is your marketing that caused the rise or if a rise or fall was due to other external circumstances.

"In the months immediately following the Science Media Fair, we noticed an increase in the use of EndNote which was demonstrated by an increase in the number of questions at the reference desk and an increase in the attendance of EndNote classes" (Soehner and Wei 2001, 90). As demonstrated in this library's measurement, an immediate increase in usage means that the electronic resource is fresh in your patrons' minds. You may find that over time the usage will slowly creep downward as patrons discover other resources that supplant the use of the initial resource. You might consider repeating your marketing plan to remind patrons of why the resource may be the best one for their needs. Repeating the plan could garner interest from those patrons who missed it the first time.

Multiple Methods

In this section, we have highlighted the three kinds of measurements we have read about being used by libraries for their e-resources marketing plans. Crenshaw (2014) thoughtfully notes in his article about marketing music databases, "The potential for influences outside the library cannot be avoided. Rather than relying solely on vendor usage statistics, then, triangulation of research methods is needed to increase confidence in the results. Surveys, interviews, and Web site log analysis are examples of additional methods that could be employed" (236). Each technique in your marketing strategy will need to be measured independently. Since each technique (and its measurement) has its own unique strengths and weaknesses, using more than one technique (and, therefore, more than one measurement) may indeed increase your confidence in your overall findings.

Assessment

The basis for assessment is using your measurements to determine how well you've accomplished your goals, giving you direction for where to head next. Assessment answers the question, "What did we learn by doing this marketing?" What you learned informs your next marketing cycle.

At the point of assessment, have your marketing team list suggestions for the next cycle of marketing, summarizing which aspects were successful and should be repeated and which need adjustment. Be sure to write this all down while it is fresh in your team's mind. Depending on the makeup of your team, members may rotate off or the entire plan may lie dormant while another plan picks up. When you're ready to come back to this one, having direction on where to begin with the next cycle will allow you to initiate the process quickly.

Now ask yourself, "Does the measurement and assessment match our goal?" Having a clearly stated goal for a marketing plan should lead to a strategy to achieve that goal, and identifying how to measure the strategy will ultimately tell a library if the campaign has helped to reach the goal. Kennedy (2010) applied the model in figure 3.5 to twenty-three articles written about library marketing plans to see if libraries efficiently designed their plans for e-resources in order to gain information about how to proceed in their next steps in a marketing cycle. Only three institutions chose a strategy that matched the goal and identified a way to measure it so that they gained actionable knowledge. You can do better! Ask yourself the same questions posed in figure 3.5 to find out if you're on the right track.

FIGURE 3.5 Efficacy Model

The contents in table 3.2 are taken directly from the three articles about institutions that did a good job identifying a goal, forming an appropriate strategy, choosing a measurement that fits the strategy, and assessing how the measurement will guide the steps in their next marketing cycle.

As demonstrated in this summary of Betz and colleagues (2009) about what worked and what needed tweaking, you can see that assessment helps to give direction for the next marketing cycle: "Future sessions will be restructured to relieve repetitive administrative work, and she will again hire enthusiastic, marketing-minded science graduate students who make the sessions fun. To further increase attendance, Brown recommends setting seminar dates earlier, and she found marketing via Facebook and Myspace less successful than expected, with e-mail being by far the most effective communication tool" (252). Broering, Chauncey, and Gomes (2006) found that their marketing cycle would need to include publicity if the plan included course instruction: "As indicated by the attendee study, publicity is an essential factor in generating class participants" (17). A fun tweak in future marketing plans would be to experiment with a variety of ways to publicize those offerings.

Roberts and Appleton (2003) possibly expected a dramatic rise in usage statistics as a result of marketing but found that the "embedding of those e-journals has taken time, so we must not be alarmed if we do not see a significant rise in use of e-books immediately" (86). The step of assessment gives you the chance to consider why your marketing plan may not have worked as you expected. Technology is definitely a consideration for marketing e-resources, as Parker-Gibson (1994) discovered about her door-to-door marketing demonstrations of the library's CD-ROMs: "If I were choosing new equipment for this application today, I would purchase a 486 machine with a larger memory for faster searching and a larger cache for quicker access to large databases such as UMI's, a brighter LCD panel projector (for rooms that can be made dim but not dark), and a cart with large wheels for smooth transit over brick sidewalks and curbs" (125). It is evident that she found the office-to-office marketing of CD-ROMs to be successful but the mechanics of the process, a bit awkward. It is the step of assessment that allows time for reflection to see which aspects of your marketing plan are winners and which will be removed from your next attempt.

Two libraries started with simple marketing plans. One found that the "survey, itself a marketing tool, is the beginning" (Hart, Coleman, and Yu 2001, 50). Another found that the "success of Awareness Week led to more

TABLE 3.2 Success in Planning

	GOAL	STRATEGY	MEASUREMENT	ASSESSMENT
1	"The goals of instructional sessions are to promote the library's resources as scholarly and reliable, highlight special features of the resources, teach literacy skills, and present the library as a welcoming place."	"Tours and introductory sessions called Smart Start Library to acquaint incoming students with the library's services and collections (including online databases and resources available via the Web site)."	"Students are asked to complete a short printed questionnaire following the session to help the library measure the effectiveness of instructional sessions."	"Of the two hundred and eighty participants who completed questionnaires in September 2005, 87% of the respondents replied either 'agree' or 'strongly agree' in response to the comment 'Orientation leaders influenced my decision to attend.' These numbers demonstrate the value of word-of-mouth advertising."
2	"Provide information to senior administrators regarding student awareness, perceptions and satisfaction of WSU's efforts to create a virtual library system."	"The research team, in cooperation with library staff, created a questionnaire with 29 questions."	"The response rate was less than expected. Of the 2,965 surveys mailed out, 271 were returned by November 22, 2000, for a response rate of 9.41%."	"From these figures, it is clear that the library's efforts to promote directly its electronic resources [are] not effective because only 18.5% of the students had learned about electronic resources from library publicity or librarians."
3	"The objectives of this research were to (1) assess the awareness and usage of current electronic resources and services by a segment of the Libraries' customer base, the faculty and teaching staff, (2) assess the obstacles to use of electronic information, and (3) determine how to increase the use of the available technologies and services."	"A random sample of 400 faculty (including teaching assistants) was generated by computer from a population of over 2,300."	"Thirty-nine percent of the recipients of the survey responded."	"The most common cited obstacle to using information technology is lack of information; to increase use of electronic resources the Libraries need to provide more information and instruction on available resources. Obviously, current promotional efforts have not been sufficient."

NOTE: Example 1: Woods 2007, 113, 112, 112, and 112, respectively; example 2: Holley and Powell 2004, 46, 46, 47, and 48, respectively; example 3: Hart, Coleman, and Yu 2001, 44, 44, 44, and 50, respectively.

ambitious plans for 2003" (Turner, Wilkie, and Rosen 2004, 266). No matter how simple or complex your plans are, the assessment step is one that should not be missed, although it may be tempting to think about this all later because the marketing involving the patrons is finished. We hope that by providing examples of what libraries have learned by marketing, and how this information can guide their next steps, we have convinced you of the importance of completing an assessment of your activities.

Marketing Your Electronic Resources Can Change Your Library

Think back to when you were a kid and learned how to ride a bike well enough that your mom or dad could remove the training wheels or to the moment you were steady enough on your roller skates that you could just concentrate on the fun rather than on remaining upright. If you never mastered these particular skills, you likely still have something in mind for which you remember the moment you realized you knew how to do it. You felt great, confident!

This kind of confidence building is exactly what your marketing plan has the potential to do for your library patrons. Your plan has the potential to change what your patrons know about what your library has to offer them, or how to use an e-resource they didn't know how to use before, or ways to do what they've always done with your collection more efficiently.

Give this quote some thought for a moment: "Effective training is one of the most valuable promotional tools of an electronic collection, because training helps to limit anxiety associated with electronic searching" (Kendall and Massarella, 2001, 31). If your marketing plan is related to education or training, then you are creating a situation that may give your patrons confidence in the place of anxiety. As a result of your marketing plan, your patrons may leave your library feeling like you did the day you rode your bike without training wheels. That's powerful!

Electronic resources exist in an environment that is about sharing—peer-to-peer, mashed up, and continually shifting. To be noticed, your marketing plan for electronic resources will need to be fun, transparent, approachable, and flexible. And why wouldn't it be all of these things? You're forging connections between active content and your patrons, who are live, enthusiastic people.

As you head into the next chapter, we encourage you to try to capture that enthusiasm in the written report of your marketing plan. The report of your planned action is a tool to convince your library's administration to approve your plan, so think positively and use powerful, upbeat language.

Recommended Resources for Further Reading

Calkins, Tim. *Breakthrough Marketing Plans: How to Stop Wasting Time and Start Driving Growth.* New York: Palgrave Macmillan, 2008. http://timcalkins.com/publications/breakthrough-marketing-plans.

> This book will get you motivated to think creatively about your marketing plan. The book provides some good guidance about branding and positioning your library's electronic resources services.

Holley, Robert P., and Ronald R. Powell. "Student Satisfaction with Electronic Library Resources at Wayne State University." *Journal of Access Services 2,* no. 1 (2004): 41–57.

> This article describes an academic library partnership with a business school class (marketing) to develop a survey for undergraduates about their use of electronic resources. This may spark an idea for how you could collaborate with student groups that use your library.

MarketingTeacher.com. "SWOT Analysis Examples." Accessed May 3, 2017. www.marketingteacher.com/lesson-store/#swot-analysis-examples.

This webpage provides some examples of SWOT analyses performed by professional organizations. Seeing how other groups have completed their SWOT analyses may give you things to think about as you conduct your own.

Row, Heath. "Influencing the Influencers: How Online Advertising and Media Impact Word of Mouth." DoubleClick.com, 2006. http://static .googleusercontent.com/media/www.google.co.jp/ja/jp/doubleclick/pdfs/ DoubleClick-12-2006-Influencing-the-Influencers.pdf.

This article has some great graphics that show the effects of word-of-mouth marketing from the "influencers" in society. You may consider how to partner with your existing library fans to act as influencers on the rest of your patron population.

References

Bancroft, Audrey F., Vicki F. Croft, Robert Speth, and Dretha M. Phillips. 1998. "A Forward-Looking Library Use Survey: WSU Libraries in the 21st Century." *The Journal of Academic Librarianship* 24 (3): 216–24.

Bartley, Bronwen, Seishi Gomibuchi, and Robin Mann. 2007. "Best Practices in Achieving a Customer-Focused Culture." *Benchmarking: An International Journal* 14 (4): 482–96.

Betz, Brie, Stephanie W. Brown, Deb Barberi, and Jeanne M. Langendorfer. 2009. "Marketing Library Database Services to End Users: Peer-to-Peer Outreach Using the Student Ambassador Program (SAm)." *The Serials Librarian* 56 (1): 250–4.

Booth, Andrew. 2004. "Introducing an Evidence-Based Approach to Marketing and Promotional Activities." In *Evidence-Based Practice for Information Professionals: A Handbook,* edited by Andrew Booth and Anne Brice, 244–58. London: Facet Publishing.

Brannon, Sian. 2007. "A Successful Promotional Campaign—We Can't Keep Quiet about Our Electronic Resources." *The Serials Librarian* 53 (3): 41–55.

Broering, Naomi C., Gregory A. Chauncey, and Stacy L. Gomes. 2006. "Outreach to Public Libraries, Senior Centers, and Clinics to Improve Patient and Consumer Health Care: An Update." *Journal of Consumer Health on the Internet* 10 (3): 1–20.

Brunner, Karen B. 2009. "A Week of Our Own: Create a National Library Week Celebration That Promotes Good Will All Year Long." *AALL Spectrum* 13 (6): 8–34.

Burkman, Amy. 2004. "A Practical Approach to Marketing the School Library." *Library Media Connection* 23 (3): 42–43.

Conduit, Jodie, and Felix T. Mavondo. 2001. "How Critical Is Internal Customer Orientation to Market Orientation?" *Journal of Business Research* 51 (1): 11–24.

For Further Information

Journals to read to keep current on marketing research:

> *International Journal of Market Research*
> *Journal of Marketing Management*
> *Journal of Retailing*
> *Marketing Research*

The articles in these journals are written by professionals in the area of marketing. Browse the journals or add the tables of contents to your RSS reader to stay current with ways to learn about your target group, issues related to serving your patrons, and how to manage your marketing tasks.

■ ■ ■

Databases to search for articles on marketing:

> *ABI/Inform (ProQuest)*
> *Business Source Premier (EBSCO)*
> *PsycInfo*

These databases point to full-text articles about marketing-related concepts such as "consumer attitudes, consumer behavior, consumer psychology" (Booth 2004, 246), and so forth. Sort your search results by date published in order to stay current with what is happening in the marketing field.

Cosgrove, John A. 2006. "Drop Them a Postcard: Another Way to Reach Your Patrons." *College and Undergraduate Libraries* 12 (1): 93–100.

Crenshaw, Clayton. 2014. "Promoting Music Library Resources—with Mixed Results." *Music Reference Services Quarterly* 17 (4): 226–36.

Delgado, Diana, and Michael A. Wood. 2007. "Get IT and Go." *The Serials Librarian* 53 (3): 125–46.

Edwards, Vilas, and Rachel Webb. 1999. "Seamless Access to Journals in the Hybrid Library: The 'Find a Journal' Service." *Serials* 12 (3): 277–82.

Ellis, Rachel. 2004. "Marketing of Electronic Resources: Projects and Experiences." *Serials* 17 (1): 57–59.

Ferriol, Ellinor. 2007. "Marketing Strategies for School Libraries." Presentation August 29 at the Manila International Book Fair, Manila, Philippines, August 29–September 2. www.slideshare.net/UPLSAA/marketing-strategies-for-school-libraries-by-ms-ellinor-ferriol.

Hart, Judith L., Vicki Coleman, and Hong Yu. 2001. "Marketing Electronic Resources and Services." *The Reference Librarian* 32 (67/68): 41–55.

Henderson, Cynthia L., Darlene P. Kelly, Joe Swanson, Roland B. Welmaker Sr., and Xiomara E. Arango. 2009. "Project Uncover Health Information Databases: A Collaboration to Promote the Use of National Library of Medicine Consumer Health Databases." *Journal of Consumer Health on the Internet* 13 (2): 135–42.

Holley, Robert P., and Ronald R. Powell. 2004. "Student Satisfaction with Electronic Library Resources at Wayne State University." *Journal of Access Services* 2 (1): 41–57.

Kendall, Sandra, and Susan Massarella. 2001. "Prescription for Successful Marketing." *Computers in Libraries* 21 (8): 28–33.

Kennedy, Marie R. 2010. "Cycling Through: Paths Libraries Take to Marketing Electronic Resources." Paper presented at the Library Assessment Conference, Baltimore MD, October 27. http://digitalcommons.lmu.edu/librarian_pubs/3.

Lai, Katie. 2015. "A Roadshow of Library Resources: Familiarize Students with What You Have." *Reference Services Review* 8 (2): 280–91.

Lindsay, Anita Rothwell. 2004. *Marketing and Public Relations Practices in College Libraries.* Chicago: American Library Association.

Manda, Paul A. 2005. "Electronic Resource Usage in Academic and Research Institutions in Tanzania." *Information Development* 21 (4): 269–82.

Metz-Wiseman, Monica, and Skye L. Rodgers. 2007. "Thinking Outside of the Library Box." *The Serials Librarian* 53 (3): 17–39.

Millet, Michelle S., and Clint Chamberlain. 2007. "Word-of-Mouth Marketing Using Peer Tutors." *The Serials Librarian* 53 (3): 95–105.

Pankl, Robert R. 2010. "Marketing the Public Library's Business Resources to Small Businesses." *Journal of Business and Finance Librarianship* 15 (2): 94–103.

Parker-Gibson, Necia. 1994. "Taking It to the Streets: Mobile CD-ROM Workshops on Campus." *Research Strategies* 12 (2): 122–6.

Pipkin, Ann Marie, and Terri Kirk. 2005. "Strategic Marketing for School Library Media Centers." Presentation at the American Association of School Librarians 12th National Conference and Exhibition, Pittsburgh, Pennsylvania, October 6–9. www.ala.org/aasl/sites/ala .org.aasl/files/content/conferencesandevents/confarchive/pittsburgh/ StrategicMarketingforSLMCs.pdf.

Ramsey, Elizabeth. 2014. "Using Slide Shows to Engage Patrons with Library Resources." *Pacific Northwest Library Association Quarterly* 79 (1): 79–83.

Roberts, Sue, and Leo Appleton. 2003. "E-texts—A Targeted Approach." *Serials* 16 (1): 83–87.

Row, Heath. 2006. "Influencing the Influencers: How Online Advertising and Media Impact Word of Mouth." DoubleClick.com. http://static .googleusercontent.com/media/www.google.co.jp/ja/jp/doubleclick/ pdfs/DoubleClick-12-2006-Influencing-the-Influencers.pdf.

Ryan, Damian, and Calvin Jones. 2009. *Understanding Digital Marketing: Marketing Strategies for Engaging the Digital Generation.* London: Kogan Page.

Saw, Grace, Wendy Abbott, Jessie Donaghey, and Carolyn McDonald. 2013. "Social Media for International Students—It's Not All about Facebook." *Library Management* 34 (3): 156–74.

Schrock, Kathy. 2003. "Promoting Your Library Media Center Program Is a Necessity." *Library Journal,* November 1. http://lj.libraryjournal .com/2003/11/ljarchives/the-abcs-of-marketing/#_.

Soehner, Catherine, and Wei Wei. 2001. "Bridge Beyond the Walls: Two Outreach Models at the University of California, Santa Cruz." *Science and Technology Libraries* 21 (1): 87–95.

Song, Yoo-Seong. 2006. "Evidence Based Marketing for Academic Librarians." *Evidence Based Library and Information Practice* 1 (1): 69–80.

St. Clair, Guy. 1990. "Marketing and Promotion in Today's Special Library." *Aslib Proceedings* 42 (7/8): 213–17.

Thorpe, Angie, and Heather Bowman. 2013. "Promoting Discovery: Creating an In-Depth Library Marketing Campaign." *Journal of Library Administration* 52 (2/3): 100–21.

Turner, Alison, Fran Wilkie, and Nick Rosen. 2004. "Virtual but Visible: Developing a Promotion Strategy for an Electronic Library." *New Library World* 105 (7/8): 262–8.

Wallace, Linda K. 2004. *Libraries, Mission, and Marketing: Writing Mission Statements That Work.* Chicago: American Library Association.

Woods, Shelley L. 2007. "A Three-Step Approach to Marketing Electronic Resources at Brock University." *The Serials Librarian* 53 (3): 107–24.

Construct Your Written Marketing Plan Report

4

IN THIS CHAPTER

✓ Write for Your Audience

✓ Address the Components in Your Report

✓ This Marketing Grant Request Form Caught Our Eyes!

✓ Wrap It Up

Early on we suggested that you write your thoughts and decisions down and keep notes for your team as you progress through the components of your marketing plan. Those notes are likely a mess, right? We'll help you get them organized during the course of this chapter. At some point, you're going to present your work externally, likely to your library's administrators, to seek their approval and support. You may have gotten verbal approval to move forward with your marketing plan and have been asked to provide a summary of your activities after the project is completed, rather than in advance. Whether you construct your report before or after your marketing campaign, you will need to package the notes you've been taking into a formal report so that it can be presented in a neat and convincing way to the stakeholders at your institution. This chapter describes the components of that report. We're thinking loosely about the word *report* in this chapter, defining it as any collocation of the components of your marketing plan into a single document. To help you visualize what a successful marketing plan report looks like, we present seven examples in part II of this book: example 1 is for an entirely online library; examples 2 and 3 are public library marketing plan reports; example 4 is from a consortium of community college libraries; and examples 5, 6, and 7 are university marketing plan reports. We'll tell you what we like about each one in the course of this chapter.

We know that the important aspect of developing a marketing plan is the planning, not the resulting plan. We don't want you to get too caught up in the details of creating your marketing plan report. We want you to get out there and put your plan in motion. To help you move forward quickly, along with the examples presented in part II of the book, we offer a downloadable blank template that you may want to use as you write your report. The template follows the organizational prompts in every section in this chapter. Visit www.alaeditions.org/webextras to access the Word version of the template, and customize it as you desire; you will also find the template at http://digitalcommons .lmu.edu/librarian_pubs/37. Happy writing!

Web Extra

Visit www.alaeditions.org/webextras to access Word versions of these reports that you can adapt for your own use.

Write for Your Audience

The format of a marketing plan report is flexible, and the components can be expanded or left off entirely to suit your needs. Customize the report to conform to the desires of your audience. Whom in your library do you need to persuade that your team has a plan that will be or has been successfully managed? Imagine that you will deliver a printed report to your library's administration; you know from experience that your administration is a no-nonsense, bottom-line kind of group. If this is the case, focus more on developing a brief, clear, and data-packed executive summary. Perhaps your administration prefers to make decisions by committee and will invite you to present your plan in person to a management team, without a request for a printed report. If this is the case, focus your presentation on buzzwords and repeated information so that the management team will be able to remember the key components of your plan. You'll also want to bring a one-page printed summary report to leave with each member of the management team.

Regardless of to whom you will deliver the report and what format it will take, there are some key questions you will want to answer for any audience. Consider the components discussed in the following section to be the basics, and plan to add more information if your audience warrants it. The downloadable template that comes with this book (available at www.alaeditions.org/webextras) includes all of the basic components as prompts for you to complete as you move through writing your own report.

Address the Components in Your Report

The components discussed in this section are designed to convince your audience that your marketing team has created a well-considered plan, taking into account big issues that they care most about, like time, staffing, and budget. The flow of your written report will follow a similar pattern to that of your marketing plan. You'll begin by outlining the report in a table of contents and then move to the following components: executive summary; current market and target market; goals, strategy, and proposed measurements; and timeline, staff, and budget.

Executive Summary

The truth is that most reports are not read all the way through. The good news is that you've already got the makings for an excellent executive summary, the most frequently read portion of a multipage report. It begins the report by asking and answering these questions:

- What's the problem?
- What's your solution?
- Why now?

The executive summary tells the reader what the rest of the report contains. It is generally brief; for a marketing plan for electronic resources, a one-page executive summary is plenty. A report summary works well as a bulleted list; use this format if reasonable. Write your executive summary as if nothing else in the report will be read, employing action words with a positive attitude. Attempt to write your summary using few acronyms and less library jargon so that it reads smoothly to a nonlibrarian audience.

What's the Problem?

You began your marketing plan by writing a project description, and much of that can be pasted right into the executive summary. The "why" component of your project description is salient for this part of the summary.

You can draw from your SWOT analysis for this section if marketing electronic resources will resolve a perceived opportunity or threat. The Galway-Mayo Institute of Technology (example 6) has chosen to reproduce the entire SWOT analysis (including the related chart) in its entirety in its report. Check it out if you would like to compare your library's strengths, weaknesses, opportunities, and threats with Galway-Mayo's. (We wonder, "Are there more similarities than differences?") In your own report, you don't have to include the complete SWOT analysis, but you can pick pieces from it as they relate to your marketing plan.

What's Your Solution?

This section allows you to toot your own horn in coming up with a marketing plan that can address a communication need for your library. Has your team branded itself, or have you named your marketing plan? How many people volunteered to be on your marketing team? Is the marketing plan important to more people than just you? Yes, it is! Stating that you've identified a need and have defined its possible solution through marketing is powerful. Be direct.

We draw your attention to the executive summary from Loyola Marymount University (example 7). The summary briefly outlines how the library plans to announce its new streaming video service, Kanopy. The last sentence is a bold one, a real selling point that tells readers up front how they will know if the marketing plan works: "Success of the rollout will be measured by analyzing usage stats and referral links."

Why Now?

It is important to convey why your marketing plan should be implemented *right now*. You want to include this in the executive summary because otherwise the decision makers might assume that the issue isn't pressing and can wait until next year, or the year after that, and all of your efforts in getting to know your target market in the current environment will be wasted.

Our advice is to write the executive summary after you write up all the other components. This way you will be sure to cover all the highlights from the rest of your report.

One reason we include the marketing plan for the Winnetka-Northfield Public Library District (example 2) in this book is to show you what an exciting marketing plan can accomplish in only six pages. The writers chose to put the information that would normally go into an executive summary into a paragraph-long introduction, and they do so quite successfully. We get a sense of the community in which the library is situated, what the potential patronage for the library may be, and how the marketing plan may increase the use of the library's resources:

> The Winnetka-Northfield Public Library District encompasses two highly educated, affluent communities on the North Shore of Chicago. The community is known for its outstanding schools, including the nationally recognized New Trier High School. The library serves a population of 17,808 with median family incomes over $100,000. Our library has great customer service and excellent resources but we needed to generate greater awareness of its online resources. While 85 percent of the district has library cards, our cardholders don't use their online resources as well as they could. This project was designed to increase both staff and patron awareness of the library's online services by revamping the way our message is delivered to busy residents.

The Milner Library marketing plan (example 5) also uses an introduction rather than an executive summary and in it references both the mission and vision statements of the library. Earlier we suggested that you use your library mission statement as your guide in developing the marketing plan for electronic resources at your library. The Milner Library plan is an example of how to prove you've done just that: you can quote it in your marketing plan report!

Current Market and Target Market

The audience for your marketing plan report is likely familiar with your library's environment, but your interpretation can help them to view it with fresh eyes. This section of your report should note all the things your team has done to find out about your library's environment as it exists today. Include a summary of where your library is, who your patrons are, what their information concerns may be, and which e-resources you have to offer them. Also describe the target market for your marketing plan, defining the group's members and convincing your library's administration why they are the people with whom you want to open a dialogue through marketing.

Web Extra

WEB

Like what you see in Winnetka-Northfield's report introduction? Visit www.alaeditions.org/webextras to access a Word version of the library's report that you can adapt for your own use.

What data-gathering methods did you use to identify your target market, and what did you learn about them as a result? Descriptions of these activities and outcomes go in this section.

You don't have to use the heading Current Market in your marketing plan. The NOVELNY marketing plan (example 1) uses Situation Analysis, and this section describes some essential pieces of information about the current market. It tells us who the patrons are ("New York State residents"), where the library is situated (exclusively online, accessed by New Yorkers "at their local public library or from the convenience of their home, school, or office"), and how the library is currently serving its population ("Of total searches, 60 percent are currently from colleges and universities with only 13 percent from New York's 1,100 public libraries"). Only one paragraph is needed to give us a sense of NOVELNY's current market.

The section describing the target market (titled Audience) of NOVELNY is quite long, spanning multiple pages. For a library that serves an entire state, the planners have to split their marketing efforts into the discrete groups they have identified as targets. They note very general audiences (General Consumer Population) and also focus specifically on smaller potential groups of users (State Legislature Elected Officials and Aides). The choice to market to an exclusive group like the legislature is a strategic one because this is presumably the group to continue to legislate funding for the library. Perhaps you should consider something like this for your own marketing plan; if you have an elite group of potential patrons for your electronic resources, you can develop an entire marketing plan for that group. Food for thought.

The 2012 communications plan for Worthington Libraries is not specifically about marketing electronic resources, but we include it as example 3 for you to review the Public Relations and Marketing section. It is clear from the first bullet point that the writers realize they do not know enough about their current market, and their plan identifies steps to take to get that information. They propose working with a consultant to help them "implement the community portion of the strategic planning process." They also plan to use focus groups and surveys to get to know their patrons better, two techniques mentioned in this book. A creative idea is to "involve the staff in trend tracking." Because staff are working with patrons throughout the day, they are a great place to start for information gathering.

The Milner Library's marketing plan report (example 5) gives us an interesting twist on identifying the target market. Realizing that the methods of communicating with the university's patron groups should be tailored to the desires of the group, Milner created a table listing the patron groups and identifying the media strategy the library will use to communicate with the groups. In the table (appendix 4 of the plan), Milner identifies "Internal" target groups as students, faculty, library personnel, and Illinois State University staff and administration; "External" groups include alumni, Friends of Milner, parents, community instructors, library consortia, citizens of Illinois, media, elected officials, and vendors. The table then indicates which

---

Web Extra `WEB`

Is your own library in the position of Worthington Libraries in realizing that you don't know your current market well enough? Visit www .alaeditions.org/webextras to access a Word version of their report that you can adapt as a guide for your own use.

of the listed media options will be used for each group. To communicate with students, for example, sixteen of the eighteen media options will be used. If your library typically communicates with as many diverse groups as Milner, developing such a table could help you narrow your options when you begin to think about your goals and strategy.

The Maricopa Community College District (example 4) has identified students as the primary audience for its plan and then notes which specific groups of students it hopes to influence, some of them being athletes, dual enrollment students, and online students. It is evident from the longer list of possible student groups that the district's Electronic Resources Committee has done the work we outlined in the Current Market section of chapter 2—to answer the question, "Who are my library's patrons?" Maricopa has gone beyond simply identifying "students" as its target market and further segmented that group into types of student groups. Smart!

Goals, Strategy, and Proposed Measurements

This is the section where a lot of your hard work can really shine. You've already read about how to create a marketing strategy that suits the goal and how to choose a measurement that will tell you if that strategy meets your goal. Here you will outline your plan for what you hope to gain from the marketing campaign. Until now you've dealt with goals, strategy, and measurements as separate components. Now you will synthesize these components.

Note in example 1 that the NOVELny marketing plan report has a number of goals, strategies, and proposed measurements (in sections titled Measures of Success) listed for each target audience. In the previous section, we noted that NOVELny's choice to develop a marketing plan for the state legislature was a deliberate one, and reading further into the NOVELny marketing plan report, we see that one measure of success for the legislative group is "sustained funding for NOVELny."

In a bold attempt at transformative impact due to marketing, one of the goals of the Maricopa Community College District Plan (example 4) is, "Students will successfully access ERC [Electronic Resources Committee] resources and become more successful." This is a powerful statement—that the library makes student achievement a goal and is taking action to help make it happen.

Marketing plan reports can be written after a cycle of marketing is finished and can act as summaries of completed work, listing the measurements of the strategy and the assessments that were done and revealing the next plans. The marketing plan report for the Winnetka-Northfield Public Library (example 2) does just this. We believe that measurement and assessment are key components to the success of any marketing cycle, and Winnetka-Northfield's plan has a good mix of measurements noted in the plan's Impact section, as well as a whole section about assessment called

Lessons Learned. In the Impact section we learn, "Thirty-four staff members and three board members were trained during seven sessions." Because one of Winnetka-Northfield's goals was to "increase staff knowledge" and the strategy to accomplish this was through training sessions, measurement of a simple count is appropriate. Another goal was to "increase . . . comfort level" in the use of databases, and measurement to discover if comfort level did indeed increase was accomplished through surveys, which "showed staff's comfort levels increased significantly over the course of the grant period." Read the entire Impact section to see how else the library measured its marketing strategy; there you'll find more simple counts, percentages, and trends over time. You'll also see that not one of the measurements is "math-y"; all the techniques are within your grasp and are powerful in conveying your efforts.

The Winnetka-Northfield plan does not shy away from reporting results that are less than desirable, and we think the authors have done it in just the right way. One of their techniques was to hand out coupons for an hour of personal consultation time with a librarian. They say in their report that "the least successful aspect was the coupon promotion. Not a single coupon for a consultation was returned. We suspect this is because people did not feel a need for a coupon and would turn to us anyway." The message is clear to readers that the authors were expecting to count (a measurement) the number of coupons cashed in; when none were, they gave a possible reason why—this is assessment. They suppose that patrons did not feel the need for the coupons because the librarians are already viewed by patrons as accessible. They have gained actionable knowledge because in their next cycle of marketing, it is unlikely that they will choose to use the marketing strategy of coupons.

The Galway-Mayo Institute of Technology (example 6) team members get it right when in preparing for their goals they first identify the marketing strategies they already have in place, in a section called Analysis of Current Marketing Strategies. Then they clearly outline their goals, objectives, strategies, measurements, and timeline in a table format. The result of using a table format is that the goals are easy to identify, and following along with the objectives and other steps is clear. The specificity in their goals is admirable. They state that in order to reach their goal of "Undergraduates will increase usage of electronic resources," their objective is that "Usage of databases will increase by 10%." They then identify three strategies to help them in their objective. At the end of their marketing plan, it will be quite easy to determine if they met their goal, simply by viewing the usage statistics for databases.

We find the Proposed Measurements section of the Loyola Marymount University plan (example 7) to be clear and effective. From this report, you can see that the marketing team members will be taking two kinds of measurements, usage statistics supplied through the vendor platform and referral statistics gathered from multiple sources. These measurements are appropriate for just launching a new subscription service. Considering that

Web Extra

Take a look at the table format of the Goal, Objective, Strategies, Measuring Outcomes, and Timeframe used in the Galway-Mayo example and download it from www.alaeditions.org/webextras if you would like to reuse that format in your own report.

one of the goals of the marketing plan was for faculty and students to use the video service, this type of measurement is a good match for letting them know if the marketing plan is working.

Timeline, Staff, and Budget

In this section, outline how long your marketing plan will take, who will be involved, and how much money and time the plan will cost. This information should be briefly noted in the executive summary, but you can describe the full plan here. For example, list each person involved and his or her time commitment throughout the project, as well as each task with which he or she is charged. In the executive summary, you will condense this information to total number of staff and total number of staff hours to complete your plan.

Also, insert an itemized list of the office supplies, printing supplies, contractor time and fees, and so forth, that you need to complete your plan, along with the costs for each item. The list will be abbreviated in your executive summary, with maybe just the total cost included there.

We especially like the section Partnerships and Outreach in the Worthington Libraries' communication plan (example 3). Consider how you may be able to expand the number of members of your marketing team in the Staff section of your marketing plan for e-resources if you're partnered with groups like the "Worthington Area Chamber of Commerce," "City of Worthington," and "Worthington Garden Club."

The Milner Library (example 5) does a nice job of outlining the timeline for its marketing plan, focusing on seasonal marketing appropriate for the university community. The marketing events are broken into Fall Semester, Spring Semester, and Summer (noted in the plan's appendix 6). The writers list annual events and conclude with a list of possible events not yet scheduled (Additional Events). Seeing your library's events broken out in a list by semester may help you gauge how many staff you will need for that semester's work. It is easy from Milner's plan, for example, to see that Fall Semester is just as busy as Spring Semester, but Summer has only a single event, making it light for the requirements of staff to assist.

The entire marketing plan for the Loyola Marymount University's (example 7) rollout of the Kanopy video product will begin in January 2016 and continue through fall 2016. It is easy to know by looking at the library's report what will be happening in the months of the plan's schedule. The work of creating flyers, e-mail templates, and social media ads is dispersed throughout a few months so that not everything is scheduled to be completed at once. We are sure the marketing team members appreciate this advanced planning on their behalf.

The Maricopa Community College District (example 4) created a Lib-Guide that coordinates with its marketing plan at http://library.scottsdalecc

Web Extra   WEB

Do you like the way the Milner Library reports its plan for events? Visit www.alaeditions.org/webextras to access a Word version of this report that you can adapt for your own use.

.edu/database_marketing. One of the tabs at the site is a calendar of annual events that lists the district's e-resources that coordinate with the events. In February, for example, for African American History Month, two databases are highlighted, African American Experience and History Reference Center. Take a look at Maricopa's calendar and borrow some ideas! Many of the events identified can be easily applied at your own library.

This Marketing Grant Request Form Caught Our Eyes!

We know we promised you marketing plans, and we're going to deliver, honest (just see part II of this book). Before we get there, though, we just had to tell you about the work of the Strategic Communications and Marketing Committee of the University Library (University of Illinois at Urbana-Champaign). The committee (charge and other information found at www.library.illinois.edu/committee/strategic/charge.html) offers grants to people in the library, specifically for marketing purposes. The reason we want to draw your attention to it relates to the form the committee uses for grant applications (reproduced here). The five questions in the application are like a mini–marketing plan report. The application prompts the applicants to think through their plan all the way to the end, with the evaluation step. Nice, isn't it?

URBANA-CHAMPAIGN GRANT REQUEST FORM

One of the awards was granted to Lisa Janicke Hinchliffe and Tom Teper, in 2014, for a postcard marketing campaign for creating awareness among students about a pilot subscription to the New York Times (online). Their application includes this response to question 5, about how the marketing strategy will be evaluated: "We will evaluate the marketing strategy through monitoring account activations and usage reports that can be derived from the NYT system administrative module. It is anticipated that sign-ups will show an immediate spike after each event at which the postcards are distributed as well as in the first two weeks of class if we are successful in encouraging faculty to incorporate aspects of the NYT service into their coursework."

ILLINOIS

UNIVERSITY OF ILLINOIS AT URBANA-CHAMPAIGN **UNIVERSITY LIBRARY**

STRATEGIC COMMUNICATIONS AND MARKETING COMMITTEE GRANT REQUEST FORM

Please complete this form and submit it to the chair of the Library's Strategic Communications and Marketing Committee (see name and e-mail address below) by **Friday, January 13, 2017**. The length of the completed form should not exceed three pages. Use 11-point font or larger.

Funds obtained through Strategic Communications and Marketing Committee grants can only be used to market or publicize Library services, innovative research tools, and public engagement events that are directly related to the University Library. These grants may not be used to purchase information resources or to augment services that are part of a library unit's ordinary activities. If you have questions, please contact one of the Committee members:

Heather Murphy, chair	hmurphy@illinois.edu	Celestina Savonius-Wroth	cswroth@illinois.edu
Susanne Belovari	belovari@illinois.edu	Nancy Taylor	netaylor@illinois.edu
Sarah Christensen	schrstn@illinois.edu	Dan Tracy	dtracy@illinois.edu
Kit Condill	condill@illinois.edu		

Today's date: _____

Unit name(s): _____

Project name: _____

Project contact(s): _____   _____

_____   _____

Estimated marketing period: Start date: _____   End date: _____

Identify the media outlets to be used for your proposed marketing strategy. Check all that apply
(double-click check box; then single-click radio button beside the word *checked* and click *OK*)

Publications (print and online)
☐ *Daily Illini*
☐ *News-Gazette*
☐ *Inside Illinois* (bimonthly for faculty / staff)

Publications (online only)
☐ *Eweek* (weekly e-newsletter for faculty / staff)

Publications (print only)
☐ *Compendium* (biannual newsletter for faculty)
☐ *Friendscript* (triannual newsletter for donors)
☐ *Postmarks* (biannual newsletter for parents)

Misc. printed items
☐ Bookmarks
☐ Flyers / brochures
☐ Invitations
☐ Postcards
☐ Other (any medium):

Radio and TV stations
☐ UI-7 (campus TV)
☐ WAND (TV)
☐ WCIA (TV)
☐ WDWS (radio)
☐ WHMS (radio)
☐ WICD (TV)
☐ WILL (radio, TV)
☐ WPGU (campus radio)

Web sites / pages
☐ UI News Bureau
☐ UI calendar / website
☐ Library calendar / website

Misc. online sources
☐ Twitter
☐ YouTube
☐ Facebook
☐ Listserv(s):

2016

1. Identify the audience(s) that your proposed marketing strategy will target (e.g., Urbana and Champaign middle school students) and the specific need(s) within this audience that your service/program/engagement initiative will attempt to meet (e.g., increase middle school student use of historic newspaper collections found in the History, Philosophy & Newspaper Library for Illinois History Day projects). **Provide as much detail as possible to ensure that the Committee understands your audience.**

2. Describe the specific Library service/program/engagement initiative that your unit will market to your targeted audience (e.g., Illinois Digital Newspaper Collections) and the specific message that you seek to convey through this marketing strategy (e.g., uncover and discover local history through the Illinois Digital Newspaper Collections). Whenever possible try to incorporate the Library's current marketing theme, *Uncover and Discover*, into your proposed message.

3. Identify the specific product(s) (e.g., print/online ads, emails, bookmarks) you will produce in order to market your service/program/engagement initiative. Also, identify the vehicle(s) (e.g., newspapers, TV, radio) you will use to deliver your message to your target audience. For example, this could be two quarter-page ads that will run in the *News-Gazette* Sunday edition in the month of March or e-mail blasts to all middle school history teachers in Urbana and Champaign that will go out in February and April.

4. Provide a detailed budget outlining the projected costs associated with the proposed marketing plan and include as part of your proposal all vendor quotes associated with your planned advertising. A general cost figure for total marketing expenditures will **NOT** be accepted. (**PLEASE NOTE**: Only one grant, for a **maximum amount of $500**, may be awarded to a single unit during a given marketing grant cycle). Awards may be used to supplement funds from other planned sources for proposed marketing projects that exceed this funding limit. When referring to wages for which funds are requested, you must describe the method of determining the amount of labor required.

5. Explain in detail how you will evaluate your marketing strategy. How will you determine whether you reached your targeted audience? (**NOTE**: A brief report must be received by the Committee at the conclusion of the funded project. Project contacts who do not submit a report may not be eligible for future grants awards.)

2016

Wrap It Up

You've been intimately involved with the development of the marketing plan, so writing a report like this may give you some objective distance to review all of the components. Such a report is deserving of an external review, a quick read by a colleague not involved in the plan, to see if your writing is clear. Having a pair of friendly eyes on the report before you submit it or present it to your library's administration can give you some added reassurance that it is sound.

Assess Your Marketing Plan

By this time you've determined the purpose of your marketing plan, designed (fashioned) it, and implemented it. Great! All done, right? Ha! You know better, since the whole point of marketing is to do *effective* marketing (otherwise we're talking empty exercise); to ensure that your marketing plan is effective, you need to assess it. And go on assessing it. The point at which you stop assessing your plan is the point at which it will be ineffective, or dead in the water. Think of Woody Allen's observation in *Annie Hall:* "A relationship, I think, is like a shark. You know? It has to constantly move forward or it dies. And I think what we got on our hands is a dead shark." Substitute the words *marketing plan* for *relationship* in the quote, and you've got our perspective on the dynamics of effective marketing plans.

First, Take a Good, Long, Hard Look at Your Library Website

Any assessment of library e-resource marketing has to consider how the library delivers those resources to its clientele. In most cases, it is via a library website or web portal. This is both a method of delivery and a major marketing tool already in place for your library's e-resources. As Hernon and Altman (2010) note:

> In addition to providing content, a library's website has a marketing function, and gives customers the opportunity to ask questions and to vent about service. If libraries fail to provide such an opportunity, they are not taking advantage of one of [the] most popular ways to find out what their customers are thinking about the library's services and online applications. (180)

And yet, how many really good, really well-constructed library websites are there, ones that do deliver the e-goods to researchers effectively? Well, since the first edition of this book was published, we have been seeing some

IN THIS CHAPTER

- ✓ First, Take a Good, Long, Hard Look at Your Library Website
- ✓ Then, Take a Good, Long, Hard Look at Your Electronic Resources
- ✓ Now, Ask Yourself Assessment Questions
- ✓ Market Your Electronic Resources Ethically
- ✓ Recommended Resources for Further Reading and Support
- ✓ References

For Further Information

Check out the "Library Website Hall of Fame" at www.libsuccess.org/index.php?title=Website_Design (last modified January 4, 2017), and see if you agree that these are particularly impressive. More important, ask some of your patrons to take a look at these websites and get their feedback on which they find to be impressive and which they find to be less so.

websites that do make library e-resources much more accessible than they were just a few years ago. For example, the Boston Public Library site (www .bpl.org) offers a direct link to electronic resources from the homepage. The link then takes you to a very well-designed page (www.bpl.org/electronic) that lets patrons search resources by subject or alphabetically by title or look for a particular article or journal (with good non-library-ese wording: "Already know the article or journal you need?"). The page also offers two very helpful resources for getting at e-material: "Need to decipher an abbreviated journal title from a citation?," coupled with a link into Genamics JournalSeek (http://journalseek.net), and "Use BPL material on your computer," which invites patrons to "Visit the Boston Public Library online collections [www.bpl.org/collections/online] to use [or] browse our digitized books, images, recordings and more." The National Library of Australia's website (www.nla.gov.au) has a conspicuous link to e-resources on the homepage under "Getting Started." The link takes you to an "eResources" page (www.nla.gov.au/app/eresources) that includes a screencast explaining how e-resources work, brief but clear explanations of different kinds of e-resources, a search box, an A-to-Z list of e-resources, a browse-by-category list, and a highlighted box of featured resources. Clear, compact, and cogent.

On many library websites, e-resources are "buried" so deeply it will take a plucky and resourceful patron to find them at all. Having found them, it will take a courageous and versatile patron to use them effectively. And we're not talking about using these files like a librarian would use them, but using them to find what the researchers are actually seeking. For example, we like the Earlham College Libraries website (http://legacy.earlham.edu/library), but if you go to the Earlham College homepage (www.earlham.edu), the only link to the libraries evident there is buried at the bottom of the screen, in a short column of not-very-prominent links (and the URL is not terribly intuitive, even for web gurus).

We came across an evaluation of university library websites in Bangladesh (Islam and Hossain 2014) and were surprised to see that, of the websites evaluated, only 54 percent of public universities and 52 percent of private universities had links to licensed e-journals. In fact, there was a greater percentage of private university websites linking to freely available resources than to licensed ones. Whether to link to freely available resources from your own library's website is a conversation for you to have at your institution, given the rise of open-access and other freely available content, but we firmly believe that linking to licensed content should be a given.

The point we're making here is that many libraries not only are missing out on the opportunity to market e-resources effectively via their websites but also are actively turning off researchers from using the resources because they are difficult to find and use. So a major portion of your marketing plan's assessment needs to include whatever means your library uses to get the e-resources to your patrons. If this sounds like an issue your library may need to address, give the 2007 article by Thompson and Schott a read; they redesigned the websites of two community colleges to give clearer access to e-resources and describe in their article how they went about it and how they determined if the redesigns were helpful to their patron groups.

For ideas on how to assess your library web presence, we recommend the following resources and examples of best practice:

- John Kupersmith's "Library Terms That Users Understand" (http://escholarship.org/uc/item/3qq499w7) is "intended to help library web developers decide how to label key resources and services in such a way that most users can understand them well enough to make productive choices. It compiles usability test data evaluating terminology on library websites, and suggests test methods and best practices for reducing cognitive barriers caused by terminology."
- *How to Design Library Websites to Maximize Usability* (Library Connect Pamphlet #5, 2004; http://digital.csic.es/bitstream/ 10261/2926/1/howtodesign[1].pdf), by Chris Jasek.
- "Accessible Design for Library Web Sites" (http://senna.sjsu.edu/ lmain/isdaccess/home.html).
- "Writing School Library Web Pages" (www.sldirectory.com/ libsf/resf/wpages.html).
- "Card Sorting: A Definitive Guide," by Donna Spencer and Todd Warfel, posted on April 7, 2004, to the *Boxes and Arrows* blog (http://boxesandarrows.com/card-sorting-a-definitive -guide).

A candid, warts-and-all assessment of your e-resources' web presence/ library research portal is so basic to any marketing that you do of your e-resources that if you don't do one, you're overlooking a key component of your marketing plan.

About Social Media for Marketing

The number of ways in which libraries are using social media (Instagram, Snapchat, Pinterest, Twitter, Facebook, etc.) varies widely. This is yet another avenue offering you opportunities to interface effectively with your patrons, if you use the right services and do it well. David Lee King's blog (www. davidleeking.com) offers ongoing, good suggestions and advice, often with specifics, about ways to explore and use social media in your library. The LMCC (Library Marketing and Communications Conference) Discussion Group on Facebook (www.facebook.com/groups/LMCC.Discussion.Group) is another good resource for using social media for marketing. The bottom line about social media use is similar to our exhortations about library websites: design, try, assess through your local users, and try again. Effective use of social media is probably even more "localized" than effective webpage design; the use of social media tools varies so much by demographics and local mores that it's going to require some library-specific trial and error to find out what will reach your institution's clientele.

Changing Your Web Presence

A consequence of assessing your library's web presence is that it will likely point to changes that need to be made for an improved patron experience. Depending on your library's politics, these kinds of changes are easy or hard. The more difficult your situation, the better off you are if you advocate for change while holding evidence in your hands. Viewing the resources listed earlier and relating them to your library's situation will give you a good basis for your advocacy efforts. Whether or not you are able to effect changes, your awareness of the environment in which your patrons access the library's electronic resources is key. You will be able to make an informed, practical marketing plan when you can empathize with your patrons' use of your library's website.

While you're thinking about the ways your patrons typically access your library's e-resources, consider whether or not you are maximizing the possibilities for your patrons to encounter those resources. When you subscribe to an e-book collection, for example, does your cataloging department put a collection record in the online catalog? Do you add a link to your e-book collections webpage? How about linking to that e-book collection via a blog post or Facebook update? Many e-book vendors will provide MARC records for their books. Have you put all the records for that e-book collection into your catalog so that patrons doing a casual keyword search can stumble upon just the resource they are seeking?

We have yet to see a focused collaboration between a department of special collections and an electronic resources department, yet this kind of collaboration can give both departments a chance to show off their resources. Suppose a special collections department plans to put together a new exhibit and contacts a staff member in electronic resources to include that department in the plans. During the planning meeting, the electronic resources librarian is easily able to identify licensed e-resources that correspond with the artifacts that will be featured in the exhibit. As the special collections staff members create the promotional materials, they are able to highlight both the artifacts and the e-resources, creating a fuller experience for viewers of the exhibit. After seeing the exhibit, viewers can follow up by looking at the corresponding e-resources, reinforcing the learning that happened when viewing the exhibit. In this way, the artifacts from the exhibit become modern, active learning tools instead of retaining their status as passive historical objects.

In addition to examining the functional ways your library communicates to its patrons, consider how your library website is (or isn't) designed to gather feedback, the "to ask questions and to vent about service" portion of the earlier Hernon and Altman (2010: 180) quote. When a patron wants to "talk" to your library via the virtual space of the website, do you have mechanisms in place to facilitate that communication?

Let's talk about e-resource problem reporting. Even the most stable of e-resources will go wonky (technical term) every once in a while. If your patrons notice a problem before you do, how do you invite them to communicate it? Does your e-resources portal have an e-mail address, a phone number, or a link to a report-a-problem page? If not, you're missing an opportunity to wow your patrons with your responsiveness to their concerns. If you do have such a communication mechanism in place, great! Do you also have a corresponding work flow for the staff member who is the primary point of contact for correcting the problem and responding to the patron? Which comes first, letting patrons know you got their message or correcting the problem? If the point person is out of the library that day, do you have a backup plan in place? How about response time? How quickly does your library think it should take you to respond to a patron's request for assistance? If you don't have all the answers to these questions, start the conversation with your colleagues. Giving your patrons the opportunity to talk to you when they need help outside of the traditional reference desk interaction builds or retains their trust in your library, a critical component to continued patronage.

What if a patron reports a problem that isn't actually a problem with an e-resource but is rather a report of difficulty using the e-resource? We view this as a golden opportunity for teaching patrons how to use the e-resource effectively as well as for providing feedback to the content provider about your patron's trouble with intuitive use of its product. Feedback from librarians about their patrons' experiences often leads to improvements in user interface design, so don't neglect this step! A simple link to an e-mail address can be the start of a perfect one-on-one communication process with a patron. Talk to any librarian who has fielded a problem report well, and that person will tell you that patrons are likely to e-mail or call again when they need help with a research project months later or a suggestion for a purchase or a kind word of support.

Figures 5.1 through 5.4 offer several examples of well-designed feedback forms on library websites. Don't re-create the wheel; if you like what you see, borrow it for your own library's use!

FIGURE 5.1 Feedback Form Example, UCSD BioMedical Library

Electronic Resource Technical Support Form

Use this form to report problems associated with the Libraries' electronic journals and databases.

Check the Electronic Resources Status Blog at http://wsulib.wordpress.com for a possible answer to the problem you are experiencing.

Date

Requestor:

Name:

○ Student   ○ Faculty   ○ Staff   ○ Other

Phone   Email

Database / Electronic Journal With Problem:

Attempted access is from:

○ Library   ○ University   ○ Home or other offsite location

Description of Problem (Be specific and include any error messages received.)

Other Information or Comments:

Attach a File   Choose File   No f...osen

Submit   Reset

Wichita State University Libraries, 1845 Fairmount, Wichita, KS 67260-0068 | Phone: (316)978-3481 | Fax: (316)978-3048 | Contact us

FIGURE 5.2   Feedback Form Example, Wichita State University

FIGURE 5.3 Feedback Form Example, Los Angeles Public Library

NEW YORK UNIVERSITY
LIBRARIES

Search: BobCat [▼] [_____] [GO]

HOME | FIND RESOURCES | RESEARCH ASSISTANCE | SERVICES | ABOUT | HELP

Services

Borrow & Renew
Computers & Laptops
Delivery Services
Digital Library
Disability Services
Group Study Rooms
Interlibrary Loan
Course Reserves
Faculty Services
Graduate Student Services
Polytechnic Institute of NYU
Alumni & Friends
Library Forms
Research Commons
Global Services
Services A-Z

Report a Database Problem

Quick Links

Report a Broken Link
Suggestions and Comments

Use this form to report technical problems accessing any of our databases or e-journals, or to report missing e-journals from our lists.

For help on how to use a particular database, how to locate a certain journal, or general questions on finding articles, Ask a Librarian.

Before reporting a problem, try:

Off-Campus Access

If you are trying to access resources from off-campus and are being asked for a password.

*Required Field
┌─ Contact Information
│ *Name
│ [_____]
│
│ *E-mail Address
│ [_____]
│
│ Telephone Number
│ [_____]
└─

┌─ Technical Details
│ *Database/Journal Name
│ [_____]
│
│ *Accessing From
│ ○ On Campus ◉ Off Campus
│ Computer Operating System
│ [Windows XP   ▼]
│ Web Browser/Version
│ [Internet Explorer 7.0   ▼]
│ *Problem Description
│ [_____]
│ [   ]
└─

[send comments]

Page last modified: October, 2009

Privacy Policy | Contact Us | Staff Resources | Career Opportunities
Search This Site | RSS | NYU Website | NYU Home

Follow us:

NEWS

- New to Bobst? Take a Video Tour
- Loan periods for students and staff
- Fall library hours
- Want your own space to study? Reserve a study room
- Upcoming Lens Replacement Project

Take a
Library Class

FIGURE 5.4 Feedback Form Example, New York University Libraries

Then, Take a Good, Long, Hard Look at Your Electronic Resources

Your patrons expect a certain level of service from your library, and this expectation is built on their experience with you and your collection. The expectations include your electronic resources, such as the ones to which you subscribe and how you provide access. You know which e-resources are more finicky than others, and your patrons know too. The e-resources in your collection that have their quirks are one thing ("Ah, you have to right-click to export a citation!"), but we're talking about the ones that seem to go belly-up for no good reason. If you're a library patron and you click on a link to an e-resource and get a "404 Not Found" message or click on a link to see the current issue of an e-journal but get access only to an archive, what would you think? You'd likely be frustrated, and you can expect that your patrons would be too. In addition to frustrating your patrons, it breaks their trust with you a little bit each time it happens. Your patrons will come to expect to not be able to access what you say they can access. In the competitive nature of today's online information resources, this is trust you can't afford to break.

Providing consistent and reliable access to e-resources, therefore, actually builds trust with your patrons. Even if the user interface of an e-resource could use some serious improvement by the provider, if your patrons know the work-arounds and can do the things they want to do with the resource, this builds trust. What does this mean for you? It means that partnering with your library's collection development department is critical so that you can advocate for the resources that your patrons find helpful. See if you can get on the committee that makes decisions about which e-resources to purchase or subscribe to and always press for a trial before subscribing so that you or the collection development team can test the user interface to see if it is satisfactory.

When you're testing access to a potential new e-resource, here are some things to consider; they may not all be deal breakers for your library, just some things to think about:

Does the e-resource work the same in all browsers? Ideally, you'd like an e-resource to be "browser agnostic," one that works the same regardless of which web browser you choose. If the e-resource works better in one than another, how will you communicate this to your patrons?

Does the e-resource require web browser plug-ins for optimal use? Plug-ins like Adobe Flash Player and Apple QuickTime often come out with new versions that need to be upgraded. Does your library have technical staff to manage those upgrades so that your patrons will have a seamless experience at your computers?

Can the e-resource be accessed only via a username and password? Often, smaller content providers will not be able to authenticate users via IP (Internet protocol) addresses and will need to confirm that only authorized users are accessing the materials via a username and password. If this is the case, how will your library manage that username/password? Will you require patrons to show a library card before they can get the username/password? Will your circulation desk or reference desk staff oversee this process?

Is the e-resource available only within the library building, or can patrons access the content off site? If they can access it off site, is their experience the same as on site? Must they use a special code or password for off-site access? Is that process clearly documented? What would your protocol be if an off-site patron reported a problem with not being able to access the content? Is that work flow clearly documented so that patrons get a quick response to their problem reports?

Your collection development team may decide that even though an e-resource is quirky, it fills a gap in the collection or is wildly popular and thus a must-have subscription. It will be up to your library to plan for how to respond to the resource's quirks. Your acquisitions staff will be critical to this plan. They'll need to have at the ready a working customer service or technical service phone number or e-mail for when things go awry. Vendors provide tutorials for dealing with quirks in using their e-resources; these canned tutorials can be your frontline staff's best friend when responding to "How do I use this?" questions. Your acquisitions staff will also often know exactly whom to contact at a vendor's office, and knowing whom to contact when you have a concern can make all the difference in providing a good experience for your patrons. If your library subscribes to e-resources as part of a consortium, know who in the consortium is the assigned contact person for vendors.

Your acquisitions or consortium staff may even keep a log of problems reported so that they can monitor the responses of vendors. This kind of evidence-based assessment will help you to keep track of the consistency of the e-resources you're providing. If at the end of a calendar year your acquisitions staff say to you, "Hey, we've had twelve problem reports this year about a particular e-resource, and they've all taken more than a week to resolve," you may want to seriously consider whether to continue to subscribe to that resource. If your acquisitions staff tell you instead that they've fielded problem reports that turned out to actually be issues with patron education (how to use an e-resource), then you'll know that it is time to decide whether the resource is too difficult for your patrons to use or if you need to provide better tutorials or learning sessions.

Even when you've made all the right decisions about which e-resources to include in the collection, they are by their nature moving targets. Vendors respond to patron feedback all the time and will often add new features to the user interfaces, like new citation export styles, RSS feeds, or an "e-mail this PDF" function. These kinds of upgrades are ubiquitous, and communicating the changes to your patrons will always be a challenge. Most libraries we have encountered will actually choose *not* to notify their patrons of small changes or additions to an e-resource platform. What we typically see are notifications about planned user interface migrations in which the entire user experience will change because the interface has been reformatted. Clearly communicating these changes to your patrons is important because patrons will choose to use an e-resource because it is the one they already know how to use. Patrons can find a change to an e-resource stressful even if they are properly notified. Making a plan for how to communicate these changes helps provide an experience your patrons can trust; they'll know you've got their interests in mind.

Now, Ask Yourself Assessment Questions

Now that you've given some thought to how you are directing your patrons to your e-resources and examined your collection from the perspective of their user interfaces, let's turn to how you've communicated with your patrons via your marketing plan. Here are some good questions to ask yourself as you undertake your marketing plan assessment (America's Byways Resource Center 2008):

1. How long has it been in place (i.e., has it been in place long enough for you to have sufficient data against which to measure its success)?
2. Reexamine what your goals were for the plan: Were they clear, and did the plan address all of them? (As you begin to assess the plan, new goals may emerge for the future.)
3. Did you identify and target the right audiences for your plan? Did you miss a significant segment of your target audience?
4. Have you changed the plan at all as you went along, according to factors that changed in your situation or resources or to meet new goals? (The ongoing success of the plan will depend on your being able to identify new goals and adjust the plan accordingly to meet them.)
5. Have you communicated well with your researchers and all those who were involved in devising and carrying out the plan? (Checking in with both researchers and staff throughout the life of the plan is a key element in your successfully "keeping your shark/plan moving forward and alive"; after all, your researchers are the reason you're securing the e-resources in the first place.)
6. What measures did you use to determine the relative success or failure of the marketing? (This could involve cost/

value analyses of how much a resource was used compared to how much it cost, done both before and after implementing your marketing plan.)

7. Have those measures revealed whether or not you met your marketing goals? (This tests your goals, your measures, and the overall effectiveness of your marketing plan; if there's a mismatch among these, or if the measures you used don't provide sufficient evidence of whether or not you met your goals, you need to change something in the equation: plan + measures = goals.)

Many of the measures already mentioned in this book should come into play in assessing your plan, including these:

- COUNTER statistics
- Patron surveys
- Focus groups

One of the main things you're seeking from these measures is information upon which you can act. You need assessment measures that can answer all the questions listed, and more: Should you continue with the marketing plan as it now exists? Should you change it? Should you rethink your goals for the plan? Is there other information missing from the group of measures you have been using, and is there a way of obtaining it?

A Rubric May Help

It seems that much of what happens in assessment is big-picture, high-level thinking, which may be a little "squishy" for your taste. Would you prefer a more concrete process? If so, then a rubric may be just the thing for you. A rubric can provide an objective way to look at the outcomes for each of the components of your marketing plan. Rubrics are designed not to help judge right or wrong, success or failure, but to show where you land on a quality continuum. Rubrics are best developed at the beginning of a project so you can have specific markers for success in mind as you move through the project.

In this section, we'll guide you through some components you may want to consider if you want to design your own rubric. We provide an example rubric in table 5.1 as well as downloadable versions in PDF and Excel formats at www.alaeditions.org/webextras (also available at http:// digitalcommons.lmu.edu/librarian_pubs/38) if you just want to get started on your assessment right away. We use the components of the marketing cycle as the main points in the rubric and have developed a scale for you to judge how well your marketing plan completed those components.

> **Project description:** To be complete, your project description should identify four things: the reasons you want to market your e-resources; what is needed to accomplish your plan;

Web Extra **WEB**

If you like the way we describe how to rank your performance on the components of a marketing plan and are eager to use it to assess your own, go to www.alaeditions .org/webextras to download our rubric in PDF format. If you like the structure of our rubric but have other ideas about the scale for measurement, you can download at the same URL an Excel version that you can revise to make your own rubric.

TABLE 5.1 Rubric for Assessment of Your Marketing Plan

MARKETING CYCLE COMPONENT	RATIONALE FOR RANKING	0	1	2	3	4
Project description	0: none written 1: 1 component addressed 2: 2 components addressed 3: 3 components addressed 4: 4 components addressed					
Current market	0: didn't attempt 1: poor understanding 2: close, but needs work 4: accurate				▨	
SWOT analysis	0: didn't attempt 1: 1 component 2: 2 components 3: 3 components 4: 4 components					
Target market	1: poor knowledge 2: some understanding 4: clear	▨			▨	
Goals	1: not reasonable 4: achievable	▨		▨	▨	
Strategy	1: poorly chosen 2: could have been better 4: well chosen	▨			▨	
Action plan, timeline	0: no plan 1: misjudged 2: wrong more than right 3: right more than wrong 4: mostly right					
Action plan, staff	0: no plan 1: choose poorly 2: wrong more than right 3: right more than wrong 4: well planned					
Action plan, budget	0: no plan 1: misjudged 2: wrong more than right 3: right more than wrong 4: accurate					
Measurement	0: didn't measure 2: poor measurement 4: good measurement		▨		▨	
Assessment	0: didn't assess 2: poor assessment 4: good assessment		▨		▨	

how much the plan will cost; and how long the plan will take to complete. In your rubric, you will judge how thorough your project description was: assign 0 to an objective measurement if you didn't write one; 1 if it addressed one of the four things; 2 if it addressed two of the four things; 3 if it addressed three of the four things; and 4 if it addressed all four.

Current market: Describing the environment in which your library functions can be a tricky business. We prompted you in chapter 2 to think about who your library patrons are, where your library is, what the information concerns of your library patrons are, how you are currently serving those information needs, and what your current electronic resources are. Put together, these details paint a complex picture. How well did you do? If you judge yourself on a scale of 0, 1, 2, and 4, with 0 being "didn't attempt" and 4 being "accurate," how did you do during this cycle of marketing? If this is your first marketing plan, don't worry if you judged yourself at a 0 or 1. Understanding your library's current market can take time. Be sure to give yourself extra time to lay your marketing foundation during your next marketing cycle.

SWOT analysis: Completing a SWOT analysis can be a complicated political process, especially if you're honest about your library's strengths, weaknesses, opportunities, and threats. Were you able to accurately reflect all four of these components? Give yourself a point for each one you think you completed in its entirety.

Target market: When you identified your target market, you had in mind a specific group of people, with certain characteristics or traits. Now that you have completed your marketing plan with that group, how well did you actually know that group? Were there people in that target market you didn't expect? Did the characteristics you had in mind exist in actuality? Did you know just the right things about the group in order to complete your marketing? Give yourself a score of 1, 2, or 4, with 1 being "poor knowledge" and 4 being a "clear" understanding of how to communicate with the group. You can see here that we're not scoring ourselves on how thoroughly we know the group overall but on whether we know enough to communicate effectively with them.

Goals: There is a predictive element to setting a goal, but a grounding mechanism is to ask yourself if the goal is attainable. Was the goal you set reasonable/achievable? If not, give yourself a 1 on the rubric; if so, give yourself a 4.

Strategy: Whether you used just one marketing technique or put together a suite for your marketing cycle, each technique was chosen specifically as part of a strategy to help you communicate to your target group. When you look back on the techniques you chose, were they appropriate for your target group and goals? The score on the rubric for this component doesn't ask if the technique actually achieved the goal you hoped for; it focuses on the technique itself. If it turns out that you chose a particular technique because of a characteristic about your target group, but the target group didn't actually have that characteristic, then the technique for communicating was a dud; give yourself a 1 on the rubric. If you know your technique (or one of your techniques) was appropriate when you began but as you conducted the marketing plan you saw that another would clearly be better, give yourself a 2 on the rubric. If the technique you chose turned out to be perfectly aligned with what you knew about your target group and their motivators, then give yourself a 4 on the rubric.

Action plan: Your action plan is composed of three separate pieces—timeline, staff, and budget. Let's score your planning for each of those separately.

Timeline: In chapter 2 we prompted you to imagine how long the short-term tasks in your marketing cycle would take to complete in order to give yourself a sense of how long the total plan would take. Time is an easy accountability measure for your library's administration, so let's use all five options on the rubric. Give yourself 0 points if you didn't make a timeline, 1 point if you seriously misjudged how long tasks would take to complete, 2 points if you were more often wrong than right in judging how long tasks would take, 3 points if you were more often right than wrong, or 4 points if you mostly timed the tasks right.

Staff: Planning for staff involvement is closely aligned with budgeting for time. Did you have the right combination of staff assigned to tasks to complete the steps in your marketing plan? It is a sign of respect for you to have managed staff properly, so use all five options on the rubric to judge your performance related to staff. Give yourself 0 points if you didn't make a plan for staffing, 1 point if you chose the wrong staff people or they abandoned the project, 2 points if some things went well but the majority of the plan related to staff was poorly executed, 3 points if some things went wrong but your overall planning for staff went well, or 4 points if you planned for staff well throughout your marketing plan.

Budget: How did you do in budgeting for all the components of your marketing plan? Give yourself 0 points if you didn't make a budget, 1 point if you made a budget but misjudged how much each piece would actually cost, 2 points if your budget was more wrong than right, 3 points if it was more right than wrong, or 4 points if your budget was accurate for each piece.

Measurement: When you conducted your marketing plan, were you able to measure your strategy as you expected? If you didn't attempt to measure your strategy, give yourself 0 points on the rubric. If you attempted to measure but it went poorly (didn't select proper measurement, measured at the wrong time, measured the wrong thing), give yourself 2 points. If you measured your strategy as expected and found the measurement accurate, give yourself 4 points.

Assessment: Did you learn enough about how the strategy you chose worked with your specific target market to know how to communicate with them further? Give yourself 0 points on the rubric if you didn't ask yourself this question. If you realize you poorly chose either your strategy or measurement and as a result have no idea how to move forward, give yourself 2 points. If your measurement makes sense with what you know about your target group as a result of your communication strategy and now you know what you will do in your next marketing cycle, give yourself 4 points.

Look over your rankings on the rubric, and you'll be able to easily see where you had more success than failure and where you need to tweak your processes during your next cycle of marketing. If you adapt our rubric for your own use or build your own, please contact us to share your version. We are always looking for improved assessment tools and would love to see what you've come up with.

Some Practical Considerations for the Assessment of Your Marketing Plan

As you developed your marketing plan, we prompted you to consider budgeting for both time and money. Let's focus for a moment on your budget for money. As you moved through your marketing plan, did you keep track of time and expenses? Are there any things you spent time or money on that you could do differently next time to economize? Perhaps you've collaborated with another group, and they have resources they're willing to contribute during your next cycle of marketing. Maybe during your first cycle you didn't anticipate needing to spend money on something and ended up using more than you had budgeted. Justifying any additional expenses of time or money by providing reasoning for why the plan would have failed if you hadn't spent the funds is an accountability measure that your library administrators can appreciate. If you didn't anticipate needing to spend money on something but you were able to get their permission to move forward with the expenditure, this shows their faith in your responsible marketing plan.

Just as you can't develop and implement a marketing plan cost-free, neither can you assess its effectiveness without spending some dollars, whether those dollars are outright cash expenses or staff time (salary). You may have done some whiz-bang marketing, but if you don't spend the time and money to find out how effective it was, it's like the proverbial tree falling in the forest—how will you know if anybody heard you? It takes some money to run focus groups (to incentivize them and to feed people), it takes money to produce marketing takeaways, and sometimes it takes money to hire somebody from outside your organization to come in and help you do the marketing. So, do build into your marketing plan's budget the money needed for assessing the plan, or don't bother to do the plan at all. (Rule 1: If you can't measure it, don't state something as a goal. Rule 2: If you can't assess it, don't do a marketing plan at all.)

We've given you a lot to consider related to assessing your e-collection and how you would assess your communication about it via a marketing plan. There is always room for improvement, and we hope that by showing you the rubric you can see how if one component of your marketing plan isn't a 4, the entire plan is not sunk. Assessment is meant to give you the tools you need to communicate the nuances of your successes and failures in your marketing, and from an objective perspective so that any success or failure is a result of the *plan,* not the *people* involved with the plan.

Market Your Electronic Resources Ethically

Finalizing your marketing plan means you're about to embark on a communication campaign. Here we give you a few things to consider to ensure that you're doing it ethically.

You've gotten phone calls or e-mails from vendors trying to sell you things, and it feels odd to have strangers contact you, doesn't it? When you're communicating on behalf of the library as part of your marketing plan, use your institution's e-mail address (if communicating via e-mail) or official library letterhead (if communicating via mail) or identify yourself as "calling from the [your library name] to talk with Mr. X" (if communicating via phone). You want the recipient of your marketing communications to know who you are so that the person knows he or she can trust you. You don't want your communications about the library's electronic resources viewed with suspicion!

A communication/marketing style that allows your library to remain a trusted entity will include giving your patrons options. To show them that you value their independence in choosing whether to participate in communications with you, incorporate opt-in/opt-out features in your strategy. If you have a list of e-mail addresses for your Friends of the Library group, the group members likely gave that information to the library in order to be contacted for social or fundraising events. If you add those e-mail addresses to your new promotional tool, your library's newsletter, without seeking permission, you will jeopardize the trust that those individuals have put in your library. If you instead send them an e-mail asking for their permission to add their names to the newsletter e-mail list and subscribe only those who respond positively, your trusted relationship status remains intact.

In addition to maintaining trustworthy communications about e-resources, also give some thought to the technological capabilities of your patrons. Dillon (2003) suggests that promoting a service that your patron group isn't ready for may breed "distrust or rejection" for those services: "maintaining library users' level of comfort, familiarity, and trust in the library is arguably the most important step in the introduction of any new library technology" (121). You have likely considered this possibility when you thought about your target group for your marketing plan, and we mention it here because of its implications for the trustworthiness of your communications. If the e-resource you are communicating about is complicated or requires a certain level of technological skill, make sure to include training as part of your communication strategy so that your patrons will be receptive to using the e-resource.

If you have been thinking of marketing as building relationships, then think about who you are as the voice of your library in those relationships. Eagle and Dahl (2015) give us some guidelines by outlining the dimensions of ethical relationship marketing:

1. Integrates ethical analysis and reduces ethical tension
2. Is relationship and customer oriented and puts the human being first
3. Is built on virtues of trust, commitment, loyalty and diligence
4. Is built on dialogue and transparency and creates co-understanding
5. Is built on giving and keeping promises and being honest
6. Exceeds the legal minimum threshold
7. Implies that the management assists with moral guidance
8. Implies that the company takes responsibility for all marketing actions (77)

If these dimensions of ethical relationship marketing pique your interest, we encourage you to dive deeply into Eagle and Dahl's book, *Marketing Ethics and Society* (included in the Recommended Resources for Further Reading and Support section of this chapter). They give their readers a lot to think about regarding how we communicate messages in today's society and how to consider the receivers of those messages.

There is potential for a great deal of data gathering about the use of and attitudes surrounding e-resources. Just as you would not share patron information about items checked out or a home address listed on an account, remove any identifying information from your e-resource data or report it only in the aggregate.

If you plan to solicit information or feedback from your patrons, try to create an environment in which the patrons feel that they retain their power and independence. To create this kind of environment, libraries will often seek feedback from an external source before they perform a survey or release a form to be completed. In an academic or medical setting, this external review is completed by an institutional review board or an independent ethics committee. If you are not in an academic or medical setting, you can seek similar feedback from someone impartial outside your library who can review your materials before you disperse them to patrons. The goal of the review is to make sure your patrons don't perceive any risk in responding to your questions, and if they do feel a risk, then they know they have the right to walk away without consequences.

To communicate the efforts you have undertaken to let your patrons know that you created the survey or form with this consideration in mind, you can give them a written statement before they take a survey that outlines all of their rights and lets them know what to expect during the survey. Alternatively, you may tell them verbally of their rights. This is called *informed consent*. The US Department of Health and Human Services (2016) notes that informed consent has three features: "(1) disclosing to potential research subjects information needed to make an informed decision; (2) facilitating the understanding of what has been disclosed; and (3) promoting the voluntariness of the decision about whether or not to participate in the research." We have seen some examples of libraries seeking feedback about e-resources from their student population, and they also turn to their student workers for information gathering. We have also seen libraries seeking information from their volunteers, knowing that they represent a sample of the larger patron population. The same kind of safe, power-retaining environment should be granted to your student workers and volunteers (the people whom you know well) that would be granted to your patrons (the people whom you would like to know better). Your own student staff or volunteers may feel more at risk in responding to questionnaires and surveys because the possibility of identification is greater, as are the perceived consequences of their responses. Be considerate of the kind of information you are gathering from these sensitive groups. We point you to a couple of resources in the following section for more information on this topic.

Once you've received feedback/communications from your patrons, what are you obligated to do with that information? We said earlier in this book that marketing is the start of a long-term conversation. If the feedback you've received is about a negative experience with an e-resource licensed by your library, difficulty using the resource (design issues), or perceived inadequacies (lack of content or user interface issues), then you may choose to take the role of advocate. In the role of advocate, you will relay to the e-resource product representatives (the vendor) the issues your patrons are having with the resource. Speaking up on behalf of your patrons can be a powerful role to take, and it's not something everyone is willing to do. If you are willing to take that leap, to extend the conversation to include the vendor, then change can happen. If a vendor hears from enough librarians that a particular component of an e-resource is troublesome, then that may lead to a fix. This type of conversation certainly has an ethical component to it—to maintain trust with your patrons. You would never reveal the name/ contact information of the patron(s) to the vendor, but just the issue itself.

Imagine the increase in trust/appreciation a patron would have for your library if the next time you bumped into him or her in the hallway you said, "Hey, I took seriously what you said about the problem you were having with that database. I called our salesperson and suggested when they make their next upgrade they consider making a specific change to the design to address the issue. Guess what, they said they would!"

Recommended Resources for Further Reading and Support

Dowd, Nancy, and Kathy Dempsey. *The "M" Word: Marketing Libraries* (blog). http://themwordblog.blogspot.com.

> For an enthusiastic and up-to-date look at marketing related to libraries, follow this blog in your RSS reader. The coauthors may give you some marketing ideas to try at your own library.

Eagle, Lynne, and Stephen Dahl. *Marketing Ethics and Society.* Los Angeles: SAGE, 2015.

> This book shines a critical eye on how to market with sensitivity and transparency in today's multicultural society. It provides good food for thought about how to respond to the challenges of marketing, related to ethics.

Harvard Library User Research Center. http://urc.library.harvard.edu.

> Since the first edition of this book was published, one of the coauthors headed a group that wrote a successful proposal for a User Research Center in the Harvard Library, which was created shortly thereafter. Although most resources available from the center are for Harvard affiliates, a section of the site, "Learn Techniques" (http://urc.library .harvard.edu/resources-training), provides some generally available information and resources that can be helpful with assessing the user experience.

Library Marketing and Communications Conference (LMCC) Discussion Group. www.facebook.com/groups/LMCC.Discussion.Group.

> This treasure trove of resources and materials that will help you market in libraries comes courtesy of a dedicated group of individuals committed to library marketing. Whenever you're feeling disheartened about doing library marketing, a perusal of this group's Facebook page will reinvigorate and motivate you.

University of Washington Libraries. "Guide to Planning and Conducting Usability Tests." www.lib.washington.edu/usability/resources/guides/tests.

> For direction on choosing an appropriate usability test and practical aspects of how to conduct one, check out this University of Washing-

For Further Information

To learn more about the standards of ethical care of humans in the research you conduct, consult the webpage of the Office of Human Subjects Research, National Institutes of Health, at https://ohsr .od.nih.gov. You can also take the National Institutes of Health's free course, Protecting Human Research Participants, by registering at https://phrp.nihtraining.com. At the end of the course, you will receive a certificate.

ton Libraries guide. The guide points to other helpful websites and books about usability.

Wallbutton, Alison. *Marketing Matters for Librarians* (blog). http://alisonwallbutton.wordpress.com.

> For a thoughtful, personal approach to concepts surrounding marketing, add this blog to your RSS reader. Wallbutton provides links to current discussions about marketing happening on the Web and comments on them.

References

America's Byways Resource Center. 2008. *Marketing: Assessing Your Marketing Plan* (podcast). Recorded December 3. 60 min. Archived at https://web.archive.org/web/20090302000226/http://www.bywaysresourcecenter.org/topics/visitor-experience/marketing/tools/1310/.

Dillon, Dennis. 2003. "Strategic Marketing of Electronic Resources." *The Acquisitions Librarian* 14 (28): 117–34.

Eagle, Lynne, and Stephen Dahl. 2015. *Marketing Ethics and Society.* Los Angeles: SAGE.

Hernon, Peter, and Ellen Altman. 2010. *Assessing Service Quality: Satisfying the Expectations of Library Customers.* 2nd ed. Chicago: American Library Association.

Islam, Md. Anwarul, and Muhammad Jaber Hossain. 2014. "Marketing Information Resources and Services on the Web: Existing Status of University Libraries in Bangladesh." *The Electronic Library* 32 (5): 742–59.

Thompson, Mark S., and Lynn Schott. 2007. "Marketing to Community College Users." *The Serials Librarian* 53 (3): 57–76.

US Department of Health and Human Services, Office for Human Research Protections. 2016. "Informed Consent FAQs: What is informed consent, and when, why, and how must it be obtained." HHS.gov. Accessed November 10. www.hhs.gov/ohrp/regulations-and-policy/guidance/faq/informed-consent/index.html.

Revise and Update Your Marketing Plan ("Lather, Rinse, and Repeat")

Once you have completed your marketing plan, it is time to reflect on what you accomplished, what could have gone better, and what you plan to do the next time around. Setting aside time for reflection is especially important when completing a major project or task. In this chapter, we prompt you to think critically about the components of your marketing plan and then apply what you learned in your next marketing cycle.

Give Yourself Time to Think

Now that you've consumed the majority of this book, learning about how to construct your marketing plan for electronic resources, focusing especially on assessment, and having drawn up your own outline of a plan, what should you do next? We suggest you sit down and think about what you've accomplished so far. This reflective process gives you time to fully synthesize your plan, to view it as a complete cycle, and to imagine if there are any tweaks you can make to it for the future.

If your marketing plan is outlined but not yet implemented, then focus your energy on thinking through your assessment plan one more time. Make sure that the strategy you've chosen is suitable for your marketing goal(s), and confirm that the measurement of the strategy will give you enough information to determine if your marketing was a success or a failure.

If you've pushed forward and completed an entire cycle of marketing, then celebrate! When your team has patted itself on the back and hopefully eaten some cake and relaxed a bit, move through a reflective summary of your plan. While the cycle is fresh in your mind, reconsider all of the components. As you consider them, make notes on your original marketing plan report. These notes will be invaluable when you get to the revision process, described in the next section.

Project Description

If you had to write your project description over again, what would you say differently? Hindsight can be a marvelous tool to implement here. Does the "why" of your original project description still apply, or have your reasons for marketing electronic resources changed based on what you learned from your first cycle of marketing?

Current Market

As you moved through your marketing campaign, did you realize that you were missing information you thought you knew about your library patrons, your library's environment, the information needs of your patrons, or the assessment of how your library is currently serving those information needs? Throughout your marketing campaign, did you learn anything about your current market that you didn't expect? If you were going to run through this exact cycle of marketing again, what about your current market would you need to update for the new cycle to be effective?

Did you confirm that the "clusters" of library patrons you imagined are accurate, or did different groups of library patrons become evident to you? Did the data you gathered about your library (such as the gate count, number of patron records, and demographic information) assist in your plan? As you develop your next marketing cycle, will any of this data need to be updated? Make sure to note where (and from whom) you got the data during your first marketing cycle to make the next gathering of it easier and more efficient.

SWOT Analysis

Performing a SWOT analysis can be a little intimidating because it lays out for "all to see" just what the library's issues are. Were you able to create an environment in which a fair SWOT analysis could be done? Do you believe your analysis got at all the factors related to electronic resources, or were there things you encountered during your marketing campaign that made you think differently? In a SWOT analysis, something that you may consider to be a strength could actually be viewed as a weakness, depending on environmental factors. Were there any opportunities revealed to you as you completed your marketing campaign that you didn't anticipate?

Target Market

How did your target market respond to your campaign? Did you learn anything about the group as a whole that will help you in your next marketing cycle with that group? Was this a receptive group, or were group members tough to reach or communicate with? Do you think the group would benefit from the same marketing campaign again, or might you change aspects if you repeat it? Depending on your strategy, it may take a few repetitions to reach and sink in with your target group. Don't be shy about using the feedback you got from your first attempt and then running a similar marketing campaign with the same group. Keep in mind that some of your patron clusters are new to electronic resources generally, and they may be overcoming their own hesitations about using them. Repetition may be welcome, depending on your situation.

In chapter 2, you read about five different formal methods to learn about your target group: (1) case studies, (2) surveys, (3) participant observation, (4) cohort studies, and (5) focus groups. Did you use any of these to discover nuanced aspects of your target group? Did the method produce satisfactory results? Maybe the method you chose gave you some information but also suggested that you still need to find out more about your group. Would you benefit from choosing another one of these methods to bolster what you already know?

Goals

How did you do in setting the goals for your marketing plan? Were you specific enough about what you hoped to achieve so that it could be measured effectively? Was the goal you chose designed to fill a short-term need, or is it part of a long-term plan? Was your goal "vibrant, engaging, and specific" enough to keep you emotionally involved in the marketing plan through completion (Collins and Porras 1996, 74)?

Strategy

Before you began developing your marketing plan, your library was already communicating with patrons in a variety of ways. As you prepared your plan, you made a list of them and chose to use either existing ways or new techniques to connect with patrons. How did the techniques work for your marketing campaign? Did you think of other techniques you could try in addition to the ones you used in this cycle? Which of the four categories—physical medium, e-communication, training, or human interaction—did the majority of your techniques fall into (see figures 3.1–3.4 for a refresher on the categories)?

Finding the right combination of ways to communicate about e-resources is probably the most difficult aspect of marketing. If you use more than one marketing technique, it may be tough to figure out how much of an effect one technique had on another. We advise you not to use complicated statistics to help you tease out these kinds of effects but to use just an informal discussion among team members to figure out the effective and ineffective communication means. Practically speaking, you just want to know if all the techniques you chose worked well or not.

Action Plan

Putting all your planning into action by deciding how much time the marketing plan will take, who should be involved in the campaign, and how much the total plan will cost is an exciting and complicated step. Let's work through each part separately to find out how you did.

Timeline

Dubicki (2007) says that "just-in-time" promotions, "when patrons can immediately utilize the information on resources in order to aid in the completion of class projects, are the most effective" (224). She suggests using your usage statistics trends as your guide for when to market, choosing to conduct your marketing campaign during your month(s) of highest use. If we used figure 6.1 as our guide in this case, we would begin our marketing campaign in October/November or March/April because those months show the highest number of full-text downloads (our metric to describe "usage" of an electronic resource).

In addition to the timing of your marketing campaign, we want you to think about how long the total development of the plan took and what the time commitment was for all staff involved. Seek some feedback from your team on this. Is it a process they could sustain over time, or do they view it as working best as a rotating effort so that the same people aren't taxed with participation every year?

If you designed a Gantt chart, you tracked how long you expected each component of your marketing plan to take. How did your predictions go? Did you have to adjust the schedule to accommodate unexpected barriers? If you ran this exact same marketing campaign again, how would you need to schedule time differently?

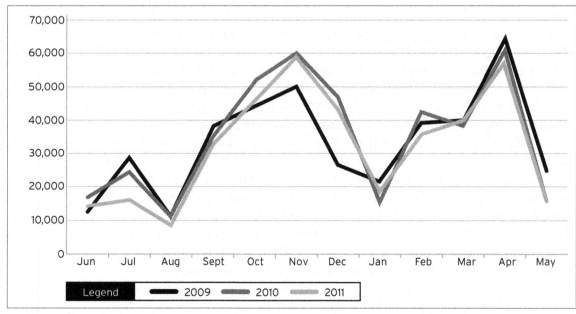

FIGURE 6.1 Usage Statistics Trend over Time

Staff

Think about the composition of your team. Looking back, do you think you had the right mix of participants overall? Were any people charged with tasks that didn't get completed? How might you address that in your next cycle of marketing?

Did you partner with a group outside your library to maximize the effectiveness of your marketing? Seek feedback from those partners at this point, or involve them in your measurement and assessment process to strengthen your relationship. Are there ways you might consider communicating differently the next time you partner on a project?

Budget

How did you fare in anticipating all the funding and hours needed to complete your marketing plan? If you had to do it again, would you need more time or more money? Reflecting about this aspect of your marketing plan is being fiscally responsible, and it shows your library's administration that you value both the time and money invested in the plan. If your marketing plan proves successful, you may be able to use this to justify an increased budget (hours or money), if needed, for your next marketing cycle.

Measurement

As you measured the effectiveness of your marketing strategy, did you think of other ways you could measure it next time? As you made the measurements, did you imagine how changing one technique might improve your overall strategy? Are there measurements you took that didn't really give you any information you could do anything with?

Assessment

Evaluating how your goals informed the strategy you chose, and what kinds of measurements you used to determine the success or failure of the strategy, leads you to know if you learned enough to prepare yourself for the next marketing cycle. If you gained good experience communicating with a new patron group and the process of marketing has inspired you to think of innovative ways to communicate with that group in the future, then your plan has succeeded. Remember to take time to celebrate the success!

Revise Your Plan

After you have thought through the components of your completed marketing plan, is it time to set it on the shelf and call it a day? Of course not! A marketing plan is a living document, one that needs consistent review to make sure you are still connecting well with your patrons.

How often should you review the components of your marketing plan? Let's be practical about this. The work flow we've outlined for you in this book is designed to be incorporated into your everyday task list. If you've done the reflective work described in the last section, thinking through what you would alter about your previous marketing plan, you are well positioned to have the briefest of reviews.

When you are ready to begin your next cycle of marketing, pull out your most recent plan and notes. Move systematically through each section, noting quickly if anything about your library has changed relative to that section since your last marketing cycle. If there have been changes in your library or your reflective notes remark that you may want to think through an aspect more deeply, these are the issues your marketing team can deal with first. The majority of the components will need little revision, and you will have the experience of having been through the entire process already. The second time you design a marketing plan, you will be poised to move much more quickly.

You can run the same marketing campaign for electronic resources over and over again. This is especially true if your patron base is cyclical in nature. If you're in a public library, for example, you may want to run a similar hands-on series of workshops on e-resources for fun summer learning year after year, as elementary school–aged children get out of school. If you're in a special library like a law library, you may want to have a marketing campaign ready for the annual target group of new hires.

Repetitive themes that occur annually, like National Nutrition Month, can give a medical library a chance to highlight the e-resource classics in nutrition as well as new databases, e-books, or newly subscribed e-journals. If the Academy of Nutrition and Dietetics has any special events as the hosting organization for National Nutrition Month that your library can tie into, you may extend the reach of your e-resources by providing a richer context on the topic. For a public or special library, National Novel Writing Month (NaNoWriMo) may provide opportunities to highlight parts of your e-collection that are hardly ever the focus; host a series of write-ins and show off your e-collection of citation manuals, thesauri, and writing guides, for example. Your library may use a whimsical approach to repetitive themes by making up some fun celebrations as an excuse to highlight parts of your e-resource collection. How about creating an annual tradition of A Month of Music, using that entire month to celebrate your e-music collection and to target your music-loving patrons?

As Murray notes (2005), "practice makes preference" (133). Learning how to use a new interface is a commitment of time on the part of your patrons, but learning builds loyalty for the interface. Your marketing plan may be to introduce a patron group to a resource for the first time. If the patrons' inclination is to use the e-resources or the interfaces they already know (and we know that this is the case), then your marketing plan is building a habit of new use. This may take replication. If you can grab your patrons' attention by creating a buzz about the e-resources while doing so, that's just much more fun for all involved, isn't it?

Communicate Your Successes or Failures in Marketing

The process we've outlined in this book for composing a marketing plan for electronic resources is a transparent one, and this includes sharing the results of your efforts. To demonstrate your commitment to and accountability for the process, you'll want to share what you learned with the people to whom you presented your written report. If your library environment is fairly informal, a verbal summary may work just as well.

The nature of the plan we've outlined in this book is cyclical, and hopefully you've gathered enough feedback in your process to inform your next cycle of marketing. Some of the feedback you received may suggest changes to the way your library functions in order to improve e-resources services to your patrons. Confronting this possibility takes courage, because now that you've asked for feedback, your patrons will expect changes to take place. To retain the trust of your patrons, you should act on their feedback. Dillon (2003) describes the long-term commitment that a library must make to a marketing campaign: "If a marketing plan is to achieve its objective, the entire organization needs to work together to effectively fulfill the user expectations that the marketing plan establishes, as well as to continue to meet these expectations over the long term" (121).

Meeting expectations over the long term is the reason you began your marketing plan to begin with, right? If so, you are well situated for a satisfactory marketing environment. Encouraging your library to pursue open and engaging conversations with your patrons is powerful and meaningful. It validates the expenses incurred by your library to provide access to e-resources if your patrons are enthusiastically learning about and using them. Early on in this book, we talked about the environment in which libraries exist today, requiring us to think innovatively about how to demonstrate our value. Marketing your electronic resources may be just the thing your library needs to make your worth highly evident.

As you embark on your own marketing plans, stay in touch! Publish your results if you can, so the larger library audience has a chance to learn from what you do. We are encouraged by Crenshaw's 2014 report of his library's attempts to market music databases: "More objective data need to be shared so that libraries can eventually develop best practices and focus their limited resources on the techniques that hold the most promise of success" (231). Feel free to drop us a line to show off your good work or to ask our advice. We look forward to learning from your own creative spins on the cycle of marketing electronic resources.

References

Collins, James C., and Jerry I. Porras. 1996. "Building Your Company's Vision." *Harvard Business Review* 74 (5): 65–77.

Crenshaw, Clayton. 2014. "Promoting Music Library Resources—with Mixed Results." *Music Reference Services Quarterly* 17 (4): 226–36.

Dillon, Dennis. 2003. "Strategic Marketing of Electronic Resources." *The Acquisitions Librarian* 14 (28): 117–34.

Dubicki, Eleonora. 2007. "Statistics Drive Marketing Efforts." In *Usage Statistics of E-serials,* edited by David C. Fowler, 215–31. Binghamton, NY: Haworth Information Press.

Murray, Kyle. 2005. "Experiencing Quality: The Impact of Practice on Customers' Preferences for and Perceptions of Electronic Interfaces." In *Contemporary Research in E-marketing,* edited by Sandeep Krishnamurthy, 1:130–48. Hershey, PA: Idea Group.

Part II

Sample Marketing Plan Reports

Marketing Plan from an All-Electronic Library

EXAMPLE

1

Statewide Marketing and Communications Plan, NOVELNY:
New York Online Virtual Electronic Library

Acknowledgment

The statewide marketing and communications plan report for NOVELNY: New York Online Virtual Electronic Library is used by permission. This NOVELNY Marketing Plan was supported by Federal Library Services and Technology Act funds awarded to the New York State Library by the Federal Institute of Museum and Library Services.

In December 2005, the New York State Library contracted with The Ivy Group to design and implement an intensified NOVELNY statewide marketing campaign.

Goals and Objectives

- Increase usage, support, and visibility for NOVELNY by multiple audiences in multiple localities and within multiple organizations across the state of New York.
- Generate future sustained funding by building brand recognition and a broad understanding of the benefits of NOVELNY.
- Promote the value of public library cards and the professional skills of librarians.
- Leverage the power of information services to raise the profiles of libraries with population segments traditionally disinclined to use the library while encouraging exploration of library online resources by loyal library customers.
- Generate favorable exposure for the New York State Library with libraries across the state by positioning NOVELNY as a value-added benefit.
- Capitalize on the NOVELNY branding and marketing program to develop new partnerships and strengthen collaboration with other state agencies.
- Make library staff across New York the best ambassadors for NOVELNY.

IN THIS EXAMPLE

- ✓ Goals and Objectives
- ✓ Campaign Planning
- ✓ Research Overview
- ✓ Situation Analysis
- ✓ Barriers to Access and Use
- ✓ OCLC Study Provides Clear Direction
- ✓ Ten Issues: Ten Strategies
- ✓ Mass Customization and Segmenting the Market
- ✓ Target Audience: General Consumer Population
- ✓ Target Audience: Executive Office, State Legislature Elected Officials and Aides, and Board of Regents
- ✓ Target Audience: Public Librarians
- ✓ Target Audience: Business and Economic Development Sector
- ✓ Target Audience: Academic Librarians, College Administrators, and College and University Librarians and Teaching Faculty
- ✓ Target Audience: Teachers, Administrators, Students, and Parents in Elementary, Middle, and High Schools; Homeschoolers and Parent-Teacher Associations
- ✓ Target Audience: Parents of One Million Plus Children in Statewide Summer Reading Program

EXAMPLE 1

- Develop a template for marketing electronic databases that can be a model for libraries across the state.

Campaign Planning

Representatives of the New York State Library and The Ivy Group have held a series of face-to-face and telephone conferences; in addition, following completion of the Himmel and Wilson NOVELNY LSTA Grant Evaluation interviews, The Ivy Group will conduct in-depth telephone interviews with librarians (not those interviewed by Himmel and Wilson), representatives of the media, and other government agencies in order to gather information that will inform the plan. Additionally, The Ivy Group will review the results of the NOVELNY LSTA Grant Evaluation for information that will guide key decisions, such as media placement and selection.

After approval by the State Library, the plan will be presented to librarians at the Fall NYLA Conference; the mass media campaign will be launched in January 2007. A statewide post-campaign CATI survey will be conducted at the end of the three-year campaign with randomly selected residents of New York State to determine the impact of the marketing initiative among the general consumer audience. Once the marketing plan is finalized and approved, benchmarks for determining the success of specific marketing initiatives in the marketing plan will also be established in consultation with the New York State Library.

Research Overview

The following research resources inform the communications plan:

- University of the State of New York, New York State Library, Division of Library Development. *Library Services in the New Century.*
- Pew Charitable Trust. *Report on Internet and American Life.*
- Himmel and Wilson. NOVELNY LSTA Grant Evaluation research.
- Connecticut State Library. iCONN Market Survey. *Measuring Current Awareness, Usages and Interest 2005.*
- EBSCO Publishing. *Customized Usage Analysis for New York State Library (NOVELNY).*
- Thomson-Gale. *NOVEL (New York Electronic Library) 2006* Annual Report.

Situation Analysis

NOVELNY is the online collection of e-journals, full-text magazine and newspaper articles, electronic books, and encyclopedias that is available to New York State residents 24/7 at their local public library or from the convenience of their home, school, or office. Currently, 5,000 libraries are actively using NOVELny databases. Of total searches, 60 percent are currently from colleges and universities with only 13 percent from New York's 1,100 public libraries. Plans are underway to expand the resources available through NOVELny and to make them even more useful to future users.

In June 2005, the New York State Library announced that NOVELny databases would be accessible 24/7 through any Internet connection. Any New Yorker can now log in with a valid New York driver's license number, a valid New York nondriver photo ID identification number, or his or her public library card.

Despite the efforts of the New York State Library and the marketing initiatives of individual libraries and library systems, New York librarians have experienced frustrations similar to those of their colleagues in other states. Awareness and use of online databases has been disappointing. Librarians have cause for concern that limited use coupled with the high licensing fees will make it difficult to move forward with developing this invaluable resource.

In January 2006, the New York State Library inaugurated the New York State Library Federated Search Portal Pilot Project. The original specifications required WebFeat to set up two "instances": one for the New York State Library (open to registered borrowers of the State Library) and one for NOVELny (open to anyone with a New York State driver's license ID or nondriver photo). The results of the pilot evaluation indicate that the pilot project should be expanded to include databases that libraries subscribe to locally as well as the basic NOVELny project. Phase 2 was developed to address this need and will be pilot tested with four libraries in the fall of 2006 through the spring of 2007.

Barriers to Access and Use

Research conducted both in New York State and in other states with products similar to NOVELny has identified several impediments to greater use of online databases. These include:

- General public, educators, and current library customers do not understand the benefits of accessing information from online databases.
- There is a general inability to differentiate research-based and peer-reviewed information found in library databases from the information found randomly surfing the Web.
- When databases are promoted, multiple databases on a subject area are often not grouped so that they will appeal to a defined target audience.
- There has been a chronic shortage of funds to support marketing initiatives, which has made it difficult for NOVELny to compete with well-heeled commercial search engines.

EXAMPLE 1

- Strategic planning and marketing efforts to date have been fragmented and inconsistent.
- Because a federated searching mechanism is not available to every NOVELny user, many become frustrated because database searching is not quick or easy.
- Library staff in many libraries are uncomfortable using and recommending databases, and training efforts are often inconsistent.
- The NOVELny website is not easy to navigate and does not stand up to its chief competitor—Google—which is attractive and well designed.
- Database vendors complicate the situation by establishing daunting access and authentication requirements and by not considering the needs or preferences of users and potential users.
- The fact that future funding for NOVELny is uncertain may undermine the commitment of librarians to the NOVELny product and motivate the development and branding of individual library and library system resources.
- While any tax-funded initiative can suffer from a funding cut, that prospect poses a problem for librarians who are being encouraged to guide their customers to use NOVELny.

OCLC Study Provides Clear Direction

The 2003 study "Perceptions of Libraries and Information Resources" conducted by the Online Computer Library Center (OCLC) solicited responses from 3,300 online information consumers, revealing that:

- 84 percent of all individuals looking for information online begin with a search engine;
- 72 percent use search engines such as Google;
- only 1 percent of the consumer respondents and 2 percent of college student respondents begin a search by going to a library website;
- 84 percent of all respondents have never used an online database;
- 70 percent of the survey participants have never used a library website;
- 39 percent of active information seekers find out about new electronic resources through advertising and promotions; and
- only 15 percent obtain information about these resources from a library website.

This study clearly indicates:

- Search engine behavior is entrenched; the marketing program can leverage these behaviors to steer users to NOVELny.
- Targeted advertising of new electronic resources can be effective.
- A campaign must begin with the understanding that the general public is not well educated about databases.
- The public does not associate libraries with online research.
- Generally speaking, library websites are currently not effective marketing mechanisms.
- Regardless of how NOVELny is marketed across the state, individual libraries must also market their online resources more proactively, especially via their websites.

Ten Issues: Ten Strategies

1. Googlization of the Marketplace

Jerry Yang, Yahoo's cofounder, contrasts the experiences of the earliest days of search engines when people were delighted to stumble across the information they sought with today's more presumptive attitudes that the information is available, but finding it easily is only a matter of technologists cutting down the number of keystrokes (*The World Is Flat: A Brief History of the Twenty-First Century,* Thomas L. Friedman, 2005, Farrar, Straus, and Giroux).

Consumers expect the same ease of access and use with library databases as they currently experience with commercial search engines. Indeed, technology has advanced beyond active and interactive search to personalization and customization based on the user's search history and actual geography according to IP address.

NOVELny cannot in any way compete with the monolithic market forces of the large commercial search engines; however, these portals offer significant opportunities to steer prospects to NOVELny.

These issues of access, searchability, and authentication are being evaluated by libraries and other organizations nationally. We would anticipate monitoring those discussions to learn how lessons learned elsewhere might apply to New York State.

Strategy

- Explore potential partnerships with Google and other search engines and/or vendors to drive information seekers to NOVELny and to simplify authentication.

2. The State Library's NOVELny Website Development

By and large, the websites of all but the largest, best-funded public libraries—not only in New York, but across the nation—have not advanced in

EXAMPLE 1

step with the rest of the e-world. In addition, it is the rare library that has applied any search engine technology or e-marketing to the promotion of a library's website or online resources.

Concurrently, commercial search engines have expanded their service offerings with more targeted search capabilities so that initiatives such as Google Scholar as well as Google's foray into online publishing and archiving trespass on territories that have been the mainstay of libraries.

NOVELny's site (www.nysl.nysed.gov/library/novel/database), although created primarily for librarians, can be reconfigured to be more user friendly and usable by not only professionals but also consumers. A streamlined NOVELny website is a critical component of a successful campaign: a new look, sparkling creative and dynamic colors, compelling graphics, flawless navigation, and ready access to all the promotional and informational tools intermediary and direct audiences need to understand, use, and promote NOVELny.

Strategies

- Create an attractive, compelling, comprehensive website that sets the standard for ease of access, navigability, and brand development. Integrate RSS feeds and other value-adds to the main page.
- Integrate a "marketing toolkit" and pressroom.
- Reserve more market-friendly URLs (e.g., newyorkknows.org).

3. Multiple Levels of Quality

Marketing communications must take into account the following access issues:

- Some New York libraries have only the twelve NOVELny databases, while other larger and better-funded libraries supplement the core database product with subscriptions to additional databases.
- All reference librarians are not created equal! Some are extremely proficient in database searching, while others are insecure using the databases and avoid recommending them to library users.
- Some libraries have resources to market databases on their own, while others have neither staff nor resources for marketing and PR.
- The ease of accessing the NOVELny databases can vary depending on the sophistication and navigability of local library websites.
- Ready access to marketing tools will narrow the funding gap between well-to-do libraries and those with fewer financial resources.

Strategy

- Create an online toolkit that offers all New York librarians
  and other "intermediary marketers" a marketing program for
  NOVELNY.

4. Tying NOVELNY to Driver's License Registration

Logic would suggest that anything that can be done to make these databases more widely used and successfully promoted is sound business practice. Even though the statistics would indicate that the driver's license campaign and its associated PR boosted usage, librarians in the field cannot help but feel bypassed by a strategy that does not link NOVELNY directly to local library services.

Nevertheless, this initiative is underway; the DMV has indicated it would be a willing promotional partner; and, despite its detractors, the program shows promise.

Strategies

- To gain more local library "buy-in," all marketing messages
  that target DMV license renewals also promote library card
  registration and the benefits of local library use in addition to
  NOVELNY.
- Include in all driver's license renewal mailings as well as those
  that go to young adults who are applying for driver's permits
  an insert providing information about NOVELNY, library card
  registration, and benefits of using a local library. Also include
  inserts with driver's permits to young adults.

5. Product Name

Although the NOVELNY product name (New York Online Virtual Electronic Library) can be readily understood by those inside the library "family," it suggests to the general public a specific literary genre.

Strategy

- In all marketing communications, restate the name (New York
  Online Virtual Electronic Library) and add a tagline (e.g.,
  "Putting New Yorkers in the Know," "NOVELNY Drives Good
  Grades," "NOVELNY Drives Prosperity," "NOVELNY Puts You
  in the Information Driver's Seat"). These positioning statements
  eliminate the confusion created by the product name and convey a ready understanding of what NOVELNY is all about (e.g.,
  "a commercial-free online channel to accurate, relevant information") and benefits statements (e.g., "save time by retrieving
  only the information you need, when you need it").

EXAMPLE 1

6. Library Jargon

Four issues impede the layman's understanding of online library resources:

1. There is a tendency in the library world to market database products by defining them with traditional library terminology (materials, resources, citations, full-text, abstracts, etc.) rather than marketing the benefits that customers will experience when they use the product.

2. The product designation "databases" is not immediately understood and, in fact, suggests to some potential users that it is a source of statistical tables.

3. There is an overdependence on respected brand names such as EBSCO, Wilson, and Gale—brands that are not, however, well-known outside the library environment.

4. Names given to individual databases within the vendor brand name are often not descriptive or easily understood.

Strategies

- Integrate results of professional research that has been recently conducted on library nomenclature into all NOVELny marketing communications materials.
- Eliminate words that confuse customers, formulate messages that stress product benefits, and use real-life examples of how NOVELny is used in situations that will resonate with individuals hearing about NOVELny for the first time.

7. Supporting Local Librarians and Other "Market Intermediaries"

Research indicates that individuals who have library cards are far more likely to access public library services than individuals who do not. In addition, librarians would embrace any efforts by the state to push card registration. Generating demand for product via "pull through" ("Ask your local librarian for more information about NOVELny") is a well-established consumer strategy that builds a "buzz" about the campaign, bolsters support among librarians for this state initiative, encourages library use, and ultimately increases NOVELny use.

Strategies

- Integrate "@your library" and card registration messages into all marketing communications.
- Include in the NOVELny toolkit in-library promotional materials so that libraries may be able to market NOVELny to their current customers.

8. Public Relations Support

The success of the AP wire story in the spring of 2006 in driving NOVELny use is evidence of the power of earned media. Well-orchestrated public relations initiatives will leverage the resources committed to the NOVELny marketing campaign.

Timing, content, and delivery of information to media outlets must be keyed at all times to other aspects of the marketing program.

Strategies

- Public relations activities will be used to support all campaign initiatives. Stories will highlight how real people use NOVELny to get information that is important in their lives and will focus on databases that are of the greatest interest to the most people.
- Include in the toolkit information that will help local libraries use public relations to promote NOVELny in their communities.
- Consider the possibility of identifying individuals who might be spokespersons for NOVELny.

9. Branding

Powerful branding will enable NOVELny to stand up to its powerful search engine competitors. The configuration and graphics quality of the current logo, color palette, and graphics treatment are inappropriate for a large media and web campaign.

Strategies

- Upgrade graphics standards; standardize all publications; create distinctive brand elements.
- Build positioning through repetition of key statements, such as:

  "Have you heard there's a great free source of answers to all your health (or business or . . . etc.) questions?"

  "Wow! That's NOVELny!"

- All marketing communications will emphasize key messages, summarized as NOVELny's "Brand Promise":

  Answers to your questions when you need them

  An all-ages product

  Commercial-free

  Complete copies of most articles obtained through NOVELny databases

  Access to almost 5,000 magazines, newspapers, and other information sources worth millions of dollars

  Superior place to find information about business, jobs, careers, investments

EXAMPLE 1

A trustworthy source of information for New Yorkers who have important questions about their health care, consumer purchases, and so forth

Library card is the most valuable card in your wallet/no limits/no fees/no unexpected charges

One of the best services you will ever get for your tax dollar

Access to a library that never closes—even on holidays

Help for students of all ages—get better grades

Invaluable resources that make good teachers even better

Help is available from thousands of highly trained professional librarians and information specialists at more than 6,900 libraries in New York State

10. Vendor Management and Relationships

Vendor policies have created significant obstacles to use; the State Library must work toward more extensive vendor support, enhanced contracts, and co-op marketing opportunities for NOVELny databases.

Strategies

- Initiate discussions with the two NOVELny vendors to solicit greater support for partnering in promoting the product.
- Negotiate co-op marketing initiatives.
- Include vendor-produced co-branded marketing materials in the toolkit.

Mass Customization and Segmenting the Market

The consumer marketplace is not homogeneous, while the assumption has always been that mass media is. On the contrary, mass media can be targeted to specific audiences in order to communicate benefits messages that are tailored to that audience's interests, needs, and culture. Nevertheless, while this plan addresses specific target segments, all individuals within each segment also "qualify" and will be exposed to other segments' messages within the larger marketplace and from the driver's license renewal marketing initiative.

Some market segments may already have direct access to a far larger range of databases and proprietary research that is not available through NOVELny. While these segments (corporate, law, finance, and medical professionals, for example) initially seem logical as target audiences, their information needs are generally being better served by channels outside the NOVELny product. Similarly, while a number of smaller markets would greatly benefit from increased use of NOVELny, limited resources and prohibitive media costs may preclude targeting these groups.

TARGET AUDIENCE
General Consumer Population

Goals

- Increase the capacity of all New Yorkers to access and manage information that is relevant to important issues in their lives such as health care, personal finance, consumer product purchases, careers and job opportunities, and so forth.
- Foster greater awareness and increased use of NOVELNY databases by the general public.
- Support efforts of individual libraries and library systems to market online databases.
- Generate sufficient use to motivate elected officials to fund NOVELNY in the future.

Issues

- NOVELNY has been underpromoted to the general public.
- The general public does not understand the difference between research-based information found in online databases and information found by randomly surfing the Web.
- Substantial costs are associated with marketing to the open consumer marketplace.
- There is a risk attached to implementing highly visible marketing initiatives at the same time that libraries are advocating for more money for basic services and operations.
- The experience of the .com phenomenon teaches us that it is very difficult to move consumers to online behaviors via conventional offline marketing.

Key Messages

- Reliable, accurate, timely information on health-related issues.
- Information available to all New Yorkers at any time of the day no matter where they live.
- Information for New Yorkers enrolled in higher education or engaged in lifelong learning programs.
- Access to a well-stocked library in your own home or office.

Strategies

- Target adults getting or renewing their driver's license.
- Target current library users who do not use the library databases.

EXAMPLE 1

- Target early adapters (defined as individuals who are comfortable with new technologies and already experienced using computers to access information online).
- Focus on subject areas of greatest interest to the largest number of New York residents.
- Continue conversations with ConEd (or National Grid) about using their in-house publications to promote to their employees/potential NOVELny users.
- Explore the potential of doing NOVELny billing inserts in cooperation with National Grid, the energy provider in the northern part of New York State.
- Explore the potential of using the mass distribution channels available through the telephone company and cable providers.
- Leverage the popularity of online health-care information.

Recommended Distribution Channels

- Insertion program to three million New Yorkers annually renewing their driver's license
- PBS channels in New York State
- Google and other search engines
- Health-care organizations and health-care providers involved in patient education

Measures of Success

- 30 percent of randomly selected New Yorkers demonstrate awareness of NOVELny.
- An increased number of New Yorkers access NOVELny using their driver's license.
- 15 percent of respondents in statewide survey report they have used NOVELny.
- 5 percent of survey respondents indicate a family member has benefited from using NOVELny.
- Survey respondents were successful in finding the information they were seeking.
- Insertion, search engine, and partnering programs were successfully implemented.
- Use of databases of most relevance and broadest appeal to general public increased.
- New Yorkers have reliable information upon which they can make decisions regarding personal finances and investments.
- PR stories were successfully placed.

TARGET AUDIENCE
Executive Office, State Legislature Elected Officials and Aides, and Board of Regents

Goals

- Increase usage of online resources.
- Make NOVELny a funding priority of elected officials.
- Position NOVELny to legislators as the State Library's "work smart" initiative that saves money at the local level. (Every $1 invested in NOVELny saves $35 at the local level.)

Issues

- Key legislators above a certain age have little experience with online research.
- Aides have access to higher-end databases that are funded apart from NOVELny.
- Funding priority is given to projects that are perceived to have a direct benefit at the local level.
- While 5,000+ libraries in the state access NOVELny, funding is from the federal government.
- Future funding is uncertain.
- Previous training for legislators and legislative staff may have confused more than it helped.

Key Messages

- NOVELny brings valuable information services to local libraries and their constituents throughout the state.
- NOVELny ensures equity in access to information by anyone with a public library card or driver's license.
- NOVELny supports the democratic process and economic development by offering access to reliable, timely information to any resident of the state and to all agencies of government.
- NOVELny information facilitates informed decision making.
- NOVELny enables citizens to be involved in the formulation and understanding of public policy issues and to be better-educated voters.
- NOVELny supports academic achievement at all levels and lifelong learning for all New Yorkers.
- NOVELny ensures that all New Yorkers have equal access to information, regardless of their economic status or the size/financial resources of their local library system.

EXAMPLE 1

- NOVELNY is excellent value, providing access to peer-reviewed research and accurate, timely information on such issues as medical care, financial planning, career exploration, consumer purchasing, and other essentials.

Strategies

- Leverage existing targeted communication channels that are created expressly for this extremely important, but difficult-to-reach and critical target audience.
- Incorporate story placement in key publications to garner visibility, use, and support.
- Marketing messages that appeal to the general public will also reach elected officials who are a component of the larger marketplace.
- Penetrate the governmental sector by targeting information that reaches aides and assistants rather than the more elusive elected officials.
- Encourage local librarians to solicit opportunities to demonstrate the value of NOVELNY to municipal officials.
- Provide opportunity on the NOVELNY homepage for librarians to voice their support for continued NOVELNY funding directly to their legislators.

Recommended Distribution Channels

- NYSED electronic discussion list
- Fax alerts to aides who research issues and write position papers and speeches
- *Legislative Gazette* (the weekly newspaper of the New York State government)
- Publications of such organizations as the Association of County Executives, City Managers, Mayors
- Integrate information about NOVELNY into orientation programs for elected officials at the state level

Measures of Success

- Sustained funding for NOVELNY is found.
- More legislative aides participate in an orientation/demo program that includes information about NOVELNY.
- Elected officials have a better understanding of how NOVELNY benefits their constituents.
- Elected officials emerge as "product champions" for NOVELNY.
- Elected officials have more reliable information upon which they can make decisions pertaining to public policy issues.

- E-mail campaign is successfully implemented.
- Stories are placed in publications that target the capital.

TARGET AUDIENCE
Public Librarians

Goal

- Increase the capacity of public librarians to promote databases in general and NOVELNY in particular.

Issues

- Public librarians have limited resources, time, and marketing expertise.
- Perceived value of NOVELNY varies according to quality of online resources available at the individual and system library level.

Strategies

- Add perceived value to support of NOVELNY by assisting librarians in marketing all online resources.
- Create an online toolkit that provides all the materials and information necessary for librarians to educate customers about the attributes and benefit of NOVELNY, with a special focus on in-library promotions and educating current library users.
- Provide toolkit training and promotion at statewide conferences.

Recommended Distribution Channels

- Statewide meetings
- Electronic discussion list
- Website

Measures of Success

- NOVELNY is presented and discussed at statewide meetings.
- NOVELNY steering committee provides informal feedback.
- NOVELNY toolkit is launched and promoted.
- Libraries use toolkit to market NOVELNY in their communities.
- More New Yorkers access NOVELNY using a public library card.

EXAMPLE 1

TARGET AUDIENCE
Business and Economic Development Sector

Goals

- Promote the wider use of specialized databases on business and finance.
- Leverage support for the continued funding of the databases by generating use among staff and aides who can influence elected officials at the local, county, and state levels.

Issues

- Marketing databases to business owners and operators who are focused on day-to-day business operations has been challenging in most states.
- Many business owners operate their businesses without accurate information and without business plans.
- The business sector is highly fragmented when considering size, maturity of businesses, and the unending emergence of new and start-up businesses.
- Business owners often "don't know what they don't know."
- Large, better-funded corporations frequently have their own research departments and subscribe to highly specialized and extremely expensive databases that are currently not within the NOVELny product.
- If NOVELny is augmented with more academic databases, the plan may be adjusted in coordination with NYSTAR.

Key Messages

NOVELny:

- provides access to information that cultivates an educated and skilled workforce;
- provides critical technical and financial information for new and emergent businesses;
- provides key information to economic development agencies throughout the state; and
- supports career exploration and professional business development.

Strategies

- Target medium and slightly more mature businesses that will be most likely to respond to NOVELny.

- Leverage contacts with chambers of commerce and other professional and business organizations in the state to identify communications and marketing opportunities.
- Target professors and instructors in business schools and departments.
- Target young professionals, career explorers, and adults who are enrolled in continuing education and professional certification programs and are currently using Google.

Recommended Distribution Channels

- Chambers of commerce newsletters
- Metropolitan business journals
- Presentations at state meetings of business, professional, and trade associations

Measures of Success

- Number of visitors to business and economic development portal increases.
- NOVELNY-related stories are placed in business publications.
- Use of business-related databases increases.
- New York business owners have more reliable information with which to make business decisions.
- New Yorkers have enhanced access to quality information for job searches and career exploration.

TARGET AUDIENCE
Academic Librarians, College Administrators, and College and University Librarians and Teaching Faculty

Goals

- Increase the ability of academic librarians to market NOVELNY to students, faculty, and administrators.
- Increase the awareness and use of NOVELNY among academic populations.

Issues

- Academic librarians have limited resources to market NOVELNY.
- Online databases are underutilized by faculty, undergraduate students, adjunct faculty, and nontraditional students such as

EXAMPLE 1

those enrolled in the Empire State College who do not use their college libraries.

- Students and faculty at institutions with more financial resources generally have access to many expensive databases that are not part of NOVELny.
- An important subset of this segment is students enrolled in library science programs.

Key Messages

NOVELny:

- supports information literacy for college students at colleges and universities in New York State by providing access to peer-reviewed, research-based information found in credible and respected professional journals;
- supports faculty development by providing access to resources that they need for research and for classroom instruction;
- supports recruitment of world-class faculty who are actively engaged in research;
- supports Middle State Accreditation;
- supports more robust undergraduate research;
- provides access to research materials for smaller and less affluent colleges and universities; and
- serves as a superior resource for distance learning and nontraditional students.

Strategies

- Leverage the distribution system composed of 120 private academic institutions and sixty colleges in the state system.
- Capitalize on the fact that there is a community college in every district that also serves the general public and the business community in the region.
- Focus on lesser-funded four-year and two-year colleges.
- Include in the toolkit materials that educate students in library science programs about NOVELny.
- Give librarians the tools to market NOVELny to faculty, students, and administrators via an online toolkit.

Recommended Distribution Channels

- Associations and consortia of school administrators and librarians at two-year and four-year colleges in New York State
- Marketing toolkit that will be promoted to academic librarians
- E-commerce to students currently using Google
- State newspaper for higher education

Measures of Success

- Stories are placed in higher education publications.
- Toolkit is used by academic librarians to promote NOVELNY to students, faculty, and administrators.
- Use of NOVELNY by students and faculty at colleges and universities increases.

TARGET AUDIENCE

Teachers, Administrators, Students, and Parents in Elementary, Middle, and High Schools; Homeschoolers and Parent-Teacher Associations

Goals

- Increase the awareness of NOVELNY among parents of school-aged children.
- Promote a higher level of awareness and use of NOVELNY by New York teachers and their students.
- Increase the awareness of the value and importance of NOVELNY among school administrators and school board members who are well positioned to lobby for continued funding.
- Increase the ability of students to plan and complete higher quality research assignments.
- Position NOVELNY as the "resource of choice" for teens who want to use services that are customized to their lifestyle—giving them what they want when they want it.

Issues

- Teachers and other school personnel do not always know about NOVELNY or recommend it to their students.
- Teachers do not always understand the difference between information found in NOVELNY databases and in less reliable sources.
- Well-established teachers are sometimes reluctant to change lesson plans to include assignments that will require the use of NOVELNY or other online databases.
- School librarians often lack the resources to promote the use of NOVELNY within their school buildings to teachers, students, administrators, and school board members.
- The educational marketplace is complex when considering gender, age, ethnicity, levels of academic achievement, geography, and so forth.

EXAMPLE 1

- NOVELNY is generally available to New York students in their school library or media center during regular school hours, but students sometimes cannot access the version of NOVELNY that is available in schools remotely from their homes and instead must use NOVELNY through their public library.
- Some schools and libraries have no Internet connection; filters create access barriers; and many schools lack certified librarians.

Key Messages

- NOVELNY makes good teachers even better.
- NOVELNY is a superior resource for teachers enrolled in continuing education and degree programs.
- Students with access to quality library resources and services generally experience greater academic success.
- NOVELNY is an invaluable resource for gifted and advanced students.
- NOVELNY is available 24/7 and ideally suited to the lifestyles and preferences of teens and other students who cannot get to their school or public library during normal hours of operation.
- NOVELNY levels the playing field for students in schools that lack financial resources.
- NOVELNY is a safe site for students of all ages.

Strategies

- Leverage the New York State Library's position within the New York State Department of Education to distribute information about NOVELNY to a targeted and defined audience that can be reached in New York schools settings.
- Capitalize on the cost efficiencies associated with using multiple in-school distribution systems such as:

  information packets distributed to classroom instructors, administrators, and librarians;

  in-service training programs for instructors and librarians;

  articles in school district newsletters;

  in-game advertising at football and basketball games;

  bookmarks in school libraries and media centers;

  banners for school libraries;

  displays at back-to-school nights and popular student locations; and

  special events for students and/or their parents.

- Cultivate a higher level of awareness and use of NOVELny by classroom teachers who can, in turn, stimulate use among their students.
- Focus on teens who are early adapters, reluctant to access information in traditional library settings, and have a lifestyle that is ideally suited to the NOVELny product and its use.
- Promote the long-range use of library databases by increasing the use of NOVELny by young schoolchildren.
- Package and promote databases with specific appeal to young children and their parents.
- Drive the use of NOVELny products for young children by tying the marketing to in-school card registration drives.
- Simplify interfaces between sites such as http://homeworknyc.org and NOVELny access.

Recommended Distribution Channels

- New York State educational newspapers and newsletters
- Homeschool networks and organizations
- New York State Association of School Boards
- New York State Teachers Association
- Online toolkit with materials for teachers, parents, students, administrators, and school board members
- Parent-teacher associations
- Promotional items and giveaways underwritten by vendors—particularly for teens
- New York City school district publications

Measures of Success

- PR is placed in education publications.
- The toolkit is used to promote NOVELny within schools.
- Use of NOVELny databases by young children and students increases.
- Students have access to reliable information for satisfying academic requirements.
- Parents of schoolchildren are more aware of NOVELny and the ways in which it bolsters academic achievement.

EXAMPLE 1

TARGET AUDIENCE
Parents of One Million Plus Children in Statewide Summer Reading Program

Goals

- Leverage the success of the statewide reading program to educate parents about NOVELNY and to encourage and build long-term use among elementary-aged children.
- Expand the perception of summer reading program attendees that libraries are for reading to include an understanding that the library is an excellent source of information for school projects and assignments.

Issues

- Young children who access online resources while in elementary school are more likely to continue to access them in middle and high school.
- In New York, to date, there has not been an effort to cross-market these library programs and services.

Key Messages

- Access to quality library resources leads to greater academic achievement.
- NOVELNY teaches children how to access and manage information—a skill that will be invaluable to them in our information-based society.
- NOVELNY puts a high-quality "reference shelf" in the home of every student.
- NOVELNY is an invaluable resource for gifted and advanced students.
- NOVELNY is available 24/7 and ideally suited to the lifestyles and preferences of time-starved parents and heavily programmed children.
- NOVELNY is a safe site for children.

Strategies

- Integrate use of databases into summer reading activities.
- Develop customized marketing materials for parents about parenting information available on NOVELNY.
- Promote the group of NOVELNY databases geared to the needs of schoolchildren.
- Capitalize on the opportunity to distribute NOVELNY information to students during in-school card registration drives.

Recommended Distribution Channels

- Directly distribute NOVELNY information packet to parents who enroll their children in summer reading and to children signing up for a library card via a statewide program
- Include relevant NOVELNY access on Summer Reading Program websites

Measures of Success

- Use of databases specifically for young children increases.
- The NOVELNY information packet for parents is successfully distributed.
- Summer reading program activities are expanded to include activities that use NOVELNY.

Web Extra

Visit www.alaeditions.org/webextras to access the original NOVELNY plan in PDF format as well as an editable version in Word that you can adapt for your own use.

Marketing Plan from a Public Library, Sample 1

Winnetka-Northfield Public Library District, "Building a Buzz"

EXAMPLE
2

Acknowledgment

The marketing plan report for the Winnetka-Northfield Public Library District, developed in part by Juli Janovicz, Head of Adult Services (julij@ winnetkalibrary.org), is used courtesy of the Winnetka-Northfield Public Library District.

Both online use and staff morale got a boost when this library focused on engaging staff:

> Our staff were excited by the incentive contests and by the database training. Once they felt comfortable using the resources they were able to pass the key message on with confidence.

Introduction

The Winnetka-Northfield Public Library District encompasses two highly educated, affluent communities on the North Shore of Chicago. The community is known for its outstanding schools, including the nationally recognized New Trier High School. The library serves a population of 17,808 with median family incomes over $100,000. Our library has great customer service and excellent resources, but we needed to generate greater awareness of its online resources. While 85 percent of the district has library cards, our cardholders don't use their online resources as well as they could. This project was designed to increase both staff and patron awareness of the library's online services by revamping the way our message is delivered to busy residents.

Goals

- Patrons of the Winnetka-Northfield Public Library District will value and use their library 24/7.
- Our staff will have exceptional customer service skills.

IN THIS EXAMPLE

✓ Introduction
✓ Goals
✓ Objectives
✓ Key Audiences
✓ Message
✓ Strategies
✓ Tools
✓ Budget
✓ Impact
✓ Lessons Learned

EXAMPLE 2

- The staff and board will deliver a clear, concise message with accuracy and confidence.

Objectives

- Increase staff knowledge and comfort level by providing training about the library's databases, word-of-mouth marketing, and customer service techniques.
- Increase the number of unique cardholder hits to the online resources by 10 percent.
- Increase the number of consultations about various online services.

Key Audiences

- Staff
- Trustees
- Influential members of the community
- Winnetka Chamber of Commerce
- Northfield Chamber of Commerce
- Winnetka Alliance for Early Childhood
- Rotary of Winnetka-Northfield
- Parents
- Elementary and middle school children

Message

We're Up When You Are: 24 Hours a Day.

Strategies

Internal

- Provide training for staff on word-of-mouth marketing and the importance of team involvement and also online resources, customer service, and one of our newest databases, Standard and Poor's.
- Encourage staff to explore these resources individually and to familiarize themselves with one or two databases on their own.
- Hold a contest to promote staff involvement in developing and delivering our message.
- Survey staff pre- and post-training to gauge comfort level with word-of-mouth marketing and the library's databases.
- Provide "cheat sheets" with talking points to help staff initiate conversations. These were designed specifically for nonreference

staff members who don't deal with reference interviews or databases on a regular basis.

External

- Develop and distribute a handy "24 Hour" bookmark/brochure that lists our online services.
- Encourage staff to talk up and demonstrate online databases to library users at every opportunity. Give notepads to those who participate. Staff members who give away the most notepads will win prizes.
- Expand database training for the public to include our newest database, Standard and Poor's. This database was added as a direct result of a conversation at the Northfield Branch during the incentive contest.
- Participate in special events, for example, first-grade reading parties, the Chamber of Commerce Annual Sidewalk Sale. Provide goodie bags with promotional materials, including a coupon for a consultation with a librarian.

Tools

- A $50 gift card for the best slogan/message submitted by staff
- Note cubes with our message on them
- Laminated "cheat sheets" with talking points
- A "24-Hour" bookmark/brochure (Worth its weight in gold, this bookmark lists all of the library's 24-hour online resources with boxes for staff to check off suggested databases when conversing with patrons.)
- Coupons for an hour of personal consultation time with a librarian

Budget

A total of $2,450 was spent on staff incentives, promo items, and staff training.

Impact

The most successful aspect of this project was the staff involvement. Thirty-four staff members and three board members were trained during seven sessions on word-of-mouth marketing, customer service, and online resources. Surveys showed staff's comfort levels increased significantly over the course of the grant period. People were excited by the incentive contests and by the database training. Once they felt comfortable using the resources, they

EXAMPLE 2

were able to pass the key message on with confidence. We continue to hold refresher training sessions.

The number of hits by unique cardholders was more than double what we had projected. It increased by 23 percent between March and April after staff training took place. Database usage increased 14.6 percent from October 2007 to October 2008.

During the incentive contest, which lasted a week, staff distributed 160 promotional note cubes to the public. Two staff members were awarded $100 gift cards from Barnes and Noble for their efforts. One distributed fifty-six cubes. She said she liked having a reason to initiate talking with customers. Hundreds of the "24-Hour" bookmarks were given out.

The least successful aspect was the coupon promotion. Not a single coupon for a consultation was returned. We suspect this is because people did not feel a need for a coupon and would turn to us anyway.

This marketing project marked the start of revamping the way the Winnetka-Northfield Public Library District delivers the message about 24/7 services to our busy residents. By continually increasing both staff and patron awareness we want to inform people that our exceptional customer service extends into their homes via our website. And then we want them to tell their friends. . . .

Lessons Learned

One challenge was to overcome staff's assumption that good customer service is enough. It was important to stress that marketing has become an integral part of everyday business at the library. The phrase "promotes library services and materials" has been added to all staff evaluation forms.

It was surprising and rewarding to see the way people responded to being part of the team. It was a positive experience for all the staff to see how their colleagues, even those who are shy, excelled at being customer service extroverts. People learned from each other. This was the perfect project to foster team building from within the ranks.

The "24-Hour" bookmark/brochure has become one of our most useful promotional pieces. It can be adapted for a variety of situations and uses by any department. It is simple and easy to replicate for any library.

Web Extra

Visit www.alaeditions.org/webextras to access the original Winnetka-Northfield plan in PDF format as well as an editable version in Word that you can adapt for your own use.

Marketing Plan from a Public Library, Sample 2

Worthington Libraries 2012 Communications
and Development Plan

Acknowledgment

The communications and development plan report for the Worthington
Libraries is used with permission of Worthington Libraries (Worthington,
Ohio).

Community Relations Department Staff

Lisa Fuller, Director of Community Engagement

Lindsey Smith, Outreach Services/Volunteer Coordinator

Hillary Kline, Communications Specialist

Lisa Bond, Graphic Designer

Rebecca Wenden, Library Associate

Plan Focus Areas

FUNDRAISING AND DEVELOPMENT
　　Encourage both public and private support of the Library.

PROGRAMMING
　　Present targeted programs designed to educate, enlighten, and
　　　　entertain people of all ages.

PUBLIC RELATIONS AND MARKETING
　　Increase awareness and understanding of the library's value in the
　　　　community.

PARTNERSHIPS AND OUTREACH
　　Facilitate and support effective library partnerships and collaborations.

IN THIS EXAMPLE

✓ Community Relations
　Department Staff

✓ Plan Focus Areas

✓ Fundraising and Development

✓ Programming

✓ Public Relations and Marketing

✓ Partnerships and Outreach

EXAMPLE 3

Fundraising and Development

Encourage both public and private support of the Library:

- Continue to work with the Friends Foundation of Worthington Libraries to identify the best organizational solution to support the short- and long-term fundraising goals of the Library. This process could include:

    creating new position descriptions for Friends Foundation board members,

    assisting the Friends Foundation with identifying new board members,

    developing an orientation procedure/packet for new Friends Foundation board members,

    setting an appropriate fundraising goal for the Friends Foundation,

    working with the Friends Foundation to identify and cultivate fundraising prospects, and

    establishing a separate organization to manage the Worthington Libraries Endowment Fund and assisting that group with everything outlined above.

- Identify the key focus areas for library fundraising (homework help, create young readers, build successful enterprises, etc.).
- Secure grant funding for key projects and initiatives (Family Reading Festival, Homework Help Centers, school technology partnerships, etc.).
- Tie fundraising efforts to Worthington's philanthropic history and the establishment of the community's first library.
- Educate the community about the giving opportunities available through the Library, Friends Foundation, and endowment fund.
- Evaluate the necessity of purchasing fundraising software to better track and record library donations and donations to the Friends Foundation/endowment fund.
- Prepare an annual budget request for the Friends Foundation.
- Coordinate the Hear & Now author series and other events to benefit the Friends Foundation.
- Update the library's Power Philanthropy Portrait on The Columbus Foundation website.
- Create a Power Philanthropy Portrait for the Friends Foundation and/or the endowment fund advisory group once they have established all necessary policies and procedures.
- Recognize donors in the library's winter newsletter.
- Research the feasibility of implementing a "fundraising days" program whereby people could sponsor a day of service at the Library in exchange for some type of meaningful recognition.

- Encourage an annual gift (outside of membership) to the Friends Foundation.
- Work with legislators and the community to maintain public funding for the Library.
- Invite legislators to attend and take part in library events (like the Family Reading Festival).
- Train key library stakeholders (Friends Foundation board, etc.) as funding advocates.

Programming

Present targeted programs designed to educate, enlighten, and entertain people of all ages.

In November, we formed a program planning ad hoc committee to address some concerns related to the number of programs we are presenting each quarter. We cannot sustain programming at current levels if we also want to meet community outreach expectations and the needs of patrons visiting the Library. We will work to reduce the number of traditional programs presented by the Library while increasing our overall impact. The following are goals of the committee:

- Work with staff to reduce the number of programs we are presenting each quarter.
- Define our programming mission and align the library's programming goals with fundraising focus areas and vice versa.
- Establish realistic programming expectations and provide enough time to make an impact before moving on to the next initiative.
- Provide program planning training for staff.
- Revise all programming forms.
- Offer more targeted programs for specific populations (one big scouting program instead of several held throughout the year).
- Increase communication among buildings to avoid duplication and share ideas.
- Create a more visitor-centered approach to engage people in "on the fly" programs whenever they visit the Library.

In addition to the committee work, we will maintain an emphasis on providing quality programs and continue the library's signature programming. Specifically, the community relations department will:

- Plan the February by the Fire concert series in conjunction with Jazz Arts Group.
- Plan Northwest Library's summer concert series (using volunteers to secure signatures for noise permits).
- Continue planning and presentation of the Hear & Now author series in partnership with the McConnell Arts Center to benefit the Friends Foundation of Worthington Libraries.

EXAMPLE 3

- Coordinate the Summer Reading League in partnership with the Columbus Clippers:

    Create all graphics and promotional items.

    Secure additional coupons to be used as prizes.

    Coordinate school visits with the Clippers, ticket distribution, and game volunteers.

    Coordinate library programming in conjunction with the Summer Reading League.

- Plan the Family Reading Festival (securing a teen author as the featured speaker).

Public Relations and Marketing

Increase awareness and understanding of the library's value in the community:

- Work with the community, library board, Friends Foundation, and staff to research and write the library's next strategic plan:

    Seek proposals and engage a consultant to implement the community portion of the strategic planning process.

    Conduct focus groups, surveys, and additional market research to learn more about how patrons view and use the Library now.

    Help the community learn more and get excited about how the Library could be used in the future.

    Involve the staff in trend tracking.

    Identify focus areas for the next strategic plan and determine future funding needs for plan implementation.

- Continue implementation of the "Find yourself here" branding campaign:

    Introduce a new series of brand messages and retire older ones.

    Develop a plan for using community members in the campaign.

    Promote individual librarian expertise with "Find" messages.

- Continue development of the library's social media presence through Facebook and Twitter and the use of QR codes.
- Coordinate website promotion of "special days" with library resources, displays, and events.
- Determine the best way for other staff members (beyond the community relations and technology departments) to get involved with promoting the Library and interacting with patrons through social media.

- Introduce a new, more visually appealing e-mail newsletter.
- Assist with the development, design, and promotion of the new Worthington Memory website.
- Publish a 2011 annual report.
- Plan the annual community breakfast during National Library Week.
- Coordinate the library's participation in the Memorial Day Parade and other community events.
- Submit articles, as appropriate, to local and national media outlets.
- Collect patron stories and record them (along with names and contact information) in a database.
- Use patron quotes to promote library programs and future levy initiative.

Web Extra

Visit www.alaeditions.org/webextras to access the original Worthington Libraries plan in PDF format as well as an editable version in Word that you can adapt for your own use.

Partnerships and Outreach

Facilitate and support effective library partnerships and collaborations:

- Coordinate the library's participation in the annual Groundhog Day Business Forecast breakfast sponsored by the Worthington Area Chamber of Commerce.
- Work with the City of Worthington to develop a series of programs to benefit library and city staff (sensitivity training, violence in the workplace, etc.).
- Participate with the City of Worthington and Worthington Schools in the planning and promotion of the 2012 community celebration of Martin Luther King Day.
- Conduct a focus group with teachers in the Worthington School District to determine how the Library can best meet the technology/research needs of students and parents.
- Retool and rebrand the library's Ambassador Program (an outreach program originally designed for classroom use to promote the library's website and electronic resources).
- Promote library outreach to daycare centers, preschools, and other community organizations.
- Continue outreach activities with the Worthington Food Pantry (and discuss ways of adding value to this initiative).
- Continue successful partnership with the Worthington Garden Club in the presentation of programs focused on community sustainability and the environment.
- As needed, continue partnership with other libraries in Franklin County to present programs related to job help and technology help.
- Plan annual recognition event to thank library volunteers.
- Create a way for staff members to recognize and reward volunteers for outstanding work.

Marketing Plan from a Community College Library

Maricopa Community College District Electronic Resources Committee Marketing Plan, 2013-2016

EXAMPLE

4

Acknowledgment

The marketing plan report for the Maricopa Community College District, developed by the Electronic Resources Committee, is used with permission. ERC Marketing Subcommittee: Stephanie Allen, Marsha Ballard, Mary Beth Burgoyne, Karen Docherty, Beth Malapanes, Kande Mikelsen, and Mercedes Miramontes (May 2015).

Introduction

The Maricopa Community College District Electronic Resources Committee (ERC) mission is "to acquire electronic content and ensure its delivery using models and innovations that best serve MCCCD students and faculty." ERC subscribes to an impressive number and array of electronic library resources. They are available online to students, faculty, and employees of all the Maricopa Community Colleges. These resource links are available at http://libguides.maricopa.edu/libraryresources. This plan will outline a strategy and tactics to promote and increase awareness of these valuable resources.

Since the late 1990s the Maricopa Community Colleges have provided an online E-Library collection of resources to support student academic achievement and success. The Electronic Resources Committee wants to raise the visibility of this collection and all it has to offer and increase its usage across the District among students, faculty, and other employees. The District expends almost $900,000 for core subscriptions accessible throughout the Maricopa District, which makes it even more important to increase awareness of their availability. Users must have an MEID and password to gain access to the E-Library resources from off-campus locations.

While not its primary focus, it is also important for ERC to promote the role, importance, and contributions of Library faculty within MCCCD.

IN THIS EXAMPLE

✓ Introduction

✓ Internal Audiences

✓ Desired Behaviors and Attitudes

✓ Communication Goals

✓ Measures

✓ Communication Channels

✓ MCCCD District System-Level Strategies/Initiatives

✓ The MCCCD 2013-2016 Strategic Planning Goals

✓ ERC Strategic Plan Objective

✓ Implementation Strategies

EXAMPLE 4

This Communication Plan is intended to do the following:

1. Implement a communication and marketing process that directly helps the Electronic Resources Committee achieve its goals.
2. Strengthen the relationships with students, faculty, employees, and other stakeholders.
3. Provide focus and direction for messages/marketing in support of the ERC's goals as outlined in its Strategic Plan.
4. Enable ERC to promote itself and its activities to students, faculty, staff, and other identified audiences within the Maricopa County Community College District (MCCCD).

Internal Audiences

Students (primary):

- AAA, CPD, career and workforce development
- English, reading, math (developmental education)
- Nursing/allied health
- Music
- Athletes
- Dual enrollment
- Online students

Faculty, staff, and other MCCCD employees (secondary)

Desired Behaviors and Attitudes

Through the implementation of this Plan, the ERC hopes to strengthen the following desired behaviors and attitudes:

- Students will find information they are seeking via ERC resources.
- Recognize the E logo as a symbol of district electronic resources.
- Increased awareness of ERC and the databases and services it provides.
- Students, faculty, and MCCCD employees will value and utilize the resources provided through ERC.
- Students will successfully access ERC resources and become more successful students.
- Employees will utilize ERC resources in support of their work.

Communication Goals

1. Announce and promote Summon/One Search tool.
2. Increase awareness about types of resources: e-books, streaming media, articles, images, etc.
3. Increase brand recognition with memorable logo/branding: become as recognizable to our audience as the F for Facebook or the S for Skype or the P for Pinterest.
4. Increase use of E-Library resources by students, faculty, and staff.
5. Increase awareness and use of E-Library by targeted populations: college success, health/nursing, business, art/art history/interior design, etc.
6. Create awareness of the connection between Ask a Librarian and electronic resources.
7. Align better with the One Maricopa: Seamless Student Experience initiative.
8. Increase database usage district-wide by a certain percentage.
9. Increase brand awareness.
10. Explore tie-in to Maricopa Millions.
11. Develop a series of promotional templates that can be used throughout the district.
12. Provide a design template for individual libraries for their college E-Library unique resources.

Measures

- Number of marketing methods used
- Number of people campuses contacted
- Increased use of resources promoted
    - Usage statistics
- Awareness of resources
    - Student surveys
    - Employee surveys
    - Focus groups
- Website hits
- Community feedback

Communication Channels

The following list describes the internal and external communication channels available to the ERC.

EXAMPLE 4

Electronic

- E-mail
- Social media: Facebook, Twitter, Pinterest
- Video
- Telephone
- Websites
- Banner ads on websites
- Online ad on district homepage
- Link to district libraries on district webpage
- Newsletters
- Combine efforts with Ask a Librarian
- An app

Print

- Intercampus mail
- Posters
- Table tents
- Flyers
- Brochures
- Career guides and transfer magazines
- Tie into "I will graduate . . ." campaign
- T-shirts

Give-Away Items

- Pens, cups, flash drives, etc.

Interpersonal

- Workshops
- Conferences
- Campus meetings
- Divisions meetings
- Open forums
- Brown bag sessions
- New employee orientations/on-boarding
- Word of mouth

MCCCD District System-Level Strategies/Initiatives

- One Maricopa: Seamless Student Experience
- Maricopa Priorities
- IMOR2

- Developmental Education
- Student Success Initiative
- Performance Based Funding

The MCCCD 2013-2016 Strategic Planning Goals

Access to Learning

Goal #1: MCCCD will improve access to learning opportunities for students and the community.

Pathways to Success

Goal #2: MCCCD will enhance educational and career pathways to support student goal attainment.

Effective Learning and Teaching

Goal #3: MCCCD will improve student learning outcomes and teaching effectiveness.

ERC Strategic Plan Objective

Promote the rich collection of Library e-resources to MCCCD students and faculty.

Implementation Strategies

STRATEGY 1: Increase brand recognition with memorable logo/branding.

STRATEGY 2: Develop a series of promotional templates that can be used throughout the district.

STRATEGY 3: Work with Instructional Councils and share relevant promotional materials.

STRATEGY 4: Develop a series of promotional materials based on student narratives: How the Library helped me succeed.

Marketing Plan from a University Library, Sample 1

EXAMPLE

5

Milner Library, Illinois State University 2012–2014 Marketing Plan

Acknowledgment

The marketing plan for the Milner Library at Illinois State University is used by permission of Toni Tucker, Assistant Dean for Enabling Infrastructure, Illinois State University.

Introduction

While plans are not usually followed to the letter, the planning process is indispensable as it enables us to answer basic questions about what we do and why we do it.

One doesn't often hear marketing and library in the same sentence. Many see marketing as a process of for-profit organizations. This document is written to enable the University Libraries (hereafter library or Milner Library) to pursue a certain process in the promotion of its activities; to complement the Library's Strategic Plan; and to assist the library's and university's faculty and staff in understanding the tactics, strategy, and procedures related to the marketing of cultural events and intellectual resources.

Milner Library plays an integral role in the university teaching, learning, and research. The library's vision and mission statements enforce the library's increasing leadership role in the life and culture of the campus and community.

In its vision statement, the library aspires "to be the preeminent center of learning, information, culture, and technology in higher education" (Vision Statement, http://library.illinoisstate.edu/library-information/about/strategicplan.php).

It also aims to "create and sustain an intuitive and trusted information environment that enables learning and the advancement of knowledge in a culturally and technologically superior setting. ISU Libraries' staff is committed to developing innovative services, programs, space, strategies, and systems that promote discovery, dialogue, learning, and the human spirit"

EXAMPLE 5

(Mission Statement, http://library.illinoisstate.edu/library-information/about/strategic-plan.php).

Objectives

The University Libraries Marketing Plan aims to:

1. increase the visibility of the library and its value in our society;
2. increase the awareness of the community of the added value of the library activities and services;
3. increase the level of participation of ISU alums and community members in the life of the university and stimulate the donation and gifting process;
4. increase the level of satisfaction among our patrons; and
5. facilitate the branding of the library activities.

Marketing Strategies

To promote the Milner Library's services, resources, and activities, the library will undertake the following strategies:

- Increase the visibility of library resources through the library's homepage, brochures, social networking tools, and other appropriate channels.
- Identify services and collections to highlight through a program or a course with one of the teaching faculty.
- Publicize special events in coordination with other colleges and programs as well as community partners.
- Seek out opportunities to work with the University Library Committee as representative of the faculty and student body.
- Work with the board of the Friends of the Library on community events.
- Sponsor and support external speakers, exhibits, and programs that highlight Milner's cultural role on campus and in central Illinois.
- Seek input from the community in relation to cultural needs.
- Establish new community partnerships to support speakers, strengthening relationships between the university and local businesses and not-for-profit organizations (i.e., bookstores, museums, and public libraries).
- Highlight Milner faculty and staff research and service contributions to the profession through professional circles as well as national media.

Web Extra

Visit www.alaeditions.org/webextras to access the original Milner Library plan in PDF format as well as an editable version in Word that you can adapt for your own use.

Forms of Publicity

- Press releases
- Informational fliers/ posters
- Advertisements
- Announcements
- Newsletters
- Brochures
- Library guides
- Articles
- Presentations
- Website highlights
- READ posters

- Electronic signs
- Signcades*
- Banners
- Campus Connections*
- *College & Main* television program*
- Social networking tools
- University calendar
- Electronic discussion lists
- Other

> * **Signcades**–Portable sandwich boards that can have events changed as needed. Used by the library on the Milner Plaza and ISU QUAD.
>
> * **Campus Connections**–Resident Hall channel to advertise services and events.
>
> * ***College & Main***–A weekly half-hour television program that promotes university events and outreach to the campus and community.

Assessment/Evaluation

All marketing strategies will be evaluated through a number of methods. These include but are not limited to surveys, focus groups, and event evaluation forms. The PR staff will use the Activity Planning Feedback and the Speaker Assessment Form (Appendixes 2 and 3) for quick feedback.

Target Audiences

Primary audiences of Milner Library are members of the Illinois State University community. This includes students, faculty, staff, and alumni. Secondary audiences include but are not limited to the Bloomington/Normal community, other institutions of higher education, families of Illinois State University students, library organizations, and elected officials (Appendix 4).

Media Contacts

The Dean of University Libraries or the Dean's designee is the official spokesperson for the library and partnership organizations stated in the library's mission. The Dean may ask the head of the Public Relations Unit to respond to media questions or to provide information as appropriate. The unit head will be responsible for providing current, accurate information or identifying the appropriate source of information to the media. The unit head will act as liaison to campus and external publications (Appendix 5).

Although the President's office serves as the ultimate spokesperson for the university, a crisis communication plan is expected to be developed through the spring of 2012.

EXAMPLE 5

Public Relations and Marketing Unit Team Members

Toni Tucker (Unit Head and Assistant Dean)
ttucker@ilstu.edu
309-438-7402

Sarah Dick
sdick@ilstu.edu
309-438-2680

Jan Johnson
jrjohnso@ilstu.edu
309-438-3897

APPENDIX 1

MILNER LIBRARY LOGO

(To be used on all publications)

AVAILABLE AT

P:\Library Coordination Groups\Public Relations Committee\
FINAL (read-only)\Graphics_Logos\milner-logos

Illinois State University Libraries adhere to the university's
graphic and editorial standards developed by the University
Marketing and Communications Department. Standards
can be found at http://universitymarketing.illinoisstate.edu/
identity.

APPENDIX 2

Activity Planning Feedback

Date:	
Event:	
Event date:	
Location:	
Message:	

AUDIENCE(S)

1.
2.
3.
4.
5.
6.
7.
8.

MEDIA

1.
2.
3.
4.
5.
6.
7.
8.

CONTACTS

1.
2.
3.
4.
5.

REPORT INCLUDED

_____

_____

APPENDIX 3

Speaker Assessment Form

Today's Event

Your responses help us improve our events and give us ideas for others.

How did you hear about this event?

☐ Newspaper   ☐ Radio   ☐ Flyer/Poster   ☐ Website   ☐ Other

Are you a student?   ☐ NO   ☐ YES   ☐ High School   ☐ College

How would you rate the event/speaker?   ☐ Excellent   ☐ Just OK   ☐ Below expectations

How far (miles) did you travel to this event?

Will you attend future Milner Library events?   ☐ YES   ☐ NO

We love your ideas! Suggestions:

Speakers _____

Programs _____

Exhibits _____

Other _____

Please use the back for any additional comments you would like to share.

Printed on recycled paper.

APPENDIX 4

Target Audience/Specific Media

Media → / Audience ↓	Daily Vidette	Campus Connections	Signcades	Flyers	Brochures	Newsletters	Bulletin Boards	Electronic Signs	Posters	TV 10	Radio	College & Main	Lib Website	ISU Website	ISU Report	Social Media	Pantagraph	E-mail
Internal																		
Students	X	X	X	X	X	X	X	X	X	X	X	X	X	X		X	X	
Faculty	X		X	X	X	X	X	X	X	X	X	X	X	X	X	X	X	X
Library Personnel	X		X	X		X	X	X	X	X	X	X	X	X	X	X	X	X
ISU Staff and Admin.	X		X	X		X	X	X	X	X	X	X	X	X	X	X	X	X
External																		
Alumni						X					X	X	X	X		X	X	
Friends of Milner					X	X					X	X	X	X		X	X	
Parents					X	X						X	X	X		X	X	
Community Inst.			X			X		X	X	X	X	X	X	X		X	X	X
Library Consortia			X			X			X		X		X	X		X	X	
Citizens of Illinois											X		X	X				
Media											X	X	X	X		X	X	X
Elected Officials													X	X		X	X	X
Vendors																		X

167

APPENDIX 5

Media Contacts

Illinois State University Marketing and Communications
438-5091

PRINT

Daily Vidette

Contact changes year to year 438-5931

Broadcast E-mail Illinois State University

See campus policy at www.ctsg.ilstu.edu/policies_faq/broadcasts.shtml

Pantagraph (Local Newspaper)

Higher Education Reporter: 820-3232

MEDIA (RADIO AND TV)

WGLT NPR Radio Station

Charlie Schlenker, News, ceschle@ilsu.edu 438-7353

Willis Kern, News Director, wekern@ilstu.edu 438-5426

Development 438-2257

WJBC Radio Station

News 821-1000, Ext. 205, newsroom@wjbc.com

HOI Television News

(309) 698-1950

Campus Connections

Closed circuit TV in resident halls, www.uhs.ilstu.edu/forms/campus_conn.shtml

COLLEGE & MAIN

Deb Wylie, Coordinator of Public Service and Outreach, dkwylie@ilstu.edu, 438-2937

ELECTRONIC MESSAGE BOARD

Prairie Room—Contact a PR committee member.

Milner—Contact a PR committee member or Jan Johnson.

SIGNCADES

Contact a PR committee member.

APPENDIX 6

Marketing Timeline for Standing Annual Activities

FALL SEMESTER

New Faculty Orientation

Banned Books Week

Homecoming

> Honored Alum

> Parade

Visiting Author Program

Illinois School Library Media Association Reception

Study Breaks

Commencement

SPRING SEMESTER

Founders Day

Bryant Jackson Lectureship

Children's Author Visit

Lincoln Speaker

Edible Book Festival

National Library Week

Science & Technology Week Speaker (partnering w/CAST)

Campus Theme (when available)

Study Breaks

Commencement

SUMMER

Preview Expo

ADDITIONAL EVENTS

Exhibits

- National Endowment for the Humanities Traveling Exhibits
- Museum Traveling Exhibits
- ISU University Galleries Exhibits
- Curriculum-Based Exhibits
- Exhibits from the Library's Special Collections
- Student Organization Exhibits
- Community Exhibits

APPENDIX 7

Public Relations/Marketing Request

Send to any member of the Public Relations and Marketing Unit—Sarah Dick, Jan Johnson, or Toni Tucker.

	Today's date:
Project name:	
Project contact(s):	
Project/event date:	
Estimated marketing period: Start date: End date:	

Describe service, program etc. to be publicized: Include attachment(s), if necessary:

Select text and delete. Field will expand as you type.

Intended target audience(s): Select all that apply.

☐ All

☐ ISU students	☐ ISU faculty	☐ ISU staff	☐ ISU administration
☐ Library personnel	☐ Alumni	☐ Parents	☐ Friends of Milner
☐ Courtesy Card users	☐ Local community	☐ Media	☐ Elected officials
☐ Other:			

Suggested media: Select all that apply.

PRINT	ELECTRONIC	MEDIA (RADIO AND TV)
☐ Flyer ☐ color ☐ B/W	☐ Milner website	☐ Press release
☐ Bookmark	☐ Electronic sign (Milner)	☐ ISU Report
☐ Brochure	☐ Electronic sign (campus)	☐ *Daily Vidette*
☐ Newsletters	☐ Campus Connections	☐ WJBC
☐ Table tents	☐ E-mail	☐ WGLT
☐ Invitations	☐ Bulletin boards	☐ Channel 10
☐ Signcades	☐ University calendar	☐ Press conference
		☐ *College & Main*
☐ Other:		

Additional information that could be helpful in promoting this event:

Select text and delete. Field will expand as you type.

APPENDIX 8

FLIER POSTING INFORMATION; MAILBOX STUFFING INFORMATION

Flier Posting Information 2012–2013

University Housing Services (UHS) allows registered student organizations and University departments to post fliers in designated public areas with the following stipulations:

1. The flier relates to events, announcements, services, or activities sponsored and sanctioned by Illinois State University or one of its departments or registered student organizations.
2. The flier does not contain references to alcohol, tobacco, or illicit drugs, or to any event, activity, program, or sponsor whose purpose or activity is the sale, use, or promotion of alcohol, tobacco, or other drugs.
3. The flier does not contain profanity.
4. The flier is printed on recycled paper and contains the recycling logo along with the statement "Printed on recycled paper."
5. The flier contains the following statement for an event: "If you need a special accommodation to fully participate in this program/event, please contact Toni Tucker, Milner Library at 438-7402. Please allow sufficient time to arrange the accommodation."
6. The flier does not exceed 400 square inches.
7. Fliers will be posted for one (1) week.
8. UHS is not responsible for items that get torn down or removed prematurely.

POSTING PROCESS

Fliers are to be taken to the reception desk of each hall for approval by a UHS staff person prior to posting. The numbers of copies needed for distribution are as follows.

POSTING NUMBERS FOR 2012–2013

Hamilton-Whitten	2
Hewett	1
Atkin-Colby	2
Manchester	1
Wilkins	1
Watterson	3

Mailbox Stuffing Information

University Housing Services (UHS) allows registered student organizations and University departments to submit stuffings for the residence hall mailboxes. The items to be stuffed must follow the same stipulations as stated for flier postings.

(cont.)

STUFFING PROCESS

UHS recommends that you bring a sample of the item that you want "stuffed" to the University Housing Services Office (in the Office of Residential Life building) for approval prior to having it printed. Once the item has been approved, have it printed and then bring a final copy to the Housing Office for an authorization form from Kristen Johnson (438-5781). An authorization form must be issued for each mailbox stuffer. The organization must present the authorization at each reception desk when delivering the stuffings for distribution. The numbers of copies needed for distribution are as follows.

STUFFING NUMBERS FOR 2012–2013
ONE FLIER PER MAILBOX

Haynie	190
Hewett	200
Wright	220
Manchester	448
Hamilton-Whitten	417
Watterson	1,111
Atkin-Colby	416
Wilkins	210
Total Mailboxes	3,212

APPENDIX 9

Table Tent Guidelines for Campus Dining Halls

- Unfolded dimensions 4¼ by 11 inches
- Printed on card stock
- Must have the statement: "If you need a special accommodation to fully participate in this program/event, please contact Toni Tucker Milner Library at 438-7402."
- Approval at the John Green Building (take a draft for approval before printing)
- Fill out application form
- One week request/distribute and take down on Saturdays
- May fill out a form for up to three weeks of display
- Watterson 175/Southside 77/Linkins 84

Marketing Plan from a Regional Technical College in Ireland

Galway-Mayo Institute of Technology Library Marketing Plan

EXAMPLE

6

Acknowledgment

The marketing plan report for the Galway-Mayo Institute of Technology (GMIT) is used with permission.

Summary

The GMIT Library Marketing Plan 2009–2012 is a three-year plan with realistic goals and achievable objectives. The plan places the library service in the context of the Institute as a whole and the Strategic Overview outlines some of the challenges facing the service and the Institute in the current economic climate. The SWOT analysis develops the context by examining the strengths, weaknesses, opportunities and threats which the library service faces. The plan examines the main competitors facing the library and looks at the current marketing strategies in which the library is engaged.

The marketing programme outlines goals with consequent objectives. The marketing programme recognizes the importance of the undergraduate cohort of the library users and directs the main part of the programme at this group.

Strategic Overview

The library service of GMIT caters to the study and research needs of the students and staff of GMIT. It provides the student with the study material necessary for the chosen course and the study environment conducive to the completion of that course. It provides the academic staff member with the books and journal articles needed to remain abreast of developments in subjects. It is a central resource and essential service of the Institute. It also serves the wider community by providing access to library resources through external membership.

IN THIS EXAMPLE

✓ Summary

✓ Strategic Overview

✓ Terms of Reference and Scope

✓ GMIT Library SWOT Analysis

✓ GMIT Library's Main Competitors

✓ Target Markets: User Groups

✓ Analysis of Current Marketing Strategies

✓ Target Market: Undergraduates

EXAMPLE 6

Declining public finances has meant that the education sector has to face budget cuts and reduced staffing levels. The library service in GMIT is not immune to this reality. This marketing plan has taken account of the economic constraints and proposes a series of activities which are largely cost neutral except in the area of staff time. We recognize the difficulty the library faces in the coming year with real staff reductions already happening. However, the Marketing Group feels these are essential measures to ensure the continued relevance of the library service and to guarantee the library user gets the maximum benefit from using the library service.

Apart from the financial constraints imposed by the current state of the public finances, the downturn has influenced students' choice of college courses. 2009 CAO figures show a sharp decline in construction based courses and a 20 percent increase in applications for science courses. The number of apprentices has also declined. These fluctuations in course preferences, and consequently student numbers, have implications for the allocation of resources. The library will have to respond to an increase in demand for resources in one area and a decrease in another. These challenges are as a result of recent economic difficulties; there are other challenges facing third level education in Ireland which all have implications for the library service in a third level institution.

Demographic changes mean that the numbers of the traditional cohort of third level students are declining and will continue to do so into the next decade. Participation rates of students from the various social classes remain a serious issue. Children from higher professional group are much more likely to attend third level than children from unskilled manual group.

Despite the challenges facing the Institute and the library service within the Institute, the library must remain focused on the individual user as the most important aspect of the work in which it is engaged. To this end, the library must ensure that the services it provides are the most appropriate to its users and that the users are aware of those services and confident in their ability to access them. This has been the abiding principle for this marketing exercise.

Terms of Reference and Scope

The mission of the GMIT Library is to:

> promote a learning culture within GMIT by acquiring, organising, disseminating and providing access to learning resources and services in a congenial environment. The library will support teaching, learning, research and regional development by providing a customer based service to our students, staff and stakeholders. (GMIT Library Strategic Plan 2006–2011)

This mission statement is aligned to the GMIT strategic plan 2004–2009 and the IoT Librarians strategy statement whose mission reads as follows: "The Libraries of the Institutes of Technology operating at National and Strategic level will foster the development of flexible, accessible learning environments, drawing on international best practice and collective knowledge." The GMIT Marketing Plan 2005–2008 recommended that marketing plans be developed for each school and campus so it is important that the library service also contributes to the process.

The GMIT Library Strategic Plan was developed to provide a strategic roadmap for GMIT Library to follow. One of the goals from this strategic plan was that "a marketing plan will be designed and implemented to promote our services." This library marketing plan was researched and compiled to achieve the following objectives:

- Prepare a market analysis of patrons for the library and target markets.
- Assess perceptions of GMIT Library by key stakeholders.
- Analyze external opportunities and competition for library services.
- Conduct an internal analysis of strengths and weaknesses of the library's capabilities.
- Summarize results of library surveys of patrons.
- Assess current marketing strategies of GMIT Library.
- Set goals and objectives for library.
- Prepare action plan to identify tasks to achieve the library's goals.
- Estimate financial projections and budget to implement marketing plan.
- Develop methods of evaluating performance of objectives.

The marketing plan covers the libraries from the Galway and Cluain Mhuire campuses of GMIT.

What follows is the result of a SWOT (Strengths, Weaknesses, Opportunities and Threats) analysis of the Dublin Road Campus Library. Strengths, weaknesses, opportunities and threats to the library were identified by:

Analyzing the results of the 2009 Student Survey

Analyzing the results of the 2007 Staff Survey

Asking library staff to identify what they perceived to be our strengths, weaknesses, opportunities, and threats.

EXAMPLE 6

GMIT Library SWOT Analysis

STRENGTHS (INTERNAL)	WEAKNESSES (INTERNAL)
• Public service orientation • Well-qualified, team-oriented and dedicated staff • Commitment to strong instruction program • Excellent physical facilities, building and study rooms • Good cooperation with other libraries • Relationship with campus departments, including collaborative collection development • Ongoing goal of building quality collections and providing access to information	• Noise in library • Opening hours • Age of print and journal collections • Impact of budget on staff, training and equipment • Temperature regulation • Continuing need for consistent communication among library campuses • Customer service (some negative comments in 2009 Survey)

OPPORTUNITIES	THREATS (EXTERNAL)
• Distance learning • Cooperation with other libraries • The intensification of information skills training of undergraduate and postgraduate students and academic staff including the L2L module • Use of new technologies in information skills delivery • Possible reconfigurations of positions • Marketing library services and collections • Support innovations in teaching and changes in learners and learning styles across campus with new collections, services and technologies	• Budget cuts/economic uncertainties • Potential loss of further positions • Limitation on services offered to External members • Student numbers may fall • More demanding students (special needs, mature, foreign, etc.) • Changing perception of students concerning the role of the Library • Challenge of staying current with rapidly changing technology and difficulty of supporting that technology with limited resources

Strengths

- Public service orientation

The public service attitude of the staff makes the Library a welcoming place. Student surveys show high satisfaction rates for service received at the library (85% for students in the GMIT Library Survey 2009). Survey respondents frequently added comments such as: "Great service, nice staff, and great 'space'" or "Excellent service provided in a very professional manner."

- Well-qualified, team-oriented and dedicated staff

Library staff, in addition to their belief in service, bring a high level of education and motivation to their positions. They are committed to providing high quality library service to not only the campus but the community as well. They are active in staff development and in voluntary and community organizations.

- Commitment to a strong instruction program

GMIT library staff are dedicated to teaching students the research process, which has become increasingly complex and can be daunting to students. Through the Library, students and other users have access to a vast array of print and electronic resources, and their ability to use those resources enhances their research and their education. Numbers of library inductions, online resource and EndNote training sessions, continue to rise. Library staff are also part of the Learning 2 Learn Module instruction team.

- Excellent physical facilities, building and study rooms

GMIT Library moved into a new Library and Learning Centre building in 2003 which is a wonderful facility for the students. The inclusion of 15 group study rooms in its design has proved to be a great resource for students in their group projects and course work.

- Good cooperation with other libraries

GMIT library is part of an Institute of Technology libraries consortium which aims to procure electronic and other resources at competitive rates through cooperative purchasing. In 2009, the Irel e-journals initiative was introduced into the IoT sector with the funding of the BSP/ASP collection of e-journals. A cost effective price for the journals has been achieved through joint procurement with the universities. GMIT Library now has access to the EBSCO journals as a result of this initiative. There has also been a Digital Mapping Project with Galway Public Library and the National University of Galway Library.

- Relationship with GMIT campuses, including collaborative collection development

Each GMIT campus spends an annual library materials allocation and is involved in decision-making on databases and journals in their fields. A subject librarian is assigned to each school to liaise with the school on all library matters and assist with any related queries.

- Ongoing goal of building quality collections and providing access to information

The Library works hard to maximize limited resources to build print and electronic collections which will support the study and research needs of students and staff. Inter-branch borrowing allows users to borrow directly from other GMIT campus libraries when required. The Interlibrary Loan department processed almost 800 ILL requests last year including journal articles, books and theses. Library electronic resources are available 24/7 remotely.

EXAMPLE 6

Weaknesses

- Noise in library

Noise in the library has been a problem over recent years. In the Library Survey 2009, comments were received such as "need more staff to keep noise levels down" and "only real problem is the amount of chatting and laughing that is allowed to go on."

- Opening hours

There have been complaints about the library's opening hours in the last two library surveys. In the Library Survey 2009, 51% of students rated the library's opening hours as "Poor" or "Adequate." 44% of respondents gave a preference for earlier morning opening times as their first choice of extended opening times. 31% indicated a first preference for longer Saturday opening and 25% gave a first preference for longer opening times in the evenings. Comments were received like "I think longer hours morning and evening would provide a better service again" and "Weekend hours are a joke."

- Age of print and journal collections

The GMIT Library Review 2007 indicated that 80% of the library's book stock is pre-2000. The library was not given an extra allocation of funding for books when it moved to the new library building in 2003. Consequently, the book stock is in need of updating. Comments in the GMIT Library Survey 2009 include "Books out-dated—need modern version" and "Books lecturers recommend for reading are not in the library and course books are not in the library either."

Journal price increases combined with flat library budgets have created serious problems in the library world. Although electronic databases, especially with linked full-text journals, increase research effectiveness and access, the switch from print indices to electronic databases incurs a large financial commitment.

- Impact of budget on staff, training and equipment

Staff: When open positions are not filled, those duties must be reassigned or dropped, and the remaining staff feel the burden. The library is in the process of losing two half-time positions and the recruitment of a replacement for the Librarian's retirement is uncertain at this point.

Training: About a quarter of the library staff give library inductions or other library resource training, but the pool is not large enough for the forecasted increasing demand for training (i.e., the Learning 2 Learn module).

Equipment: Funds are insufficient to replace the PCs on the library floor for students. These computers are now 6 years old and the Library Survey 2009 showed many complaints about the slowness of these computers.

Comments were received like "Computers always freezing" and "Computers in the library are very slow."

- Temperature regulation

The heating and ventilation system is controlled electronically via the copper sails. The library building is naturally ventilated to comply with BRE guidelines. However, the temperature in the GMIT Library varies considerably from very cold in some parts to very warm in others. Comments from the GMIT Library Survey 2009 include "Library cold frequently" and "Too hot or too cold."

- Continuing need for consistent communication among library campuses

No campus library works in isolation, and what one group does may affect other parts of the Library, sometimes in unexpected ways. The sharing of new projects, policy changes, new services, committee minutes, and news benefits the whole Library.

Opportunities

- Distance learning

There are two courses in the School of Science that are run through distance learning. While this number of students is small relative to the total student body, it is likely that GMIT will operate more courses in this manner in future years. GMIT will need to support remote services for distance learners, promote electronic access to the library and offer inductions on library services to students when they visit the college.

- Cooperation with other libraries

While GMIT Library has good relations with other libraries, it is important to maintain these relationships. There may be opportunities for future partnerships with some of these libraries in acquiring resources. For example, the Digital Mapping Project with Galway Public Library and NUIG Library, the Irel Project, the National Digital Repository and the possibility of a Union Catalogue.

- The intensification of information skills training of undergraduate students, postgraduate students and academic staff

The Learning 2 Learn module (L2L) is due to roll out in September 2009 for all first year students. There is a Library Information Skills section in this module which involves 6 hours of instruction. This kind of training could be expanded in future years to include other undergraduate students, postgraduate students and academic staff. As more patrons become aware of our EndNote software for creating and storing references, they may avail of training on this software also.

EXAMPLE 6

- Use of new technologies in information skills delivery

New technologies in delivering information skills training can be explored such as Moodle and Camtasia. The library can also use Moodle for its course details and assignments.

- Possible reconfigurations of positions

Although loss of experience and knowledge is a concern, retirements afford the Library the opportunity to evaluate the overall staffing patterns and workflow and change positions as the Library's needs have changed.

- Marketing library services and collections

The Library does not have a history of promoting its services in a systematic manner, although marketing has always been carried out. With vast and changing Library resources available for use, outreach to the campuses and larger community would increase awareness and use of these resources. Assessment of what our users and non-users need and want could lead to targeted marketing.

- Support innovations in teaching and changes in learners across campus with new collections, services and technologies

Libraries are evolving from repositories to active partners in the teaching mission of the Institute. Today's learners need services and spaces that support their collaborative learning styles. Living in a world of almost constant communication and social networking, students would benefit from Library assistance in learning and evaluating new methods of researching. The Library could assume a leading role in helping students conduct research using Web 2.0 technologies.

Threats

- Budget cuts/economic uncertainties

Lack of sufficient funding has already affected many areas of the Library as detailed under "Weaknesses" above. The current recession in Ireland and the likelihood of further cuts undermine the development of long-range plans.

- Potential loss of further positions

As well as the current proposed job cuts, further decreases in staff numbers cannot be ruled out. Pressure on individuals will increase as the number of library staff drops, leaving little time for developing new initiatives. Further loss of staff would increase stress and burnout for the remaining individuals.

- Limitation on services offered to External members

There are no I.T. facilities or access to electronic resources available for external members of the library who are physically visiting the library. While they can access library electronic databases at home on their own computers once they have set up a PIN number, the same facility for browsing the Internet on one of the student PCs is not available.

- Student numbers may fall

With population numbers falling in GMIT's target age group coupled with increased competition from other colleges, undergraduate student numbers attending GMIT may fall. There is an increased impetus for stronger marketing and targeting of other patron types to ensure continued exploitation of library resources.

- More demanding students (special needs, mature, foreign, etc.)

The age group of GMIT's students varies from young to mature. There are also students with special needs and foreign students attending the Institute. Staff need to be trained in customer service to ensure appropriate service to these patrons.

- Changing perception of students concerning the role of the Library

The Library is not the first stop (even virtually) for many students doing research. Many students resort to web search engines (Google, Yahoo, etc.) as their first port of call for research assignments. 68% of students in the Library Survey 2009 used Library Electronic Resources occasionally or frequently.

- Challenge of staying current with rapidly changing technology and difficulty of supporting that technology with limited resources

Given the accelerating rate of technical change, it is becoming increasing difficult for staff to stay informed and become proficient in working with new technologies. Electronic resources coordination has become more complex and time-consuming. Changing technology requires hardware and software replacements with the consequent budget increases and staff retraining.

GMIT Library's Main Competitors

Three main sources of competition have been identified and explored.

1. The Internet as a source of information

The ease of a Google search of the Internet as opposed to library-based research is obvious. The library must convince patrons that the quality, range and depth of the information gleaned from the use of library electronic resources is superior to a general web search.

Users need to be made aware that library.gmit.ie is a gateway to more relevant information than that found on Google or other search engines. The GMIT Library website gives access to much more valuable and reliable

EXAMPLE 6

information via subscription databases, alongside information on where to locate books on a particular topic, and order full text articles through ILL.

General Google and other web search engines can be accessed from the GMIT Library website as can Google Scholar for more academic information. A trial of LibraryThing is currently getting underway for GMIT. The library already has the Syndetics catalogue enrichments which are of benefit to users. Reviews are also possible through LibraryThing. A Google Analytics account has also been set up for the Library. This will demonstrate how and when the Library is being accessed through Google and will also make staff aware of possible keywords they can add to the website to make it more retrievable via Google.

The Library blog puts it on the Internet in another way and will encourage participation and discussion on topics of users' interest (http://gmitlibrary.blogspot.com). It is linked through from the main library page and library main menu on GMIT library web pages. RSS Feeds also make the library website more interactive. Rather than regarding the Internet and the various search engines as a threat, the library must use the technologies available and integrate them into the library service options, but all the while stressing that accessing library electronic resources will give a richer return than general web searching.

2. Competition from other libraries

GMIT library patrons may also make use of other libraries. The reasons for patrons' use of other libraries should be explored: they may be better stocked for their subject area; more conducive to study or in a more convenient location.

GMIT Library welcomes co-operation with other libraries. It is already part of a PARTNERS consortium with other IoT libraries; GMIT patrons may use any of 11 other institute libraries for study or lending, once they have a Partners card from their own institution.

GMIT Library also cooperates with the James Hardiman Library in NUIG. Students may use the NUIG library if they provide a letter signed by a GMIT Librarian. GMIT has already joined forces with NUIG in participating on the 1842 OS map digitization project for Galway County.

Public libraries may be sought after as places to do research and study and may be located more conveniently to some patrons. GMIT could promote its external membership using public libraries, making patrons aware of what is available to them from online databases, for example. Its existing multi-campus approach means GMIT library has an established ethos of resource sharing which can be broadened to include other libraries.

GMIT Library also has a good history of involving itself with public libraries through the Library Association of Ireland, particularly the Western Regional Section. At least one staff member from GMIT has been an officer on the WRS committee for many years.

GMIT Library has also run a number of successful WRS activities in recent years. Other libraries should be seen as opportunities for cooperation.

3. Competition from Home Study

Using home instead of the library for study may be a more viable option for patrons for any number of reasons: they do not live near the library, home is quieter for study or that a good Internet connection for home gives access to all GMIT's online resources. It is important for those studying outside the library to be aware of services both in-house and online, that they get access to news from the library and that they are aware of the range of services and facilities available to them.

It is important to get patrons to talk to library staff, either via telephone, e-mail, blogs, Facebook, etc., so that they know what these users want and how best they can meet their needs. The library online suggestions box and Ask a Librarian should be promoted for this purpose.

TARGET MARKETS
User Groups

Undergraduates

Undergraduates form the largest group of library patrons. 3954 students registered in 2007/08, representing 50% of total library patrons. Library needs of undergraduates vary according to their course year. First years need induction tours and more assistance from staff at the Issue Desk. They may also need instruction on how to use the photocopiers. First years access books as their main information resource. Second, third and fourth year students are more experienced in how to use the library and their library needs include researching theses, multimedia, journals and online resources. They are given more detailed research assignments and so require some guidance from library staff on how to access information. Many are still unaware of the depth of information available from GMIT's journal collection (both print and electronic) and may need to be guided to those resources by staff at the Issue Desk if help is requested. All undergraduates look for past exam papers and many print them off from the library catalogue.

Most of the reported library requirements of undergraduates from the GMIT Library Survey 2009 are for studying, checking out books, getting exam papers, using the photocopiers and computers and for availing of group study rooms for group work. Other library facilities such as maps, multimedia, getting inter-library loans, using EndNote software and accessing online resources are currently under-utilized by undergraduates.

Although this group is advanced in Internet usage, their level of research skills and comfort utilizing library services can be relatively poor. Many rely on Google and have no sense of evaluation of results. The library can teach them skills that they will be able to use not only during college, but also throughout their lives.

EXAMPLE 6

Post-graduates

Post-graduates represented 1% of GMIT library patrons in 2007/08. This group has different requirements for library services than the undergraduates. They are all acquainted with how to find books in the library and have some awareness of its journal collection. Post-graduates use inter-library loan service and access the electronic databases more frequently than other patrons. Library staff may need to assist in the search for information for these patrons, although many do not ask for it. As these patrons are undertaking Masters and Ph.D. degrees, they are strongly motivated to seek out information for their research and theses. They have a greater awareness of evaluating Internet sources than their undergraduate counterparts and access the subscribed databases with more regularity. This can be aided by library staff offering subject specific guidance on electronic resources and other library services. Citation and referencing are a necessary part of this process and the library provides training on using EndNote Referencing software to this end. Post-graduates have also access to the dedicated library research space, the Research Room.

Staff

GMIT staff constitute the second largest patron group. There are currently 853 staff patrons, with academic staff making the highest proportion.

All GMIT staff have automatic membership of the Library and can borrow up to ten items at one time. All library members have online access to all GMIT databases from both on and off campus and staff engaged in research are heavy users of databases.

Academic staff are aware of the benefits of subscription databases over the general Internet, but many are not aware of the scope and coverage that GMIT online resources offer.

Academic and administrative staff have access to information from the Library via e-mail. This information is usually about new online resources or products on trial. It is possible that there are many staff, particularly non-academic administrative and support staff, who are unaware of the extent of services and facilities that the Library has to offer and that this marketing programme should address this issue.

Apprentices Motor (Mechanics and Electricians)

They make up approximately 5% of the total number of GMIT students comprising two groups twice a year. Their needs differ from mainstream students in so far as they use the library for a limited portion of the academic year. Exam papers and study spaces are their main request; online journals and databases are a lesser priority for them. They also borrow books and use the study rooms.

Adult Education–Short/Hobby Courses

Adult Education is founded on the belief that learning is a lifelong and life-wide process. Courses are offered on a variety of levels across a diverse range of subjects, from Computing to Interior Design with approximately 1500 people enrolled.

The services required by the Library are the photocopiers, computers, access to books and journals. The courses start towards the end of September when the library is open from 9:30 a.m. to 9:30 p.m.; therefore any students wishing to visit the Library can do so before or after class. This group of students is not a high user group of library services.

Adult Education–Professional Courses

There are approximately 200 students studying Professional Courses, examples of which include the Diploma in Quality Management and The Institute of Accounting Technicians. These students are Library members and have access to books, databases, study rooms and photocopiers. They do not have access to computers on campus but once a pin number is set up, they can access databases at home.

Distance Learning Membership

Distance Learning students of GMIT are users who receive their education via electronic formats and by self-study learning materials. At present GMIT offers two science courses by distance learning. This user group comprises a small proportion of the total student group. A library induction tour is offered at the start of a DE course to enable patrons to use the library resources and services effectively. The library provides access to a high number of titles from the core reading lists. They also have access to the general library collection for other books that they may wish to borrow. Borrowing privileges include five books at any one time for a one month period. A postal loan service is provided to those unable to visit the library in person.

Remote online access to the electronic resources is essential for these students for their researching purposes. Partaking in the Learning 2 Learn Module would provide these students with the necessary skills to carry out their research more effectively at home.

It is important that the library continues to promote electronic access to distance learners and to support and enhance remote services for the distance learners as outlined in the GMIT Library Strategic Plan 2006–2011.

External Membership

GMIT library offers and supports external membership. External patrons consist of members of public from the Galway environs who are interested in the library's broad subject areas or specific collections such as the Western Theological Trust collection. The library has developed an extensive local

EXAMPLE 6

history section and the fiction section would include works from popular authors. Daily newspapers are also available, while in the last year regional newspapers have been introduced for patrons to browse.

Library staff may need to assist external members with use of OPACs, explain how the items are classified and with the general layout of the library when they join initially. The library recognizes the importance of external membership in promoting the regional remit of the Institute, one of the strategic drivers of the GMIT Strategic Plan.

Alumni

The library also supports Alumni membership; these former students of the college are able to continue to utilise the library's vast resources and facilities.

Retired Staff

The age profile of GMIT staff has meant that large numbers of staff have retired in the last few years. Many of these would have been regular users of the library during their time in GMIT and may still want to keep up with developments in their subject area or may want to use the library for recreational reading using the fiction or general non-fiction collections. Retired staff are entitled to free membership of the library.

International Students

International students make up less than 1% of the total number of our students. They come here through the Leonardo and Socretes programmes. In this sector, one would have to pay particular attention to their cultural differences and language would be a huge part. They would need assistance in finding books. However they would be focused and inquisitive about services in general.

Innovation in Business Centre

Some members of the IiBC are members of the library as they are classed as staff members. Use of the electronic resources for product and market research is seen as a vital reason for library membership for this group. The marketing group feels that a section of this report should be directed to this user group to maximize their knowledge of library resources and services.

Wider Community—Schools

GMIT Strategic Plan lists as one of its strategies for developing its regional focus to "develop programmes for linkage and collaboration with secondary and primary schools in the region." GMIT library liaises with the Schools Liaison Office to bring school groups into the library, particularly during

Library Ireland Week, but also at other times throughout the year. These groups usually have a tour of the library and a talk about the library given by one of the staff. A PowerPoint presentation is also available for schools groups who visit the library. School visits to the library are often conducted as part of a visit to the Institute as a whole.

Analysis of Current Marketing Strategies

Question 12 of the 2009 User Satisfaction Survey asked: "How do you keep up with library developments?" The percentage of respondents who used the following communications means are listed below where applicable.

Marketing Strategies

Library Website

The library webpage contains a comprehensive collection of library information on all aspects of library services and is the access point for all library electronic services.

> Used by 21% of Survey respondents, Dublin Road
>
> Used by 20% of Survey respondents, Cluain Mhuire

Library Newsletter

The purpose of the Newsletter is to inform library patrons of service developments and highlight existing services. It includes information on new services, reviews of new book and journal titles, changes in staff. The Newsletter is produced at the start of every term and is available on the library webpage.

> Used by 13% of Survey respondents, Dublin Road
>
> Used by 16% of Survey respondents, Cluain Mhuire

Students Union Newsletter

Web-based newsletter produced every fortnight. This includes a page or ½ page of library information highlighting changes to opening hours, reminders of current service options and alerts to new services.

> Used by 22% of Survey respondents, Dublin Road
>
> Used by 12% of Survey respondents, Cluain Mhuire

Staff Newsletter

Occasional submissions to the Staff Newsletter produced by the GMIT Communications Office.

> Used by 4% of Survey respondents, Dublin Road
>
> Used by 0% of Survey respondents, Cluain Mhuire

EXAMPLE 6

E-mail Updates

E-mail updates are used to alert staff on new electronic services or database trials.

> Used by 25% of Survey respondents, Dublin Road (?)
>
> Used by 19% of Survey respondents, Cluain Mhuire (?)

Ask a Librarian

E-mail link from the library homepage to staff member regarding any matter of library services.

Brochures

Brochures are available from the library website and in paper format in the library in the following areas:

- Subject guides for each school, e.g., Science Guide, Humanities
- Membership guides for the different membership categories, e.g., Distance Learners Guide, External Membership Guide
- Electronic Services guides, e.g., Endnote Web Guide, Online Databases
- General Library Guides, e.g., Code of Conduct, Inter-Library Loans
- Room Guides, e.g., Research Room, Independent Learning Unit

> Used by 15% of Survey respondents, Dublin Road
>
> Used by 33% of Survey respondents, Cluain Mhuire

Library Ireland Week Activities

GMIT Library hosts activities for the nationwide Library Ireland Week promoted by the Library Association of Ireland since 2005. Activities are targeted internally and externally. Lectures, readings and concerts are part of the activities focused at GMIT students and staff. The wider community is served by bringing school groups to GMIT library for a morning's activities. These groups are shown the library and given a talk on the building. Also included is a library quiz. The Schools, particularly Engineering and Hotel and Catering, give demonstrations and tours of their departments. This broadens the focus of the visit, gives a taste of life in GMIT.

GMIT Open Day

The library has a stand in the Café Foyer during Open Day with a selection of brochures and a PowerPoint presentation running. Tours of the library are available but generally groups of students just wander in for a look.

LCD Display in the Library

This electronic display gives updates on library opening hours or events.

Staff

Staff should be aware that they are marketing the library in all their dealings with library patrons.

Display Cabinets

Themed displays of books and journals are housed in three large display cabinets, situated opposite the Library Information desk. Examples of recent displays are travel books towards the end of term when students and staff may be thinking of holidays, collection of Seamus Heaney titles to celebrate his 70th birthday and astronomy books to mark 2009 as the International Year of Astronomy.

Blogs

Blogs are being used increasingly by libraries as a communications tool. GMIT has just started a library blog.

TARGET MARKET
Undergraduates

Marketing Programme for Undergraduates

Undergraduates are the largest cohort of library patrons and are the main target for this marketing exercise. They range from the First Year student who starts in September with little knowledge of the working of the Institute or the Library and its services to the Fourth Year student who may be very familiar with library services or alternatively who may not have used the library service to the optimum. For the purpose of this marketing plan, the First Year student group will be viewed as a separate cohort of patrons. The Library will focus marketing strategies on this group with particular reference to the initial Induction period.

Goal

The First Year experience, including the perception of the library and its services, is widely acknowledged as vital in the students' positive perception of college life. A GMIT Partnership Project completed an integrated programme for New Students to GMIT in 2004. The purpose of this programme is to make the initial impression of GMIT as positive as possible and to ease the transition to third level education.

The goal of the Library is that First Year students will perceive the library as an integral part of college life and central to the successful completion of their studies.

GOAL	OBJECTIVE	STRATEGIES	MEASURING OUTCOMES	TIMEFRAME
First Year students will perceive the library as an integral part of college life.	**1.** The First Year student will know where to seek information and be comfortable doing so from library staff.	**1.** A friendly greeting at the library desk. **2.** The presentation for the First Year Institute Induction programme will emphasize the welcoming atmosphere in the library and the value of the library Service. **3.** The Library Newsletter will include information targeted at new students.	A survey of First Years will be undertaken in November to assess outcomes. One class from each school will be surveyed.	**1.** November 09 **2.** September 09 **3.** Library Newsletter
	2. The First Year student will be familiar with the library services and Facilities.	**1.** Welcome desk near library entrance for Week 1 of term where staff will demonstrate library website, OPAC, and answer general queries. **2.** All First Year students will complete a Library Induction programme. **3.** Staff will demonstrate the Self Service machine at selected times during the first 2 weeks of term.	Comparison of circulation figures using Self Service option	**1.** January 2010
	3. The First Year student will see the library as a congenial location in which to engage in their studies.	**1.** Welcome message to First Years on Electronic notice board. **2.** All staff to wear name badges. **3.** Staff will be particularly aware of the needs of First Year students. **4.** Staff will endeavour to keep noise levels to a minimum.		
Undergraduates will increase usage of electronic resources.	**1.** Usage of databases will increase by 10%.	**1.** Continue promotion of electronic resource training. **2.** Evaluation sheets will be introduced for training sessions. **3.** Offer open training session on a weekly basis for a trial period–times to be decided.	Database statistics by June 2010	**1.** June 2010
	2. Usage of IReL databases will increase by 20%.	**1.** Emphasise the quality of the IReL suite of databases. **2.** Library Newsletter will promote the IReL databases. 3. Academic staff will be urged to promote IReL to students.		
	3. Undergraduates will increase their use of EndNote.	**1.** EndNote training will be advertised more widely. **2.** More library staff will become familiar with EndNote. **3.** EndNote will be promoted particularly to Postgraduates.		
Undergraduates will increase usage of Self Service.	Use of Self Service unit will increase by 50%.	**1.** Staff demonstrations of the Self Service unit will be undertaken on an ongoing basis.	Self Service statistics by June 2010	
Undergraduates will increase usage of library book stock.	Undergraduates will exploit a core element of the library service.	**1.** The library will address the age of collection issue. **2.** The library will ensure that copies of core text materials and reading lists are available.	Circulation statistics	**1.** June 2010– ongoing

GOAL	OBJECTIVE	STRATEGIES	MEASURING OUTCOMES	TIMEFRAME
Identify and implement opportunities and outlets to inform users about GMIT Library resources and services.	**1.** Enhance the library's current publications into an integrated communications plan.	**1.** Update format of GMIT Newsletter. **2.** E-mail all staff on its publication and provide link to online version. **3.** Formalize distribution policy, including distribution to external lists. **4.** Encourage wider library staff input to Newsletter. **5.** Continue to develop library contributions to Students Union Newsletter. **6.** Liaise with Communications Officer re: publication dates for Staff Newsletter. **7.** Ensure library input to Staff Newsletter. **8.** Assess guides/brochures for updating and currency of information.		**1.** January 10 **2.** Ongoing **3.** January 10 **4.** Ongoing **5.** Ongoing **6.** September 09 **7.** Ongoing **8.** Each Summer
	2. Enhance the library's current communications outlets into an integrated communications plan.	**1.** Enhance library staff awareness of the Library website as a marketing tool. **2.** Monitor and assess the Library blog. **3.** Continue to highlight Ask a Librarian e-mail link. **4.** Continue e-mail alerts of new resources to GMIT staff list.		**1.** Ongoing
Develop strategies to involve GMIT Library staff in marketing efforts.	**1.** Encourage a shared responsibility for promoting GMIT Library to users and potential users.	**1.** Staff are aware that all encounters with patrons are marketing opportunities. **2.** Encourage staff promotional ideas.		
	2. Enhance commitment of all GMIT Library staff to providing and promoting excellent service.	Continuous emphasis on customer service in staff training.		
	3. Heighten appreciation and support for developing GMIT Library relationships with others.	Encourage library staff participation in Institute-wide activities and wider community groups.		
Align the Library with the concepts of lifelong learning and love of reading.	**1.** The library will be the cultural centre of the Institute.	**1.** Investigate the feasibility of starting a library-based book club. **2.** Promote library collections for recreational reading.		
	2. Promote library activities and resources by showcasing collections, services, exhibits and events.	**1.** Update displays in display cabinets more frequently. **2.** Tie themes of displays to current events, celebrations and anniversaries in a more vibrant manner.		
	3. Develop Library Ireland Week activities.	**1.** Develop activities relevant to library users. **2.** Promote Library Ireland Week as an Institute event. **3.** Liaise with Communications Officer re: promoting Library Ireland Week.		

GOAL	OBJECTIVE	STRATEGIES	MEASURING OUTCOMES	TIMEFRAME
Increase the visibility of the Library in the GMIT campuses.	Expand upon existing liaison activities with academic departments on campus.	**1.** Subject Librarians will enhance promotional activities within their areas. **2.** Partner with the GMIT Communications Office to link library marketing with relevant campus events and initiatives.		
All GMIT staff are aware of the range and extent of library services and facilities.	**1.** All new GMIT staff receive a library induction session.	Liaise with Staff Development re: Staff Induction Day.	Staff Induction attendee numbers	Ongoing
	2. Existing staff will be kept up to date with new developments.	**1.** General communication channels. **2.** Subject Librarians will enhance communications with lecturing staff.		
	3. Distribute Library Newsletters to support staff.	Newsletters to be delivered to canteen, café, cleaning staff rooms, porter's office and administration offices.		From January 10
That liBC members will be aware of and use library services.	30% of liBC members will become library members.	**1.** Library Newsletter will be circulated to liBC. **2.** Library information leaflets and application forms will be left at liBC Reception area. **3.** Library will offer a library induction session to all liBC members. **4.** Information e-mails to be directed through liBC Reception.	Survey of liBC membership numbers	January 10
Unemployed persons who require access to GMIT Library will be aware of, and in a position to avail of, library services.	**1.** Unemployed persons be aware of GMIT Library services.	**1.** Distribute library information re: membership to FAS offices, Dept. of Social Welfare offices, Galway Peoples Resource Centre, Galway County Library.	Measurement of Concession membership at May 2010	**1.** October 09 **2.** October 09
	2. Concession membership will make access easier for unemployed.	**1.** Finalize the introduction of Concession membership policy. **2.** Liaise with Communications Office re: press release for Concession membership fee for unemployed persons.		October 09

Marketing Plan from a University Library, Sample 2

Marketing Plan for Kanopy, William H. Hannon Library,
Loyola Marymount University, Spring-Fall 2016

EXAMPLE

7

Acknowledgment

The marketing plan for the William H. Hannon Library is used by permission of John Jackson, Outreach & Communications Librarian, Loyola Marymount University.

Executive Summary

In Spring 2016, the Loyola Marymount University's William H. Hannon Library (LMU) purchased access to a new streaming video platform, Kanopy. Kanopy provides access to online video content, including award-winning documentaries, training films, and theatrical releases, utilizing a patron-driven acquisitions model. It is our hope that it will not only supplement our physical video collection but also provide a more sustainable and accessible option for faculty seeking to incorporate films into their courses.

The rollout of the product will begin in January 2016 and continue through the Fall 2016 semester, beginning with a round of targeted communications and ending with a steady stream of timely reminders about topical films of interest. All the promotional materials will be created in-house and utilize the time and expertise of three full-time librarians. Success of the rollout will be measured by analyzing usage stats and referral links.

Current Market

While Kanopy is not our library's only video streaming service, it is the first one that is truly interdisciplinary and has the potential to appeal across disciplines at the university. The main competition comes from already established streaming video platforms that offer enough content to satisfy users and prevent them from seeking additional sources.

IN THIS EXAMPLE

- ✓ Executive Summary
- ✓ Current Market
- ✓ Target Market
- ✓ Goals
- ✓ Strategies
- ✓ Proposed Measurements
- ✓ Timeline
- ✓ Staff
- ✓ Budget
- ✓ Summary
- ✓ Appendix A: Kanopy Flyer for Circulation Desk
- ✓ Appendix B: Sample E-mail to Faculty Library Representatives
- ✓ Appendix C: Digital Signage
- ✓ Appendix D: Library Blog Post Draft
- ✓ Appendix E: Kanopy Social Media Post

EXAMPLE 7

External competitors

Netflix, Amazon, Hulu, Apple iTunes, Google Play, YouTube

Internal competitors

Films on Demand, our own DVD collection (i.e., relating to course reserves)

Both students and faculty at LMU utilize streaming video services in the classroom for educational use as well as outside the classroom for personal use. Students are more likely to access streaming video for non-curricular use and are most familiar with these platforms.

Target Market

Audience #1: Faculty

This product should appeal to faculty in all disciplines, but especially those in the social sciences. The subjects of the videos relate to coursework offered at LMU and the videos can be embedded in Blackboard. Faculty at LMU mostly utilize library collections (vs. services and spaces) and the level of use for print vs. electronic varies by discipline. This audience primarily accepts communication via e-mail and print mailers and is most responsive to new communications at the beginning of the semester.

Audience #2: Undergraduate and Graduate Students

This product should appeal to students in all disciplines, though the appeal is not necessarily connected to the student's field of study. This product may appeal to students looking for a resource that provides both entertainment and/or edification. Students mostly utilize library spaces (vs. services and collections), though the use of services is likely higher than that of faculty. This audience primarily accepts communication via digital promotion on our website and digital displays, but the most impactful communication comes via their instructors. This group is most responsive to new communications at the moment of need (i.e., when needed for an assignment or looking for a film to watch on personal time).

Goals

For Faculty

Instructors will utilize Kanopy streaming video in class and/or require viewing of Kanopy titles for class assignments.

For Students

Students will utilize Kanopy for academic research and personal edification.
Primary messages to convey:

1. Kanopy is easy to use.
2. Kanopy provides access to exclusive content.

Strategies

Voice and Style

The voice and style of communications about this product should depend on the audience. For students, it should be simple and direct, similar to Apple's approach to their user's guide (i.e., it's so easy you don't need a guide). For faculty, we should utilize a step-by-step guidelines approach for how to use the resource in courses. The overall feeling that we are trying to convey is "simple," "fun," and "You never know what you will find!"

Frequency/Saturation

The library website and digital signage should advertise the product for the entire semester (with a student audience in mind). Targeted communications to faculty (via e-mail or announcement channels) should happen 2–3 times during the semester; at least one of these should happen via the faculty library liaisons.

Internal communication channels/partners

- Librarian/staff meeting
- ITS/ITA staff meeting
- Info Desk student workers
- Faculty library liaisons
- Ethnic and Intercultural Services
- Office of International Students

External communication channels/partners

- MyLMU staff/faculty announcements feed
- Library newsletter
- Social media
- Digital signage in library and on campus

Deliverables

- Digital promotion in library, academic units, and residence halls
- E-mails to Faculty Library Representatives and partners, plus announcements/social media blasts
- Step-by-step guide for embedding films in Blackboard (for faculty)

EXAMPLE 7

Proposed Measurements

Kanopy Use Statistics

In coordination with the system administrator, monitor usage of Kanopy monthly, giving specific attention to usage patterns (numbers of hits, number of films watched) immediately following targeted communications.

URL/Referral Statistics

Using website traffic data (Siteimprove), social media URL stats (Hootsuite), and e-mail newsletter click-through rates (Constant Contact), gather information about how many users (and, where possible, what type of users) access Kanopy directly from our communications.

Timeline

January–February 2016: Internal Rollout

- Present about Kanopy at library staff meeting and ITS/ITA meeting.
- Create flyer for student workers at the Information Desk (Appendix A).
- Create e-mail template for faculty library liaisons (Appendix B).
- Remind librarians to include links to subject collections in LibGuides.

March 2016: External Rollout

- Post ads to library and campus digital signage (Appendix C).
- Send announcement to all faculty via MyLMU.
- Post ads to social media (Appendix D and Appendix E).
- Create blurb for library e-newsletter.
- Contact specific programs and other non-discipline-specific units on campus (e.g., Ethnic and Intercultural Services, International Students, etc.).

Summer–Fall 2016

- Create flyers for new faculty orientation.
- Create "New Resource" highlight for library homepage.
- Continue to highlight timely films on library social media.

Staff

Internal Partners

- Outreach and Communications Librarian

- Collections Assessment Librarian
- Subject Liaison to School of Film and Television

External Partners

- Faculty/instructors who typically assign films in courses
- ITS/ITA staff

Budget

The cost for creating promotional material will be measured in staff time and labor. No financial or physical resources are necessary to create the deliverables. It is expected that 4–5 hours of time (divided among three librarians) will be required to create the visual and textual materials necessary.

Summary

It is our hope that Kanopy with become a useful supplement to our physical film collection and, where possible, a replacement for assigned DVDs in courses. Following the initial rollout, it would be beneficial to survey faculty to identify if specific films within Kanopy have been assigned (though this data could be inferred from usage statistics) and to survey students about their awareness of the product (again, this data could be inferred from usage and referral statistics).

Kanopy Flyer for Circulation Desk

We've made it easier for you to access streaming video through a service called *Kanopy*. Kanopy's extensive offerings include thousands of award-winning documentaries, educational and training films, and theatrical releases. The collection includes a number of leading producers, such as the Criterion Collection, PBS, Kino Lorber, New Day Films, The Great Courses, California Newsreel, and hundreds more.

Watch now: lmu.kanopystreaming.com

You can search films by subject, filmmaker, and year. You can create playlists and clips. You can even share videos on social media. Best of all, the makers of Kanopy constantly update the homepage with collections of films relevant to current events. For example, this month Kanopy is highlighting films about the African American experience and the history of race in America.

[Created by Rhonda Rosen, Circulation Services Librarian]

Sample E-mail to Faculty Library Representatives

Dear <Name>,

I am pleased to announce that the William H. Hannon Library has recently added a new online video streaming service—Kanopy—to our collections. Kanopy's extensive offerings include thousands of award-winning documentaries, educational and training films, and theatrical releases. Each video is available in HD and accessible to an unlimited number of simultaneous viewers.

The collection includes a number of leading producers, such as the Criterion Collection, PBS, Kino Lorber, New Day Films, The Great Courses, California Newsreel, and hundreds more.

You can bookmark and browse the homepage here: http://lmu.kanopystreaming.com; or you may also discover individual titles through our library catalog.

You and your colleagues in <insert department name> may also be interested in exploring the following subject collection(s):

    <identify one or more links to subject collections in Kanopy>

You'll find that you can easily share films, create clips or teaching playlists, and embed them into MyLMU Connect. We hope you, your colleagues, and your students will find these an exciting addition to our library collections.

Thank you for sharing this with your department—please don't hesitate to get in touch with me if you have any questions!

<Salutation of choice>,
[Name]

[Created by Jamie Hazlitt, Librarian for Collection Development and Evaluation]

Digital Signage

Campus Digital Screen Ads

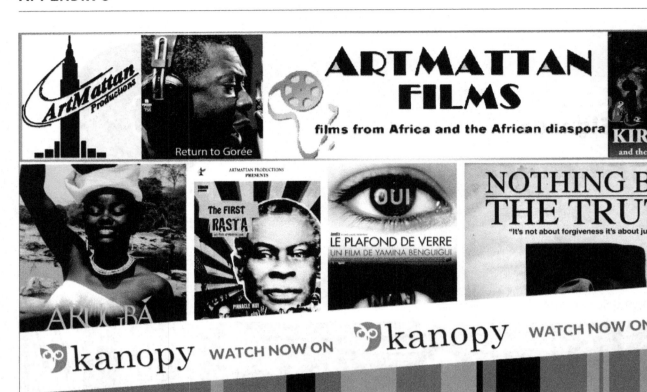

Library Blog Post Draft

Link to post: http://librarynews.lmu.edu/2016/02/new-streaming-video-service-kanopy/

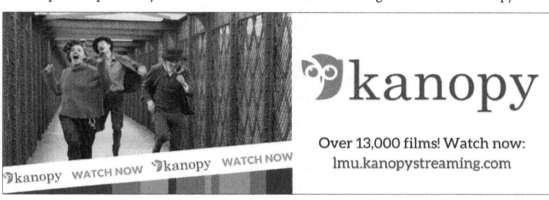

Over 13,000 films! Watch now:
lmu.kanopystreaming.com

We've just made it easier for you to access streaming video through a new service called Kanopy. Kanopy's extensive offerings include thousands of award-winning documentaries, educational and training films, and theatrical releases. The collection includes a number of leading producers, such as the Criterion Collection, PBS, Kino Lorber, New Day Films, The Great Courses, California Newsreel, and hundreds more.

Watch now: lmu.kanopystreaming.com

You can search films by subject, filmmaker, and year. You can create playlists and clips. You can even share videos on social media. Best of all, the makers of Kanopy constantly update the homepage with collections of films relevant to current events. For example, this month Kanopy is highlighting films about the African American experience and the history of race in America.

We'd like to recommend Through a Lens Darkly: Black Photographers and the Emergence of a People, a film that explores the role of photography in shaping the identity, aspirations, and social emergence of African Americans.

[embedded film]

Kanopy Social Media Post

LMU Library
Published by John Jackson [?] · October 14 · 🌐

Bob Dylan was recently awarded the Nobel Peace Prize for Literature. LMU Lions can check out this amazing film of Bob Dylan from our Kanopy collection: http://lmu.kanopystreaming.com/video/dont-look-back

Bob Dylan is captured on-screen as he never would be again in this groundbreaking film from D. A. Pennebaker. The legendary documentarian finds Dylan in England during his 1965 tour, which would be his last as an acoustic artist. In this wildly entertaining vision of one of the twentieth century's greatest artists, Dylan is surrounded by teen fans, gets into heated philosophical jousts with journalists, and kicks back with fellow musicians Joan Baez, Donovan, and Alan Price.

Featuring some of Dylan's most famous songs, including "Subterranean Homesick Blues," "The Times They Are A-Changin'," and "It's All Over Now, Baby Blue," Dont Look Back is a radically conceived portrait of an American icon that has influenced decades of verite behind-the-scenes documentaries.

(h/t Librarian Rhonda)

Watch Don't Look Back - Bob Dylan's 1965 Tour

Bob Dylan is captured on-screen as he never would be again in this groundbreaking film from D. A. Pennebaker. The legendary documentarian finds Dylan in England during his 1965 tour, which would be his last as an acoustic artist. In this wildly...

LMU.KANOPYSTREAMING.COM

About the Authors

MARIE R. KENNEDY is a Librarian at Loyola Marymount University, where she coordinates serials and electronic resources. She has written and presented widely on the development and use of electronic resource management systems. In her spare time she makes photographs and creates taste experiments in her kitchen. Marie also writes the *Organization Monkey* blog about organization and librarianship. She is the codirector of the Institute for Research Design in Librarianship (http://irdlonline.org).

CHERYL LaGUARDIA is a Research Librarian at Widener Library, Harvard University, where she is the library liaison to the Center for Jewish Studies, the Center for Middle Eastern Studies, the Committee on Regional Studies—East Asia, the Department of East Asian Languages and Civilizations, the Department of Near Eastern Languages and Civilizations, and the Freshman Seminar Program. Previously she worked in reference, research instruction, online services, collection development, interlibrary loan, and circulation at the University of California, Santa Barbara, and at Union College in Schenectady, New York. She writes the *Not Dead Yet* blog and e-reviews for *Library Journal.* She was awarded RUSA's highest honor, the 2016 Isadore Gilbert Mudge Award, as well as the 1996 Louis Shores/Oryx Press Award for reviewing. She has edited ProQuest's *Magazines for Libraries* since 2000 and is also the editor of the online-only *Magazines for Libraries Update.* She is an editorial advisor to CC Advisor (Choice Charleston Advisor) and is on the editorial board of *Reference Services Review.* She has published a number of books, including *Becoming a Library Teacher; Finding Common Ground: Creating the Library of the Future without Diminishing the Library of the Past;* and *Teaching the New Library* (Neal-Schuman, 1996–2000).

Index

Lightning Source UK Ltd.
Milton Keynes UK
UKOW05f0501111017

310777UK00006B/45/P